THE DOLLAR FAULT LINE

How America's Currency Became the World's Single Point of Failure

JOSH LUBERISSE

The Dollar Fault Line: How America's Currency Became the World's Single Point of Failure

Josh Luberisse

Published by Fortis Novum Mundum, 2025.

THE DOLLAR FAULT LINE: HOW AMERICA'S CURRENCY BECAME THE WORLD'S SINGLE POINT OF FAILURE

First edition. June 16, 2025.

ISBN: 979-8231562978

Written by Josh Luberisse.

“The Americans have the exorbitant privilege of being able to run up deficits without tears.”

— Valéry Giscard d'Estaing, Finance Minister of France, 1960s

The Dollar Fault Line: How America's Currency Became the World's Single Point of Failure

By

Josh Luberisse

Table of Contents

Preface

At 04:17 on a mist-coloured Tuesday in in northern New Jersey, the first tremor of daylight finds a lean team of technicians watching a wall of numbers scroll across twin monitors at the Federal Reserve Bank's East Rutherford Operations Center—a silent annex to the Manhattan financial empire. Within the next twenty-four hours Fedwire will settle roughly **US $4.3 trillion** in wholesale payments—rent for a fleet of tankers idling off Fujairah, interest on a Zambian Eurobond, collateral for a Chicago soybean-futures spread. Forty-five blocks downtown, the private CHIPS platform will net another **US $1.8 trillion** before Wall Street breaks for lunch. These rivers of money appear orderly on a dashboard, yet their smooth flow masks a dependence so concentrated that engineers would never tolerate it in any other critical infrastructure: there is no parallel channel, no emergency bypass. If the lights dim on the Hudson, commerce in Lagos, Seoul, and São Paulo stalls within minutes.

That vulnerability is not an accident of under-investment; it is the unintended consequence of success. In the eighty years since Bretton Woods the **U.S. dollar has become the invoice on roughly four-fifths of world trade, the unit for most cross-border bank lending, and the numeraire for almost every derivative hedge** a corporate treasurer inks to survive volatile markets. The network effects that once looked like elegant efficiency now resemble an airline that has routed every trans-Pacific flight through the same single-runway island. When headwinds rise, congestion metastasizes into crisis.

I began this project during the first pandemic spring, when the Federal Reserve's emergency swap lines ballooned from zero to almost **US $450 billion** in eight weeks—more dollar liquidity than the entire

IMF could command—while Congress debated whether an American central bank should be bailing out foreign credit markets at all. The episode crystallized a paradox: Washington wields unmatched leverage because only it can print the currency everyone else must scramble to obtain, yet that same privilege chains U.S. domestic policy to the anxieties of distant banking systems. The world's lifeboat is tethered to a single captain whose own vessel is subject to partisan squalls.

The pages that follow trace how that tether was forged—through gold-backed promises abandoned in 1971, through petrodollar recycling deals that turned oil shocks into Treasury-bill demand, through the euro-market deregulation that exported Wall Street's appetite for leverage to the City of London, and through a lattice of correspondent accounts that placed a handful of clearing banks at every arterial junction of global finance. The narrative then dissects the plumbing: Fedwire's settlement clock, CHIPS's liquidity-saving algorithm, the off-balance-sheet alchemy of FX swaps and prime-broker repos that create synthetic dollars beyond regulatory radar. It shows how **illicit fortunes, sanctioned state entities, and perfectly legitimate multinationals all converge on the same clearing channels**, rendering anti-money-laundering compliance a geopolitical choke hold and, simultaneously, a potential catalyst for systemic seizure.

But the book is not a polemic against American power, nor a eulogy for a lost multilateral ideal. It is an examination of structural risk: of a world that has engineered its commercial metabolism around a network whose resilience rests on a single legislature's tolerance, a single central bank's balance-sheet and a single city's fibre-optic loops. It argues that **climate-driven catastrophe losses, cyber intrusions capable of freezing high-value payment rails, or a debt-ceiling impasse on Capitol Hill are no longer local shocks but instant global margin calls.** They reach you—wherever you live—through the mundane act of settling payroll, rolling trade credit, or refinancing a mortgage denominated in a currency you do not even use at the supermarket.

Readers will encounter three recurring motifs. First, efficiency is indistinguishable from fragility when it concentrates optionality in one node. Second, leverage is reciprocal: the United States commands extraordinary influence, but the obligation to rescue the same system on which its own prosperity rests can narrow that influence at critical moments. Third, redundancy is expensive in the short run and indispensable in the long run; yet no market participant, acting alone, will pay the premium to build it.

This book therefore closes by asking not how to dethrone the dollar but how to craft an architecture that can survive its temporary unavailability—whether for an hour, a day, or, in the darkest scenario, a season of political paralysis. The answer will require choices as uncomfortable in Beijing and Brussels as in Washington, for the present constellation persists because it suits too many interests too well. To see the urgency one need only revisit the swap-line spike of 2020 or observe the way sanctions on a handful of Russian institutions reordered commodity collateral chains from Amsterdam to Qingdao in forty-eight hours. These are foreshocks. The main quake will make 2008 look like a rehearsal conducted on half-strength instruments.

I write in hope, not in pessimism. Systems can be redesigned—painfully, incrementally, but decisively—once their fault lines are mapped in daylight. My task in the chapters ahead is to chart those lines, to show how they criss-cross the Atlantic cables and the desert pipeline valves, the data centers of suburban New Jersey and the state-owned banks of coastal China. Only then can policymakers, financiers, and citizens choose whether to reinforce the bridge, reroute the traffic, or build the parallel span that history now demands.

Josh Luberisse

New York City,

April 2025

Introduction – The Manhattan Bottleneck

Anatomy of a Single-Point-of-Failure System

AT FIRST GLANCE THE global payments grid seems a triumph of distributed design. Banks from Lagos to Ljubljana route messages across SWIFT; multinationals hedge exposures in Singapore before New York opens; a Kenyan mobile-money platform settles millions of retail transfers without a single server on U.S. soil. Yet zoom into the final stage of value transfer and the façade of dispersion gives way to an alarming singularity. Every weekday, shortly after five-thirty Eastern Time, two high-security buildings separated by the Hudson River begin absorbing the world's commercial heartbeat. By midnight Fedwire Funds will have pushed more than **US $4 trillion** through its mainframe, while the private CHIPS network nets another **US $1–2 trillion** for its forty-seven member banks. Whether the underlying transaction originates in a Seoul ship-yard advance, a Zambian copper-royalty payment, or a German insurer's Treasury roll, the dollar leg must pass these Manhattan-centric rails before the day can close.

The geography is not merely symbolic. Fedwire's dollar leg confers legal finality only when reserve balances at the Federal Reserve Bank of New York are updated; CHIPS, in turn, depends on intraday Fedwire cash to settle its multilateral positions. CLS—the consortium that secures ninety per cent of global foreign-exchange settlements—hinges on an identical mechanism for its "PvP" dollar leg. Remove or even delay that single vector and what the BIS calls payment-versus-payment symmetry collapses into asymmetry: sterling can change hands in London, yen in Tokyo, but the dollar side of the trade remains in limbo, suspending title transfer and freezing margin. The world's financial metabolism therefore lives and dies by server racks that sit, quite literally, atop the bedrock of Lower Manhattan and the fibre conduits that spider beneath the Hudson to New Jersey co-location centers.

Network science teaches that the same topology which minimizes friction in tranquil states maximizes fragility under shock. Nowhere is that paradox starker than in dollar clearing. **Roughly eighty-eight per cent of global trade invoices and more than half of all cross-border bank claims are denominated in dollars**, even when neither buyer nor seller is American. The Ghanaian cocoa cooperative that sells beans to a Swiss chocolatier, the Qatari LNG exporter collecting payments from a Taiwanese utility, and the Ukrainian agribusiness drawing on a revolving credit line at Rabobank all meet inside the dollar corridor, funneling their liabilities through correspondent accounts at Citi, JPMorgan, or their European equivalents' U.S. branches. What looks like choice is in fact lock-in: liquidity begets liquidity, and the deepest pool lies in New York.

Dependence might be tolerable were resilience commensurate with scale, yet a glance at incident logs reveals how thin the margin has become. A three-hour Fedwire outage in February 2021—caused by an unremarkable application restart—forced banks to extend daylight overdrafts and trapped collateral at tri-party agents after the repo cut-off. Six months later a software error at a CHIPS participant halted end-of-day funding for dozens of Asian exporters, compelling an unscheduled liquidity infusion from the firm's New York branch.

Cyber-security red-teaming at the Treasury's Office of Critical Infrastructure Protection now models a ransomware assault that corrupts payment-instruction integrity rather than blocking access outright; the resolving mechanism still requires Fedwire to reopen clean and on time, a contingency that collapses if backup facilities share code bases or power grids with the primary.

European mega-banks provide an additional layer of complexity. Deutsche Bank, BNP Paribas, and Barclays each intermediate hundreds of billions in offshore dollars, yet their ultimate liquidity backstop is the Federal Reserve's foreign-bank branch window in New York. During Turkey's 2018 lira implosion, French and Spanish lenders scrambled to obtain dollar funding overnight when FX-swap spreads blew past internal tolerance, underscoring how shocks in emerging-market assets canalize through European balance sheets only to resurface in Manhattan before Asian markets open. Geography, once again, overrides nationality.

China's designers of alternative rails confront the flip side of the same physics. The Cross-Border Interbank Payment System (CIPS) offers renminbi settlement without SWIFT codependency, and the mBridge prototype records live CBDC transfers among four central banks. Yet together they clear in a month what Fedwire and CHIPS handle before New York coffee breaks. Liquidity's first-mover advantage is brutal: until reserve managers believe they can exit at scale in non-dollar assets during stress, invoicing inertia will continue to push trade and finance back along the Manhattan bottleneck.

This book opens here—at the servers beneath Liberty Street and the cable trenches of Weehawken—because understanding their centrality is prerequisite to grasping every downstream phenomenon: the Federal Reserve's reluctant role as offshore lender of last resort, the Treasury's capacity to weaponize sanctions, the ease with which climate-insurance settlements in Jakarta morph into daylight overdrafts in Jersey City. The chapters ahead chart how this architecture emerged, why it persists, how it confers both power and liability on the United States, and why attempts to duplicate it, bypass it, or weaponize it define the next era of monetary statecraft.

The bottleneck is not destiny. It is a design, and designs can be re-engineered. But redesign first demands that citizens, legislators, and bankers recognize the concentration they have inherited. A single street in Lower Manhattan is not merely hosting the world's traffic; it is underwriting the world's assumption that money itself cannot get stuck. To test that assumption is to invite crisis; to ignore the possibility is to guarantee one.

Part I – The Rise of Dollar Dominion

Chapter 1: Bretton Woods and the Gold–Dollar Synthesis

1.1 Geopolitical Victory Translated into Monetary Privilege

THE DELEGATES WHO ARRIVED in the White Mountains of New Hampshire in July 1944 confronted a ruined world economy but an unmistakable power asymmetry. By that summer the United States was supplying almost two-thirds of the Allies' matériel, financing three-quarters of Lend-Lease shipments, and sitting on roughly **70 percent of the planet's official gold stock**—the hoard accumulated as Europe shipped bullion to New York in exchange for tanks, wheat, and aviation fuel. Washington's wartime industrial surge had turned a continental power into the undisputed creditor of every major combatant. Its leverage at Bretton Woods derived not from abstract ideology but from control of the only balance sheet capable of restarting global trade.

John Maynard Keynes arrived determined to limit that leverage. He proposed an International Clearing Union with a new supranational unit of account—the *bancor*—whose built-in penalties would restrain both chronic debtors and chronic creditors. Harry Dexter White, speaking for the U.S. Treasury, countered that stability could be achieved more simply: fix exchange rates to the dollar at **$35 an ounce of gold**, oblige Washington alone to convert on demand, and require all other countries to adjust by tightening domestic policy when reserves dwindled. The argument was unequal from the start. Britain's reserves were exhausted; France, the Netherlands, and China were dependent on U.S. military aid; the Soviet Union declined to participate. White's design prevailed, institutionalized in the Articles of Agreement that created the International Monetary Fund and the International Bank for Reconstruction and Development. Formal gold parity remained, but in practice the gold link served chiefly to crown the dollar as the pivot of the system.

Victory in war thus translated into a privileged peacetime balance-sheet position. Under the new rules only the United States could settle foreign deficits by supplying dollars in excess of its gold outflow, because everyone else needed to *earn* dollars before they could import. When Western Europe's supply chains lay in rubble, the **Marshall Plan's $12–13 billion** infusion (roughly $150 billion in today's money) arrived not merely as humanitarian aid but as the working capital of a dollar-centric order: European governments spent U.S. grants on American equipment, the dollars recycled into European central-bank reserves, and the circle closed with renewed imports of U.S. grain and machinery. Each transaction deepened habit. By the time currencies became fully convertible in 1958, invoicing conventions, commercial contracts, and the back-office software of fledgling multinationals already defaulted to dollars.

The privilege carried a structural corollary: so long as foreign authorities held the dollar's value credible, Washington could run external deficits without confronting the immediate constraint that gold-standard orthodoxy had once imposed. European and later Japanese exporters earned dollars, but rather than redeeming them for bullion they reinvested in Treasury bills, financing America's own Cold-War expansion. What Keynes had labelled the "transfer problem" flipped; the balance-of-payments strain now fell on surplus nations obliged to absorb a currency they could neither reject nor easily spend elsewhere. The gold–dollar synthesis was, in effect, an IOU system guaranteed by the geopolitical insurer of last resort.

For American policymakers the arrangement proved irresistible. It cemented the dollar's role as reserve asset, unit of account, and settlement medium all at once. It tethered the reconstruction of Europe and, later, the export-led growth of East Asia to U.S. fiscal-monetary policy, giving the Federal Reserve an outsized influence over distant business cycles. And it established a template for leverage: the promise of convertibility in theory, the convenience of paper promises in practice, and a built-in presumption that no alternative anchor possessed the legal, military, or financial credibility to challenge the American claim.

That synthesis would endure for a quarter-century—long enough to embed the dollar in the sinews of global commerce, long enough for world trade to quintuple, and long enough for the first cracks of credibility to appear as the United States itself began to run persistent deficits. Those tensions, and the Eurodollar escape valves they spawned, occupy the next phase of our story. But they all originate in the geopolitical arithmetic of 1944: unequal gold reserves, a devastated Eurasian continent, and a negotiating room where the only creditor with surplus resources wrote the operating code of the post-war monetary world.

1.2 Fixed-rate Discipline and the First Cracks in Convertibility

FOR THE SYSTEM'S FIRST decade discipline appeared automatic. Countries that imported more than they exported surrendered gold or dollars to the U.S. Treasury; surplus nations accumulated reserves and, by the Fund's design, were expected to ease monetary conditions so demand would shift back toward deficit states. The architecture seemed symmetrical, but only as long as the United States retained the bulk of global bullion. By the late 1950s Europe's factories were humming, Japan's shipyards were winning orders, and the flow of trade surpluses reversed. Dollars streamed abroad faster than gold returned, eroding the stock that guaranteed the solemn promise of redemption at thirty-five dollars an ounce. In 1960 economist Robert Triffin told a U.S. congressional committee that the very dollars the world needed for liquidity would, if issued in excess, eventually destroy confidence in their value—a contradiction soon branded the *Triffin dilemma*.

Pressure migrated first to the London bullion market. Private demand for metal rose whenever speculators sensed that U.S. gold reserves were thinning; to defend the peg the Bank of England and seven other central banks formed the London Gold Pool in 1961, jointly selling from their vaults to cap the market at the official price. The arrangement consumed nearly a fifth of pooled stocks in frantic interventions between November 1967 and March 1968, after sterling's devaluation signaled that fixed parities could break. France quit the consortium, dispatching a naval frigate to New Jersey to collect bullion and denouncing the "exorbitant privilege" that let Washington finance guns and social programs with overseas IOUs. The pool collapsed on 14 March 1968; two days later markets were closed, and when trading resumed a two-tier system separated official settlements from a free price that promptly traded above forty dollars.

Convertibility now rested on faith rather than arithmetic. Between 1949 and 1969 U.S. monetary gold fell from roughly twenty-four thousand to twelve thousand metric tons, even as foreign central-bank dollar holdings tripled. Each French or Italian request for bullion, lawful under the rules, amplified doubt that the window could stay open. Yet any U.S. attempt to contract the external supply of dollars risked starving the very liquidity that underpinned post-war recovery and Cold-War alliance politics. Fixed rates thus became a confidence game: the United States issued liabilities it could not fully honor, and its allies pretended not to notice so long as export booms continued.

The Eurodollar market, inadvertently born from this tension, offered private actors a way around official constraints. Soviet and Latin-American deposits parked in London banks created offshore dollars beyond the Federal Reserve's reserve requirements. By the mid-1960s those balances reached into the tens of billions, supplying short-term funding to European banks that recycled the cash into long-term U.S. Treasury holdings—a leverage loop that magnified the disparity between on-shore gold cover and off-shore dollar claims. Convertibility still existed on paper, but the plumbing of global finance was already mutating into a credit system whose ultimate collateral lay in Fort Knox while its liabilities multiplied in Basel and the Bahamas.

By 1968 the contradiction Triffin had warned about was visible to anyone tracking weekly Treasury statistics. The fixed-rate discipline that once conferred credibility now accelerated reserve depletion, because every defense of parity required selling gold or raising U.S. interest rates high enough to trigger domestic recession—politically untenable in the Great Society era. The first cracks had widened into fractures; all that remained was formal acknowledgment, an act that would arrive three summers later when President Nixon closed the window altogether. The world learned then what the numbers had whispered for years: a currency system can live on trust long after its mechanical guarantees have rusted, but once that trust buckles, convertibility ends not in negotiation but in unilateral decree.

1.3 The Eurodollar Escape Valve and Offshore Dollar Multiplication

THE MOMENT FIXED-RATE discipline began to bite, global finance invented a side door. A Eurodollar was, at the outset, nothing more exotic than a dollar deposit lodged at a bank branch outside the territorial jurisdiction of the United States. But that small legal distinction—dollars booked in London or Nassau rather than New York—released the funds from every domestic constraint that U.S. regulators had designed to keep credit growth measured and interest costs low. Regulation Q's ceiling on deposit rates did not apply offshore, nor did reserve-requirement ratios, nor the interest-equalization tax meant to deter foreign borrowing from New York underwriters. The result was a regulatory vacuum into which dollars could multiply at will, provided the market trusted the issuing bank's balance sheet and the implicit readiness of the Federal Reserve to preserve systemic stability if matters ever got out of hand.

The initial supply came from political circumstance. Soviet and East-European trade banks, wary of U.S. asset freezes during the Cold War, shifted hard-currency takings from commodity sales into London branches of British banks. Chinese state entities followed, and before long Latin-American commodity exporters discovered the same channel offered higher yields than anything available through correspondent accounts in Manhattan. London—still the world's most liquid foreign-exchange centre—welcomed the inflow. Sterling's convertibility troubles had reduced the City's pre-war status; Eurodollars offered a fresh franchise. British supervisors, eager to revive the Square Mile, drew a simple regulatory perimeter: if the liabilities and assets were denominated in foreign currency and conducted with non-residents, UK prudential rules would be light-touch and Bank of England liquidity assistance would be minimal. In practice that meant the market could expand without matching capital cushions or binding liquidity ratios so long as transactions cleared through London book systems.

Once a critical mass of deposits had formed, the money-creation dynamic resembled onshore banking—only faster. A Swiss commodity house placed ten million dollars at a London branch of a New York bank; that branch, unencumbered by reserve requirements, lent eight million to a Dutch shipping concern; the shipping concern's payment landed in a Paris subsidiary of an Italian bank, which re-lent six million overnight to a Scandinavian broker dealing in U.S. Treasury bills. Each step created a fresh claim on the original dollars, ballooning gross balance sheets without a single dollar note crossing the Atlantic. By the late 1960s measured Eurodollar deposits exceeded forty billion, eclipsing the entire stock of U.S. gold several times over, and the number was almost certainly an undercount because off-balance-sheet interbank lines rarely appeared in published filings. What had begun as a political safeguard for Communist exporters became a self-reinforcing pool of liquidity to which every multinational now turned for working capital and trade finance.

Crucially, these offshore dollars remained functionally pari passu with domestic ones. A company drawing on its Eurodollar credit in London could settle an invoice in Chicago the same afternoon; correspondent networks reconciled the ledger entries overnight. No prudential firewall separated the two domains. The Bank of England, Bundesbank and Banque de France therefore discovered that a tightening of domestic money conditions merely pushed borrowers to offshore desks, while an easing delivered surplus reserves that leaked straight back into Euro-markets in search of higher spreads. Monetary sovereignty, a cornerstone of the Bretton Woods vision, became porous.

The Federal Reserve, for its part, monitored the boom with a mixture of curiosity and complacency. So long as Eurobanks recycled their surplus into U.S. Treasury bills the arrangement financed America's external deficit on attractive terms. The gold cover ratio continued to erode, but each foreign-held bill was politically less alarming than a formal call on Fort Knox. Robert Triffin's warning acquired a new dimension: the dilemma was no longer merely that global liquidity needs might outstrip U.S. gold; it was that the world had discovered how to manufacture its own synthetic dollars, effectively outsourcing seigniorage while leaving ultimate lender-of-last-resort duties in Washington.

With the collapse of the London Gold Pool and the two-tier gold market in 1968, Eurodollar dealers gained an additional role as the transmission channel for speculative shifts between official and free bullion prices. Banks sold forward contracts in offshore dollars, hedged exposures through New York futures, and in doing so knitted onshore and offshore funding desks into a single, time-critical web. The creation of LIBOR in 1969 codified the link: a daily fixing of London interbank rates became the benchmark for syndicated loans, floating-rate notes, and—decades later—the notional reference for quadrillions in swaps. Every extra knot tied the world's financing costs more tightly to overnight sentiment in a market the Federal Reserve did not supervise but would inevitably have to rescue if sentiment broke.

By the time President Nixon suspended gold convertibility in August 1971, the Eurodollar system was too entrenched to unwind. The fixed-rate architecture had lost its lynchpin, yet the multiplier effect offshore ensured that dollar liquidity remained abundant, even excessive. Freed from the discipline of gold redemption, U.S. fiscal-monetary policy could now indulge deeper deficits without immediate funding stress because London, Luxembourg and Nassau desks stood ready to absorb the paper. What ended was the formal promise of conversion; what began in its stead was an era of dollar dominance rooted not in a metallic peg but in the private credit machinery that the Eurodollar market had pioneered.

The escape valve thus became the engine. Offshore dollars financed petro-recycling after the 1973 oil shock, underwrote the Latin-American debt boom, and eventually morphed into the repo-driven shadow banking complexes that would transmit the subprime crisis four decades later. Each evolutionary turn preserved the core feature first revealed in the 1960s: the world could mint claims on Federal Reserve money faster than the Fed itself expanded its balance sheet, yet when those claims threatened to unravel the only balance sheet large and credible enough to halt contagion was, once again, the Fed's. The Eurodollar experiment had solved the short-term need for more liquidity; it also laid the foundation for the single-point-of-failure dilemma that frames this book.

Chapter 2: The Nixon Shock and the Petrodollar Accord

This chapter opens on Sunday evening, 15 August 1971, when President Richard Nixon interrupted prime-time television to announce that the United States would "temporarily" suspend the dollar's convertibility into gold. The speech lasted eighteen minutes, but it rewrote the operating code of the international monetary system in less time than it took most viewers to digest the televised baseball scores that followed. Within hours every central bank governor from Frankfurt to Tokyo realized that the core legal promise underpinning Bretton Woods—the right to exchange accumulated dollars for bullion at thirty-five dollars an ounce—had vanished by unilateral decree. In Washington the decision was framed as a defensive maneuver against "speculators." In reality it was the culmination of a decade-long contradiction: the United States could no longer honor both its domestic policy priorities and its external gold commitment, and domestic priorities—full employment, Vietnam War finance, the politics of wage–price controls—prevailed without contest.

The immediate market response was confusion rather than collapse. Foreign-exchange desks closed, reopened under a Smithsonian patch that widened parities, and soon discovered that speculative pressure simply re-emerged at the new bands. Without the mechanical anchor of gold redemption, confidence in fixed rates became a wager on Washington's policy discipline, and the wager faltered each month that the Federal Reserve monetized larger fiscal deficits. Exchange-rate realignments cascaded through 1972 and early 1973 until, by March, the world's major currencies had floated de facto if not yet de jure. The dollar's legal supremacy survived, but its price now moved with the political weather—an unsettling prospect for countries that still invoiced most of their trade in greenbacks.

Just as the monetary order began to drift, another rupture struck the real economy. In October 1973 Egypt and Syria launched the Yom Kippur War against Israel; the United States rushed military aid to Tel Aviv, and Arab members of the Organization of the Petroleum Exporting Countries responded with an embargo on oil shipments to America and its allies. Crude prices quadrupled within months, flipping the global balance of payments on its head. Overnight, petroleums exporters accumulated surpluses measured in tens of billions of dollars—surpluses they needed to park somewhere liquid, safe, and denominated in a currency accepted by pipeline contractors from Houston, shipbuilders in Yokohama, and arms merchants in London. The Nixon administration, sensing both peril and opportunity, dispatched Treasury Under-Secretary William Simon and National Security Adviser Henry Kissinger to engineer a solution with the Kingdom of Saudi Arabia, the only producer large enough to stabilize supply and the only monarchy sufficiently dependent on U.S. security guarantees to accept the bargain offered.

The accord that emerged in 1974 was deliberately unstated yet meticulously executed. Riyadh agreed to price all future oil sales exclusively in U.S. dollars and to invest the resulting surpluses in U.S. Treasury securities and New York money-market instruments. In return Washington promised advanced weapons, military training, and an explicit commitment to defend the kingdom against external threats. Legally, nothing prevented Saudi Arabia from diversifying into Deutsche Marks or Swiss francs; strategically, the arrangement locked oil flows and financial recycling into a dollar loop that no rival currency could match for depth or convenience. Within five years the phrase "petrodollar recycling" had entered Wall Street vernacular: Gulf surpluses arrived in Manhattan each morning, passed through

Eurodollar desks in London by afternoon, and re-emerged as syndicated loans to Latin-American and African borrowers by evening. The dollars that had once rested on a gold foundation now rested on an energy foundation, underwritten not by metallurgical scarcity but by America's naval presence in the Persian Gulf.

This shift solved one problem and created several others. It guaranteed an enduring external bid for U.S. Treasury debt, allowing Washington to finance deficits on terms unavailable to any other sovereign. It entrenched the dollar as the medium for virtually every barrel of crude traded on the seaborne market, which in turn compelled every energy-importing nation to accumulate dollar reserves as a matter of national security. At the same time it exported U.S. monetary policy to the entire oil-consuming world: when Federal Reserve Chairman Paul Volcker lifted interest rates in 1980 to crush domestic inflation, the cost of servicing petrodollar loans to Mexico and Brazil escalated catastrophically, seeding the Latin-American debt crisis that would dominate the decade.

More subtly, the accord reinforced the geopolitical dimension of dollar hegemony. To guarantee uninterrupted oil pricing in dollars, successive U.S. administrations extended military protection not only to Saudi Arabia but to smaller Gulf monarchies whose shipping lanes and pipeline infrastructures were strategically indispensable. The dollar, once justified as a neutral medium for post-war reconstruction, now derived part of its acceptability from a security architecture policed by American aircraft carriers and missile batteries. Monetary privilege and martial commitment fused: global commerce paid seigniorage to the United States, and the United States promised, in effect, to patrol the sea-lanes that made that commerce possible.

The Nixon Shock and the Petrodollar Accord therefore completed the transition from a gold-anchored fixed-rate regime to a credit-driven, energy-anchored dollar order. Where Bretton Woods had relied on tangible collateral, the new system relied on network momentum and geopolitical enforcement. Dollars circulated not because they were redeemable but because they were indispensable—for oil, for debt service, for Eurodollar interbank settlements that cleared trillions before most Americans finished breakfast. This transformation set the parameters for every subsequent episode in modern financial history, from Latin America's lost decade to the Asian crisis, from the rise of sovereign-wealth funds to the machinery of targeted sanctions. The architecture was flexible enough to survive gold's demise and volatile oil shocks, yet its flexibility masked a new fragility: the entire edifice now depended on the continuous recycling of petro-surpluses through U.S. capital markets and the implicit pledge of American power to keep the Strait of Hormuz open. In seeking freedom from the gold constraint, the United States had traded one anchor for another—less visible, more political, and ultimately just as binding on the future path of the world economy.

2.1 Closing the Gold Window, Opening Global Demand for T-bills

THE DECISION TO SUSPEND gold convertibility on 15 August 1971 severed the last mechanical tether between the dollar and any finite reserve asset, but its most immediate systemic effect was to reroute global savings into the only liquid, credit-risk-free substitute the market recognized: short-dated U.S. Treasury securities. In the Bretton Woods era central banks that wished to trim dollar exposure could do so anonymously by exchanging greenbacks for bullion at the New York assay office. Once that window slammed shut, the choice narrowed to holding dollars outright—subject to depreciation risk—or recycling them into Treasury bills, which at least paid interest and carried the implicit backing of the American polity. Within six months the foreign official share of outstanding T-bills doubled; by 1974 overseas institutions owned more than a third of the entire market, a proportion that would climb higher still once petrodollar surpluses began to flood in after the OPEC price shock.

This surge in demand was driven by several feedback loops. First, the Smithsonian realignment of December 1971 devalued the dollar by a modest 8 per cent, convincing reserve managers that further moves were likely and that only the Treasury market offered both depth and a near-term exit. Second, the Federal Reserve, eager to restore credibility while avoiding a domestic credit crunch, allowed short-term rates to rise above the ceilings still capping retail bank deposits under Regulation Q. Eurodollar branches, not subject to that ceiling, bid aggressively for funds; U.S. primary dealers in turn financed growing inventories of T-bills through those same Eurodollar deposits. A triangular arbitrage emerged: offshore banks borrowed dollars at LIBOR, lent them overnight in the New York repo market against Treasury collateral, and pocketed the spread—an innovation that multiplied the demand for bills as collateral, not merely as reserve assets.

For the Treasury, foreign uptake solved a looming fiscal headache. Vietnam expenditures and Great Society programs had pushed the federal deficit toward unheard-of post-war levels. Prior to 1971 the Treasury had relied on captive domestic demand—banks, life insurers, and savings institutions restricted by regulation to a diet of government paper. The arrival of foreign central banks and, soon after, OPEC-linked sovereign-wealth entities transformed the demand curve. Auction methodology shifted from predominantly fixed-price offerings to competitive tenders, lowering average funding costs even as nominal issuance accelerated. In effect, closing the gold window replaced one form of seigniorage—redeemable dollars backed by bullion—with another: an elastic supply of Treasury IOUs purchased by counterparties that had scant alternative for deploying their surpluses at comparable scale or safety.

The change reverberated beyond official reserves. Corporate treasurers, wary of exchange-rate volatility, adopted the T-bill as the canonical parking spot for working capital. Newly invented money-market mutual funds, beginning with the Reserve Fund in 1971, channelled household savings into the same instruments, bypassing Regulation Q restrictions and deepening the secondary market. Dealers needed balance-sheet space to warehouse the flow; the tri-party repo market, formalised in the mid-1970s, provided the leverage, using bills and notes as the universal pledge. By decade's end the bill had become not merely a funding tool for Washington but the base-layer collateral for a modern wholesale money system that spanned Tokyo, Zurich, and the Cayman Islands.

None of this was foreordained. In principle surplus nations could have diversified into Deutsche-Mark bills or gilt-edged securities, but neither the Bundesbank nor the Bank of England was willing to expand supply sufficiently to absorb oil-financed inflows. Moreover, only the United States offered the full package—deep issuance calendars, a vast and liquid secondary market, and a monetary authority prepared, when crisis hit, to lend freely against its own sovereign paper. The result was a path-dependent lock-in: every new tranche of foreign-held dollars reinforced the liquidity of the Treasury curve, and that superior liquidity, in turn, attracted the next tranche of foreign capital.

By the time the petrodollar accord with Saudi Arabia crystallized in 1974, the machinery was humming. Gulf producers deposited their windfalls in New York correspondent accounts; U.S. banks recycled a portion through London euro-branches as syndicated loans to energy-hungry emerging markets; but a growing share was simply parked at weekly bill auctions, giving the federal government a captive foreign bid that cushioned domestic borrowing costs even as inflation neared double digits. The inversion of Bretton Woods was complete: where once gold had backed the dollar and dollars backed world trade, now Treasury bills backed both, serving as the ultimate settlement asset for central banks and as the bedrock collateral for private-sector leverage.

This new equilibrium was stable so long as two assumptions held: that the U.S. Congress would never jeopardize the full faith and credit of its obligations, and that the Federal Reserve possessed both the means and the political autonomy to liquefy the system in extremis. Future chapters will show how often those assumptions have been tested—and how global reliance on the bill market turned what had seemed like a technical funding arrangement into the second pillar of the dollar trap. For the moment, it is enough to see how a single Sunday night announcement, justified as a temporary defense against speculators, redirected the torrent of international savings into a narrow trench of short-term Washington debt. Gold convertibility died in 1971; the world's appetite for the Treasury brand of paper money was born the next morning and has not waned since.

2.2 Saudi Oil, OPEC Pricing, and Compulsory Dollar Recycling

WHEN OPEC'S OIL MINISTERS convened in Kuwait City on 22 December 1973, the geopolitical drama of the Yom Kippur War had already quadrupled crude prices. What remained to settle was the currency of account for that new windfall. Some members floated basket pricing or even payment in gold; the Iranians hinted at accepting yen. Yet by the close of negotiations the cartel affirmed what American envoys had worked feverishly to secure: every barrel would continue to be invoiced exclusively in U.S. dollars. From that day forward, any nation that wished to keep the lights on had first to obtain greenbacks, and the only place to obtain them at scale was through the very financial markets Washington underwrote.

The diplomatic architecture behind that decision took shape in a series of discreet meetings between Treasury Under-Secretary William Simon, National Security Adviser Henry Kissinger, and Saudi Crown Prince (later King) Fahd. The bargain was elegant in its simplicity. Riyadh would (1) maintain dollar-denominated pricing for all Saudi crude sold worldwide, (2) invest the bulk of its surpluses in U.S. Treasury securities or New York money-market instruments, and (3) coordinate production policy to avoid destabilizing spikes or collapses inimical to American interests. In return the United States would (1) provide advanced weaponry and formalize a security umbrella for the Kingdom, (2) facilitate preferential access to American capital goods and technology, and (3) treat Saudi Arabia as OPEC's "central banker," consulted on any strategic stockpile or international energy initiative. No treaty was ever signed, yet Treasury documents from 1974 show non-marketable "special issue" bills purchased directly by the Saudi Arabian Monetary Agency—an arrangement so sensitive it was initially withheld from the public auction calendar.

The financial implications were immediate. OPEC export earnings jumped from roughly $23 billion in 1972 to $140 billion in 1978, with Saudi Arabia alone capturing close to forty per cent. Because every dollar Riyadh received went back into U.S. assets or dollar-clearing Eurodollar deposits, the oil shock that threatened to bankrupt importers simultaneously underwrote Washington's deficits. Indeed, the Treasury discovered that the larger the current-account hole created by higher oil prices, the larger the capital inflow that returned via Saudi and Kuwaiti investment channels. The petrodollar loop thus transformed a raw-material cartel into an involuntary financier of U.S. fiscal policy.

Commercial banks were the next link in the chain. Citibank, Chase, and British lenders such as Midland and Barclays opened dedicated "sovereign advisory" desks to court Gulf deposits. They booked the funds overnight in London, paid a basis-point sweetener over Treasury yields, and scrambled to relend the money—often by arranging syndicated loans for energy-poor, commodity-rich governments in Latin America and Africa. The term "petrodollar recycling," coined by Congressman Henry Reuss, captured the circular motion: dollars flowed from consumers to producers, then from producers to New York and London, and finally back to consumers in the form of hard-currency loans that imported inflation and exchange-rate risk to the developing world. What looked like liquidity relief in 1975 morphed into debt service nightmares by 1982, when Volcker's anti-inflationary rate hikes pushed LIBOR into the high teens.

At the centre of the loop sat a simple operational fact: oil was priced in a currency the producers themselves could not spend domestically. Saudi budget outlays were riyal-denominated; new petrochemical complexes in Jubail and Yanbu paid contractors in dollars, true, but wages, subsidies, and social programmes required local currency. Converting export proceeds into riyals meant selling dollars back to the Saudi monetary authority, which in turn had to park the dollars somewhere. Given limited appetite for European sovereign paper and unresolved questions about Deutschmark liquidity in crisis, the safest option remained the T-bill. Thus compulsory recycling was less a policy choice than a balance-sheet necessity encoded in the pricing decision.

The international ramifications were profound. To pay for oil, importers needed dollar reserves; to obtain reserves, they either exported surpluses to the United States or borrowed in Eurodollar markets. Japan ran structural trade surpluses in consumer electronics; Brazil borrowed against future iron-ore exports; both channels enlarged the external claim on U.S. monetary policy. When the Federal

Reserve tightened, energy importers felt the squeeze twice—once through higher financing costs, again through softer global demand for their exports. Saudi oil revenues therefore acted as a transmission belt for American interest-rate decisions, magnifying the dollar's reach far beyond what gold convertibility had ever achieved.

Security considerations cemented the arrangement. By the early 1980s Saudi Arabia had become the largest purchaser of U.S. military hardware, a de facto linkage of petro-surplus recycling to the American defense-industrial base. Washington, in turn, expanded its naval presence in the Persian Gulf, ensuring that the physical flow underpinning the financial loop could not be disrupted without confronting U.S. forces. Dollar dominance was no longer anchored merely in a financial promise; it was patrolled by carrier strike groups and AWACS squadrons flying over desert airspace.

None of the OPEC members were legally forbidden to diversify, but inertia and network effects proved overwhelming. Attempts by Iran and Venezuela to invoice limited cargoes in yen or Deutsche marks faltered as buyers balked at the basis-swap costs and liquidity gaps in non-dollar forward markets. Even after the petrodollar windfall exposed them to U.S. sanctions leverage, producers discovered that shifting the pricing unit would require not only a new benchmark contract but also a wholesale retooling of trade credit, shipping insurance, and derivatives hedging—each of which depended on dollar-settled margins. The system's architecture made exit theoretically simple and practically impossible.

Compulsory dollar recycling thus locked two resource flows—oil and capital—into a self-reinforcing circuit whose choke point remained the New York clearinghouse. Every geopolitical shock that rattled the Gulf thereafter—whether the Iranian Revolution, the Tanker Wars, or Saddam Hussein's invasion of Kuwait—threatened not just energy supply but the stability of global money markets, because any interruption forced producers to draw down dollar deposits while importers scrambled for emergency funding. What had begun as an expedient to stabilize prices after the gold window's collapse matured into the second structural pillar of the dollar trap: a commodity-backed liquidity machine run on American rules, defended by American arms, and indispensable to every economy that burned hydrocarbons to generate growth.

2.3 Wall Street's Swift Capture of the New Liquidity Torrent

SAUDI PETRODOLLARS did not drift passively into the United States; they were intercepted, packaged, and re-exported by New York banks that sensed in the gush of oil revenue the makings of an entirely new business model. Until the early 1970s the big money-center institutions—Citibank, Chase Manhattan, Bankers Trust—had lived mainly on corporate cash management and the conservative spread between insured deposits and prime loans. Regulation Q ceilings suppressed the rate they could pay to households, and Glass-Steagall kept them clear of the capital markets. The quadrupling of oil prices rewrote every line of that script. Tens of billions of dollars arrived each quarter in correspondent accounts; the sums dwarfed domestic deposit growth and, crucially, bore no regulatory cost. Offshore branches could credit them at a whisker below T-bill yields, free of reserve requirements. The question was how to redeploy the torrent at a margin fat enough to please shareholders without triggering domestic supervisors. Wall Street's answer was syndication.

Syndicated Eurodollar loans had existed in embryonic form since the late 1960s, but after 1974 they exploded. The key insight was that one bank alone could not—or would not—place an OPEC deposit wholesale with a single Latin-American sovereign or state utility.

Assemble a consortium of twenty lead managers, however, and a $500 million credit facility became routine. Citibank pioneered the "rolling club" format: the borrower paid a front-end fee of one-and-an-eighth percent, interest reset every six months at LIBOR plus two hundred basis points, and the paper traded informally in secondary grey markets that sprang up along the Dealing Room corridor of Midtown. The arrangement delivered a triple benefit for New York: deposits stayed onshore just long enough to be transformed into fee income, the credit risk migrated to a geographically diverse pool of banks hungry for higher margins, and every rollover reaffirmed the dollar benchmark because borrowers had no realistic alternative currency in which to refinance.

The torrent reshaped the mechanics of funding as well. The traditional Federal Funds market, once a sleepy overnight venue for reserve adjustments among domestic banks, became a throat for channeling petrodollar balances back to the Treasury market via repurchase agreements. Bankers Trust and Salomon Brothers refined "matched book" repo operations: they borrowed overnight from OPEC-linked foreign branches, lent term to U.S. securities dealers against Treasuries, and pocketed the spread. By 1978 aggregate repo balances exceeded $80 billion, a fivefold increase in four years, and the instrument's evolution from collateralized loan to de facto money accelerated. Each night's close left trillions in claim tickets all referencing the same collateral set—short-dated U.S. government paper—quietly reinforcing the habit of treating Treasuries as the only universal pledge.

Wall Street also captured the torrent through innovation at the margin of legality. Bankers Trust devised the first stand-alone interest-rate swap in 1981 between IBM and the World Bank, but the intellectual seed lay in the floating-rate Eurodollar loans of the previous decade. Traders realised they could strip the LIBOR component from syndicated debt and trade the residual risk—effectively sculpting bespoke cash-flow exchanges that required almost no initial capital. Notional volumes jumped twentyfold in the decade; every swap booked against LIBOR created embedded demand for bank term funding in the same benchmark, indirectly deepening the Eurodollar curve that petrodollars had already saturated.

The cultural shift inside the banks was equally swift. Treasury operations, once back-office cost centres, became "balance-sheet management" units tasked with arbitraging global rate differentials minute by minute. Careers were made by traders who could juggle Riyadh time-zone inflows against São Paulo drawdowns and park the remainder in Frankfurt repos before New York's close. The revolving door between trading floors and policy circles began to spin: alumni drafted into Treasury or the Federal Reserve brought with them a worldview in which global liquidity management and U.S. national interest were indistinguishable.

Yet every triumph etched a deeper groove of fragility. Syndicated loans were rarely provisioned for sudden hikes in LIBOR; when Volcker's disinflation drive sent the rate above eighteen percent in 1980, much of Latin America's annual export income evaporated in debt service. Repos assumed that Treasury collateral would remain zero-risk and infinitely rehypothecable; the 1979 failure of Drysdale Government Securities exposed how a single mis-marked position could detonate daylight-overdraft exposures at half a dozen clearing banks. And swaps, while capital-light, embedded counterparty chains that regulators barely mapped until the Long-Term Capital Management rescue thirteen years later. Wall Street's capture of the torrent thus locked the world into a structure where dollar liquidity was abundant in fair seas, yet prone to tsunami-like withdrawal when confidence wavered—because the same handful of institutions acted as deposit-takers, market-makers, and last-mile correspondents.

By the close of the 1970s the petrodollar surge had sculpted a landscape no planner at Bretton Woods could have imagined: OPEC surpluses recycled through Manhattan shaped the cost of capital in Mexico City; Eurodollar LIBOR fixings in London governed mortgage resets in Kuala Lumpur; repo desks on Liberty Street set the overnight rate that would guide Federal Reserve policy deliberations in Washington. Wall Street had alchemised a geopolitical shock into an enduring franchise, proving that in the dollar era the fastest banks did not merely ride global liquidity—they wrote its routing instructions. The consequences, benign and malign, would reverberate through every subsequent crisis examined in the chapters ahead.

Chapter 3: Deregulation and the Age of Financial Engineering

The oil windfall that cascaded through New York in the mid-seventies did more than fatten balance sheets: it exposed the increasingly awkward fit between Depression-era banking statutes and a marketplace that now spun trillions through Eurodollar cables before Congress had settled breakfast. By 1978 every money-center treasurer knew where the statutory bottlenecks lay—reserve requirements, deposit-rate caps, geographic branching limits—and each constraint invited a work-around that blurred the boundary between ordinary intermediation and outright alchemy. Policymakers faced a stark choice: either police an expanding archipelago of offshore and shadow maneuvers or rewrite domestic rules to let Wall Street compete on equal terms. They chose the latter, and in doing so opened a decade in which regulation retreated faster than technology advanced, leaving creativity to flourish in the interstices.

The first breach came with the Depository Institutions Deregulation and Monetary Control Act of 1980, a title as prosaic as its consequences were volcanic. Phased abolition of Regulation Q ceilings unleashed a scramble for yield that money-market mutual funds had already begun to exploit; thrifts, stripped of their captive deposit base, reached for higher-yield assets that regulators neither fully understood nor, after Garn-St Germain in 1982, could easily curb. At the same moment the Federal Reserve's switch to reserve-quantity targeting sent short-term rates soaring into the high teens, a level at which interest-rate futures—traded only since 1975 on the Chicago Board of Trade—became a lifeline rather than a curiosity. Traders discovered that what could be hedged could just as easily be leveraged; the boundary between insurance and speculation dissolved in a matter of weeks.

Innovation followed deregulation like heat lightning along a desert ridge. Salomon Brothers and Bank of America stitched together the first pass-through mortgage-backed security in 1977; by 1983 Fannie Mae was guaranteeing collateralized mortgage obligations with ten tranches, each tuned to a different duration and prepayment profile. Michael Milken's high-yield syndicate at Drexel rewrote the risk calculus of corporate finance, proving that junk bonds could pry open hostile-takeover gates that stodgy bank credit committees would never breach. Across the Atlantic, London prepared for its "Big Bang" abolition of fixed commissions; Wall Street houses crossed the ocean, scooped up member firms, and married American market-making technology to the City's time zone, knitting a seamless twenty-four-hour trading day for the dollar.

Derivatives provided the connective tissue. Bankers Trust's bilateral interest-rate swap between IBM and the World Bank in 1981 showed how mismatched funding needs could be netted through a single off-balance-sheet contract. Within five years notional swap volume exceeded the stock of U.S. Treasury debt; dealers passed risk around the globe like a compressed-air baton, confident that netting agreements and collateral calls would hold the chain together. Options on stock-index futures, program trading, and portfolio insurance turned capital markets into laboratories where algorithms, not portfolio managers, set the closing price. Each layer of complexity rested on the same assumption that had validated petrodollar recycling: so long as dollar liquidity was infinite and market makers stood ready at every tick, position unwinds could always be financed.

Basel I, signed in 1988, was meant to tighten the rails, yet it, too, embedded a bias toward engineered leverage. Risk-weighted capital encouraged banks to securitize mortgages, insure corporate loans with freshly minted credit-default swaps, and warehouse the residual slivers in Cayman conduits that never met a Basel examiner. Off-shore branches wrote stand-by letters of credit that converted yen or deutsche-mark funding into synthetic dollars, locking foreign banks into the benchmark they had hoped to escape. By the decade's close a money-market investor in Tokyo, a pension fund in Amsterdam, and a thrifts officer in Kansas City all priced risk off the same three-month LIBOR curve—a globalized chassis welded together by deregulation and wired to a single American power source.

Financial engineering delivered lower spreads, deeper markets, and the seductive belief that risk could be sliced thin enough to disappear. It also cemented the architecture whose fault lines this book will trace through subsequent crises. The Eurodollar torrent had shown that liquidity begets dominance; deregulation proved that dominance invites leverage; financial engineering ensured that leverage would migrate to precisely those corners of the map where macro-prudential flood-walls could not reach. What began as a pragmatic quest to modernize New Deal statutes ended by giving Wall Street the tools to manufacture capital in forms no nineteenth-century banker—or 1940s Bretton Woods delegate—could have imagined, all denominated in a currency whose stability was now inseparable from the perpetual motion of its own synthetic progeny.

3.1 Volcker, LIBOR, and the Deepening of Swap Markets

PAUL VOLCKER'S APPOINTMENT as Federal Reserve chairman in August 1979 coincided with a moment of existential doubt for the dollar order. Consumer-price inflation was racing toward fourteen percent, gold had pierced six-hundred dollars an ounce, and OPEC's second price shock was feeding an anxious narrative that the United

States had lost not only fiscal grip but monetary credibility. Volcker's response—the 6 October "Saturday-night revolution" that shifted policy from targeting the federal-funds rate to controlling the supply of non-borrowed reserves—detonated interest-rate volatility unlike anything in the post-war era. The funds rate, which had averaged ten percent, lurched to twenty-plus within months, then fell back below ten, then spiked again. The violence of those swings reshaped every balance-sheet decision from Des Moines to Düsseldorf, and in the process elevated an obscure London benchmark—three-month Eurodollar LIBOR—into the nerve signal of world credit.

Domestic banks caught in Regulation Q's final convulsions could not pay enough on retail deposits to match money-fund yields, so they tapped the Eurodollar market by issuing negotiable CDs through Cayman or Nassau affiliates. The cost reset every quarter at LIBOR plus a spread; suddenly a rate set each morning by a handful of London banks determined the marginal funding cost of institutions chartered in Ohio and Texas. Corporations confronted a mirror image: floating-rate bank loans priced off LIBOR reduced the sticker shock of Volcker-era coupon levels, but they transferred all future rate risk to borrowers who manufactured cars or refined oil, not arbitrage interest curves. The demand for a hedge was obvious; the supply required only a dealer willing to intermediate.

Bankers Trust supplied the template in August 1981 when it arranged the now-legendary swap between IBM and the World Bank. The logic was textbook: IBM could issue fixed-rate debt more cheaply than floating, the World Bank the reverse. By exchanging cash-flows—the Bank paying IBM's fixed coupon, IBM paying the Bank's LIBOR floaters—both parties trimmed overall financing cost without issuing new securities. What looked like a bilateral accommodation hid a scalable revelation: any two balance sheets with complementary comparative advantage could swap risks through an off-balance-sheet contract whose only capital consumption was the dealers' mark-to-market buffer. As Volcker kept monetary screws tight, more corporates lined up—first Texaco and ARCO, then Swissair and Toyota—while supranationals such as the European Investment Bank used currency swaps to match dollar funding with local-currency lending programs.

Every trade enlarged the reference universe for LIBOR. In the late 1970s daily fixing drew on fewer than a dozen quotes and served mainly interbank CDs. By 1983 it underpinned floating-rate notes, mortgage pass-throughs, adjustable-rate preferred stock, and the fledgling market for interest-rate caps and floors. Dealers needed a common discount curve to price ever-longer maturities; London Clearing Banks developed forward-rate agreements, Chicago pits listed Eurodollar futures, and arbitrage knit the futures strip to the cash curve within a basis-point. From Tokyo to Toronto, treasurers discovered they could synthetically transform fixed into floating or dollars into Deutschmark merely by phoning a swap desk and signing an ISDA master once the association was founded in 1985. The overlay economy—contracts not recorded as debt yet altering its economic substance—grew at geometric pace: notional outstanding interest-rate swaps rose from zero in 1980 to nearly $900 billion by 1987, dwarfing the underlying government-bond markets of most advanced economies.

Volcker's policy regime was thus paradoxical. By attacking inflation he restored faith in the dollar; by inducing wild rate gyrations he created the very volatility that made hedging indispensable and swap spreads lucrative. U.S. banks, newly freed from Glass-Steagall revenue caps by the Office of the Comptroller's "Section 20" reinterpretations, built global swap books that meshed naturally with their roles as custodians of petro and export-surplus deposits. European and Japanese rivals followed—Barclays, NatWest, Deutsche, Fuji—each booking trades through London branches to bypass domestic restrictions, tying yet another slice of world finance to a single benchmark quoted at 11 a.m. local time on Bishopsgate.

What began as a defensive maneuver against inflation therefore deepened the private-credit superstructure atop the dollar core. LIBOR ceased to be a mere price; it became the metronome to which floating-rate capitalism kept time. Swaps, futures, and options stitched national money markets into one continuous term structure, so that a tremor in Fed policy transmitted, via arbitrage, to mortgage coupons in Madrid and railway bonds in Melbourne before local central banks convened breakfast meetings. Volcker conquered the inflation dragon, but in doing so he confirmed a deeper transformation: the dollar system could now manufacture its own volatility hedges in quantities no central bank could match, and the benchmark that made those hedges possible did not reside in Washington at all but in a daily whisper network on a London trading floor. From that point forward the global cost of money would be set as much by the private algorithms of swap desks as by the deliberations of any monetary committee, binding the fate of sovereigns, corporates, and households ever tighter to the evolving plumbing of financial engineering.

3.2 Securitization, Derivatives, and the Spread of Dollar Balance-sheet Logic

THE EARLY 1980S PROVED that a single benchmark—LIBOR—could knit disparate funding markets into one elastic, dollar-denominated term structure. The next step was to manufacture assets tailored to that structure, instruments whose cash-flow geometry matched the needs of global investors but whose underlying risk was sourced from the humblest corners of the American household balance sheet. Securitization delivered exactly that. Freddie Mac's first participation certificate in 1971 had shown how fixed-rate mortgage payments could be pooled and passed through to investors; by 1983 Salomon Brothers and First Boston had refined the model into the collateralized mortgage obligation, carving a single mortgage pool into tranches that appealed to Japanese life insurers hungry for duration, to Swiss banks craving short average lives, and to leveraged bond funds chasing the exotic "inverse-floaters" whose coupons rose when LIBOR fell. Every slice referenced dollar cash-flows, every remittance cleared through U.S. servicers, and every bond was, in effect, a portable slice of the American suburb sold on the Luxembourg Eurobond market.

Derivatives amplified the reach. A German bank purchasing the senior tranche of a Ginnie Mae structure could strip prepayment risk with a swaption, convert the dollar coupon into marks through a currency swap, and finance the position in the repo market against U.S. Treasury collateral—all without booking a single asset on the German on-balance-sheet loan register. The engineering propagated a distinct balance-sheet logic: fund short at floating LIBOR; hold long, tranched assets whose convexity could be managed with options; neutralize currency exposure via swaps; and mark the entire structure to market daily. By decade's end the same toolkit was applied to auto loans, credit-card receivables, aircraft leases, and—infamously—to the leveraged loan strips that would form the raw material for collateralized debt obligations a generation later. The more heterogeneous the collateral, the more the alchemy relied on dollar-denominated tranching, ratings arbitrage, and swap overlays to render the bonds palatable to Basel capital calculations.

Basel I, finalized in 1988, inadvertently turbo-charged the process. Because senior AAA-rated securities attracted a mere twenty per cent risk weight, U.S. banks discovered they could originate mortgages at eighty-five cents equity per hundred dollars of face value, securitize them, retain the servicing strip, and free capital for the next cycle of origination. European and Asian institutions, keen to earn a spread over sovereign bonds without sacrificing regulatory capital, became eager buyers. Dollar collateral thus migrated abroad in securitized form, while foreign savings migrated to Wall Street in repo or swap form, completing a feedback loop in which American credit creation and foreign reserve accumulation became two sides of the same trade.

Credit-default swaps sealed the architecture. J.P. Morgan's Broad Index Secured Trust Offering (BISTRO) in 1997—the prototype synthetic CDO—demonstrated that one could replicate exposure to a diversified loan book without funding the loans. A Cayman vehicle sold super-senior protection on a defined portfolio of corporate names; investors posted dollar collateral, received LIBOR plus a premium, and bore only the tail loss once defaults breached a high attachment point. The trade alchemized illiquid commercial-bank credit into marketable dollar securities that asset managers in London, Zurich, and Hong Kong could finance overnight in repo, re-pledging the same Treasuries that underlay the mortgage machine. What began as risk transfer morphed into risk multiplication: each synthetic vehicle referenced the same underlying corporate obligations, yet regulators counted the super-senior exposure at negligible capital weight, mistaking correlation for diversification.

By the early 2000s the logic had spread far beyond U.S. shores. Korean savings banks held triple-A tranches of Nevada subprime pools; Norwegian municipalities bought leveraged super-senior positions on Icelandic banks; German Landesbanken warehoused conduits funded with three-month asset-backed commercial paper secured by Florida mortgage liens. Every structure spoke the same language—dollar collateral, LIBOR funding, swap overlays—and every structure relied on two clearing channels: the American repo market for daily liquidity and the dollar swap market for term transformation. The spread of securitization thus did not merely internationalize American credit risk; it imposed an operating system in which banks, insurers, and money-market funds everywhere managed assets and liabilities according to dollar-centric conventions, even when their ultimate stakeholders spoke euros, yen, or kronor.

Critics often reduce this era to a morality tale of greedy bankers and inattentive supervisors, but the deeper point is architectural. Securitization and derivatives allowed risk to be priced, sliced, and sold across jurisdictions at the speed of a Bloomberg keystroke, yet the settlement of cash and collateral still funneled through the same Manhattan bottleneck—Fedwire, CHIPS, CLS. Dollars created by Florida borrowers were recycled through Frankfurt conduits and Japanese life insurers before returning as repo funding for New York broker-dealers, all in the space of twenty-four hours. The balance-sheet logic of the dollar had become a planetary standard: mark-to-market; margin daily; fund overnight; hedge with swaps whose benchmark is set in London but collateralized in the United States. Efficiency reached its zenith, and with it fragility: a margin call in the repo market or a basis blow-out in swaps now reverberated through tranches held on five continents, forcing synchronized deleveraging that no national central bank—save one—was equipped to offset.

That singular backstop would be tested soon enough. For the moment, what matters is the asymmetry baked into the age of financial engineering: global savers embraced securitized dollar assets to pick up yield; global borrowers drew on dollar swaps to lower funding cost; global banks arbitraged capital rules by parking risk in dollar tranches. The privilege of issuing the reserve currency enabled the United States to finance both domestic consumption and Wall Street innovation on a scale unmatched in history. But privilege was indistinguishable from liability: the same plumbing that delivered limitless foreign demand for securitized paper would, under stress, demand limitless dollar liquidity in return. The balance-sheet logic the world had adopted came with an emergency instruction manual printed only at the Federal Reserve.

3.3 How Basel Rules Locked Non-US Banks into the Greenback

THE BASEL CAPITAL FRAMEWORK arrived with high-minded intent: harmonize prudential standards so a French, Japanese, or Canadian bank held roughly the same loss-absorbing cushion for equivalent risks. Yet the details of Basel I (1988) and its successors quietly entrenched the dollar at the centre of global balance-sheet management, because the rules treated **supply-rich dollar assets as "risk-free" collateral** while imposing steeper capital charges on most alternatives.

Basel I's headline innovation was the risk-weighted asset grid. A zero-per-cent weight applied to OECD sovereign bonds—meaning no capital against U.S. Treasuries, Bundesbonds, or JGBs—while a 20 per cent weight covered claims on OECD banks and triple-A securities, including the new generation of **agency-backed U.S. mortgage bonds**. The catch was availability and market depth: outside the United States few governments issued short-dated paper in volumes large enough to support repo, derivative-margin, and liquidity needs. Non-U.S. banks therefore bought Treasuries and Fannie/Freddie pass-throughs not for yield but for regulatory efficiency: every $100 million parked in those instruments required only $8 million of tier-one capital versus $100 million in corporate loans that consumed four times as much. The rulebook converted dollar assets into capital arbitrage fuel.

Funding followed collateral. A London subsidiary of a Dutch bank financing its Treasury hoard needed dollar liabilities. The cheapest source was the **Eurodollar wholesale market**, rolling three-month

CDs or overnight repos priced off LIBOR. Basel imposed no maturity-mismatch penalty; as long as the asset carried a zero weight, supervisors ignored liquidity risk. By the mid-1990s European and Japanese institutions were issuing **$500 billion in Eurodollar CDs every quarter**, a liability chain ultimately backstopped by the Federal Reserve's discount window even though the borrowers lay beyond U.S. jurisdiction.

Basel II (2004) deepened the tie. Its internal-ratings approach rewarded banks that could model granular credit risk—yet the easiest asset class to model statistically was the vast, transparent pool of U.S. consumer securitizations. Spanish and German banks filled conduits with dollar credit-card ABS and home-equity lines, funding them with asset-backed commercial paper that money-market funds would buy only if it cleared in dollars. Once again the greenback became the cheapest denominator for regulatory capital efficiency.

After 2008, Basel III's Liquidity Coverage Ratio was meant to curtail such loops, but its definition of **High-Quality Liquid Assets" placed" Level-1 U.S. Treasuries at the apex**: a zero-haircut, freely repo-able instrument available in trillions. Euro-area sovereigns under stress lost full Level-1 status, and sterling gilts were simply too scarce. Asian banks hunting for LCR buffers therefore stockpiled more Treasuries and financed them with **FX swaps—rolling tom/next into three-month tenors—creating structural demand for dollar funding at each quarter-end**. The notorious "cross-currency basis," which spikes whenever global stress tightens swap markets, is the direct artefact of that rule: non-U.S. institutions must bid aggressively for short-term dollars to maintain Basel-compliant liquidity books.

Even Basel's leverage ratio, introduced as a backstop to gaming, reinforced dollar dependence. Because the ratio treats all assets equally, banks favor the most repo-able collateral to minimize funding cost;

again U.S. paper dominates. The Federal Reserve's reverse-repo facility and tri-party market provide a standing bid that most other sovereigns cannot match.

In sum, what looked like neutral, multilateral prudence evolved into a **regulatory subsidy for holding and funding dollar assets**. Each new Basel layer intensified the pattern:

- *Risk weights* made Treasuries and agency MBS capital-light.
- *Internal models* steered banks toward data-rich U.S. securitizations.
- *Liquidity rules* canonized Treasuries as the universal buffer.
- *Leverage caps* pushed balance sheets toward the most liquid collateral—again dollar-denominated.

The loop is self-reinforcing. Foreign banks buy U.S. paper to satisfy Basel; they fund it in dollars via swaps and repo; that funding creates further demand for reliable short-term dollar instruments, enlarging the Treasury and commercial-paper curves; Basel committees observe the deep liquidity of those curves and enshrine them anew as risk-free benchmarks. By the late 2010s non-U.S. banks collectively held **more than $4 trillion in U.S. dollar assets**—a size so large that any disruption in Fed-supplied liquidity forces immediate deleveraging abroad long before strains surface in American deposit data.

Thus, the Basel accords, drafted to stabilize international banking, inadvertently welded the rest of the world's balance sheets to the greenback. Compliance demanded dollars; safety required Treasuries; funding chased LIBOR and, later, SOFR. When the dollar engine hums, the system purrs; when it stalls, every regulated institution from

Seoul to Stockholm feels the jolt, and only the Federal Reserve holds the jumper cables.

Part II – Plumbing the Dollar Machine

Chapter 4: Clearinghouses: Fedwire, CHIPS, and CLS

Every structure described so far—Eurodollar funding loops, securitized mortgage tranches, Basel-driven liquidity buffers—rests on one unglamorous layer of plumbing: the real-time ledgers that say when money has irrevocably changed hands. In the dollar world three systems dominate that function. Together they move more value before lunch than all the retail card networks settle in a year, yet they operate from a handful of data centers concentrated along the Hudson and a mirrored cluster of servers in suburban New Jersey. Their names rarely appear in headlines, but they are the mechanical heart of the single-point-of-failure problem.

Fedwire is the sovereign core, a real-time gross-settlement network run by the Federal Reserve Bank of New York. Every payment on Fedwire uses reserve balances; once transferred, it is final, uncontestable, and immune to daylight reversal. For large banks Fedwire is how reserve management and collateral substitution happen minute by minute: a Treasury bill moves from a tri-party repo custodian to the central bank, reserves flow in the opposite direction, and a new repo trade closes in seconds. Late each afternoon Fedwire settles margin calls from the futures exchanges and variation payments on cleared swaps, synchronizing the trading day's mark-to-market reality with legal finality before Asian markets wake. If Fedwire pauses, collateral cannot migrate, margin cannot be paid, and liquidity buffers everywhere freeze.

CHIPS—the Clearing House Interbank Payments System—sits one layer above. Unlike Fedwire it is private and nets payments multilaterally, compressing a typical US $1.5 trillion gross queue into perhaps US $300 billion of final settlement. That efficiency makes CHIPS the preferred route for correspondent banks handling corporate trade, syndicated-loan disbursements, and large FX trades whose dollar leg need not post instantly. Netting, however, introduces dependency: each member must prefund its daily position with Fedwire reserves, and queued payments release only when bilateral and multilateral conditions align. A credit or operational failure at one participant can slow the entire ring until collateral top-ups restore equilibrium. The system therefore substitutes lower liquidity cost for higher operational coupling—an attractive trade most days, a latent contagion channel on the worst day.

CLS (Continuous Linked Settlement) was created after the 1990s Herstatt and Barings scares to solve "time-zone risk" in foreign exchange. It settles both legs of a currency pair simultaneously—payment-versus-payment—across eighteen currencies. Yet the design still hinges on the dollar: the single greatest share of tickets are euro-dollar, yen-dollar, or sterling-dollar trades, and final multilateral pay-ins for every member bank occur in a two-hour window just after New York opens. If Fedwire hiccups during that window, CLS cannot complete its pay-in schedule; if CLS cannot complete, global FX desks face open positions they believed were flattened. A liquidity shock in São Paulo or Seoul thus resolves, in the final analysis, inside a Manhattan server farm where both legs must be stamped "settled" before the sun sets in Singapore.

These three rails interact constantly. A corporate bond issue might clear its dollar proceeds through CHIPS, use Fedwire to pledge Treasury collateral against an intraday bridge loan, and rely on CLS to swap a portion into euros for equipment purchases—all within an hour. Each hop assumes the previous hop's finality, creating a cascade that is invisible until a node stalls. And because every node's busiest window overlaps with New York's morning, a single-region power, telecom, or cyber outage threatens a payment grid on which global inventories, margin engines, and overnight funding rollovers all depend.

The clearinghouses are not unsophisticated; each runs hot-hot redundancy, dark-site back-ups, and layered cyber defenses. Yet resilience still bottlenecks at two choke points: the Federal Reserve's ability to provide emergency daylight liquidity, and the operational integrity of a handful of third-party service providers—data centers, telecom carriers, interface vendors—whose logos are unknown outside infrastructure circles. The world learned this in miniature on 24 February 2021 when a routine Fedwire application restart failed; for three hours banks extended unsecured daylight overdrafts, repo auctions were postponed, and CLS invoked contingency protocols. Nothing systemic broke, but the drill hinted at scale: if hours ever stretched into a day, derivatives variation calls would stockpile unpaid, mutual funds would miss redemption windows, and a sell-to-meet-cash spiral could begin before policymakers convened a press conference.

The pages ahead will dissect the crises that have already tested these rails—9/11's market closure, the 2008 tri-party panic, the pandemic dash-for-cash—and explore the cyber and climate scenarios that haunt today's contingency planners. For now, it is enough to see the architecture: Fedwire as the sovereign spine, CHIPS as the efficiency layer, CLS as the global linker. Strip away their acronyms and what remains is a simple fact: every modern dollar, whether born in Eurodollar swaps or securitized mortgages, must eventually pass down one of these pipes to achieve finality. They are narrow, they are centralized, and they hold together the vast latticework of contracts described in earlier chapters. Understanding their mechanics is therefore indispensable to understanding how a local shock can rip across jurisdictions at light speed—and why, in a system optimized for speed and cost, operational resilience remains the ultimate form of trust.

4.1 Technical Choreography of Settlement Finality

EVERY WEEKDAY AT 7:00 A.M. Eastern Time Fedwire's core mainframe releases an electronic gong—the so-called "first-in window"—that lets member banks begin submitting MT103 and MT202 messages through proprietary FedLine channels. The choreography from that instant resembles a ballet in which each dancer's misstep can halt the entire corps. A payment hits the switch, the system verifies that the sending institution's master account at the Federal Reserve holds sufficient daylight balance or collateralized overdraft capacity, and—if so—marks the reserves irrevocably transferred within milliseconds. That atomic timestamp is legal finality: property rights change, collateral pledges transform, and every downstream contract keyed to "good funds" becomes enforceable.

Throughout the morning the flow accelerates. Dealer desks aggregate triparty-repo unwinds; custodians mobilize Treasuries for securities-delivery-versus-payment windows at 9:00 and 11:30; options exchanges dispatch variation-margin sweeps aligned with futures-closing prices. Liquidity pulses in one-minute cycles as high-value queues clear, then momentarily plateaus while back-office validators reconcile confirmations and reject syntactically invalid messages. Should a bank's outgoing queue exceed its available reserves, Fedwire suspends the item and issues a negative acknowledgement, forcing the participant either to pre-position additional collateral or to re-sequence the payment—choices that treasury managers make in a control room illuminated by dashboard latency monitors.

CHIPS joins the dance at 9:00. Members upload thousands of MT103 payments encrypted over a SWIFT interface and tagged "hold," allowing CHIPS's liquidity-saving algorithm to assemble bilateral offset chains. Once the algorithm detects a closed loop with sufficient pre-funded balances, it simultaneously releases every leg, often collapsing a gross queue of US $5 billion into a net settlement of a few hundred million. That net figure fires across Fedwire as a single payment from CHIPS's omnibus account to the net receiver; the reserves settle, and CHIPS flips its ledger flags from "provisional" to "final." In practice this means that a dollar entrusted to CHIPS attains full legal finality only after Fedwire silently stamps its counterpart—a two-step cadence invisible to originators but critical to systemic synchrony.

CLS operates on a different beat yet still cues off Fedwire's bass line. By 6:30 A.M. New York time, participant banks transmit multilateral pay-in schedules covering the twenty-three currencies settling that day. CLS's engine nets those schedules into eight distinct funding windows, the most voluminous of which is the US-dollar tranche. At 10:00 A.M. Eastern, dollar pay-ins fire through Fedwire from each member to CLS's Federal Reserve account; only after every leg arrives does CLS execute payment-versus-payment across its internal ledger and release offsetting outflows in yen, euros, sterling, and the rest. If a single dollar pay-in misses its window—whether through a cyber outage, mis-keyed message, or intraday liquidity squeeze—CLS defers the entire cycle, forcing banks worldwide to reopen VaR calculations, extend daylight credit to counterparties, or scramble for overnight swaps to roll unmatched positions. The system's safety therefore depends on continuous high-availability links between three continents' RTGS networks and one clearing account in Manhattan.

Underlying these routines is an elaborate risk governor: the Federal Reserve provides daylight overdrafts at a penal rate, collateralized by Treasuries delivered via Fedwire Securities. A participant burning through its collateral headroom triggers automated caps that throttle outgoing traffic and flash red alerts at the Reserve Bank's National Settlement Service console. Treasury desks then triage: they can repo in fresh securities, postpone non-time-critical corporate payments, or call trading desks to flatten positions until margin settlements pass. In normal markets the maneuver is mundane; under stress it becomes a race against cutoff clocks. The 6:30 P.M. Fedwire close is immovable—any residual obligation unsettled at that tick cascades into overnight overdrafts, forcing emergency borrowing at the discount window and, potentially, reputational fallout that rating agencies notice by dawn.

What appears to outsiders as a seamless torrent is, from within, a perishable choreography of hardware latencies, escrow algorithms, queuing heuristics, and human triage. Every element assumes real-time communication among banks' core-processing systems, SWIFT gateways, and liquidity dashboards; every element assumes the Federal Reserve's ledger is online, time-stamping with nanosecond precision. Finality is therefore less a legal abstraction than a physical event—a transistor flip in a secure facility on the east bank of the Hudson. The genius of the design is its speed; the vulnerability is its singular geography. Should fibre be severed, code corrupted, or political authority withheld, the entire ballet halts mid-pose, leaving trillions in limbo and the global derivatives pyramid dangling—collateral unpaid, margins unmet, traders unable to exit. In the dollar era, trust in money settles not in marble vaults of gold but in the uninterrupted choreography of these circuits—circuits that, by design, converge in Manhattan.

4.2 Correspondent Banking as Global Capillary System

IF FEDWIRE, CHIPS, and CLS are the arteries of dollar settlement, correspondent banking forms the capillary network that no algorithmic bypass has yet replaced. A correspondent account—often called a *nostro* by the foreign bank that owns it and a *vostro* by the U.S. bank that hosts it—is little more than a demand deposit on the books of a New York clearing institution. Yet that mundane ledger entry is what allows a cotton cooperative in Côte d'Ivoire to receive payment from a textile mill in Bangladesh without either party holding a direct Fedwire connection. The Ivorian cooperative banks locally, its domestic institution holds a nostro at, say, Citi; Citi transfers reserves through Fedwire on the cooperative's behalf; the Bangladeshi buyer's bank settles the dollar leg through its own correspondent at JPMorgan; and within milliseconds a commercial transaction spanning three legal systems, two time zones, and one currency reaches finality. The architecture hides complexity behind the illusion of directness.

Scale is staggering. Fewer than fifty banks enjoy direct CHIPS membership, and an even smaller subset maintains Fedwire master accounts. All other institutions—thousands worldwide—daisy-chain their payments through layers of correspondents that ultimately converge on the same handful of New York giants. A Jamaican credit union, a Sudanese commodity trader (if not under sanctions), and a Finnish fintech start-up all rely on those giants' willingness to host their upstream banks' accounts. The operational result is a hub-and-spoke topology so dense that major correspondents process upwards of a million cross-border messages daily, embedding dollar legs even in transactions that are notionally non-U.S.: a peso-euro swap executed in Mexico City may still route through Manhattan because the intermediary banks clear dollars intraday to square positions.

This dependency grants the host banks extraordinary gatekeeper power, a fact that became explicit after 9/11 when successive rounds of AML and counter-terrorist-financing rules raised the compliance cost of maintaining exotic nostros. Risk officers began to rank corridors not merely by fee income but by reputational hazard. Between 2011 and 2020 the number of active U.S. dollar correspondent relationships fell by nearly a quarter, a phenomenon dubbed "de-risking." Entire regions—Pacific micro-states, parts of Sub-Saharan Africa, segments of the Caribbean—found themselves one compliance policy away from effective exclusion from the dollar circuit. When a correspondent severs ties, local banks must reroute through more remote hubs, elongating settlement chains and inflating costs for perfectly lawful commerce. The systemic irony is acute: rules intended to police illicit finance can, by shrinking the capillary map, force remaining channels to concentrate even more flow through even fewer nodes, magnifying single-point vulnerability.

Operational risk travels the same channels. An outage at a major correspondent's payment interface instantly ricochets through dependent banks that have no direct Fedwire access, freezing their ability to honor import letters of credit or margin calls on exchange-traded futures. The 2021 Fedwire hiccup exposed this leverage when several Latin-American banks, reliant on a single U.S. correspondent, triggered local liquidity squeezes because intraday dollar positions could not be squared before regional cut-off times. No cyberattack was involved; the mere impossibility of reaching the correspondent's back-office queue threatened payroll disbursements a hemisphere away.

Sanctions transform the capillary metaphor into a choke chain. When the Office of Foreign Assets Control adds a party to the Specially Designated Nationals list, the command reaches implementation not through the State Department but through correspondent banks that police their own ledgers. A single "reject" flag at JPMorgan or Bank of New York Mellon can strand oil-tanker charter payments in limbo, prompting shippers in Dubai and insurers in London simultaneously to refuse cargoes they had no political quarrel with twelve hours earlier. The functional sovereignty of the dollar thus resides less in

Washington's formal legal reach than in the risk committees of five or six New York and London institutions that decide which nostros live or die.

Technology has not dissolved the reliance. Fin-tech challengers promising real-time global settlement still anchor ultimate funds movement in traditional correspondents because only they sit on Fedwire. Stablecoins, for all the rhetoric, require commercial-bank custody for their fiat backing; an operational freeze on those accounts strands the token supply. Even central-bank digital-currency pilots such as mBridge anticipate off-ramps into commercial-bank nostros when trades graduate from proof-of-concept to real invoices. The plumbing remains stubbornly physical.

The consequence is a structural paradox: correspondent banking globalized the dollar by enabling distant institutions to piggyback on New York access, yet by funneling ever-growing volumes through a shrinking set of gatekeepers it intensifies the very fragility the broader system labors to contain. As long as businesses in Accra or Phnom Penh must pray that compliance teams in lower Manhattan or Canary Wharf keep their nostros alive, the dollar's reach will continue to equal its risk. A rupture—in the form of a major technical failure, a sweeping sanctions episode, or a sudden wave of de-risking after a compliance scandal—would not merely inconvenience peripheral markets; it would back-propagate liquidity stress into the same New York corridors whose balance sheets and payment rails anchor global finance. The capillaries feed the heart, and when they constrict, the pulse everywhere falters.

4.3 Operational Risk, Cyber Exposure, and Single-Hub Vulnerability

THE FINANCIAL SYSTEM'S public mythology imagines a redundant, cloud-era web of mirrored servers humming in far-flung bunkers; the reality is a tight cluster of data halls straddling the Hudson, stitched together by the same fibre conduits that carry cable news. Fedwire's production boxes sit in East Rutherford and a mirrored site upriver; CHIPS and CLS run primary engines inside the very same carrier hotels—165 Halsey Street, 60 Hudson, Equinix NY4—that handle high-frequency equity orders and social-media traffic. A single metropolitan power grid, a single telecom backbone, and a handful of shared facilities supply life support to the settlement arteries that determine legal ownership of the world's reserve currency. In most industries such geographic concentration would be filed under "business continuity red flag"; in dollar clearing it is accepted as legacy fact, rationalized by the argument that proximity minimizes latency. Efficiency, once again, is purchased at the price of correlated failure modes.

Operational risk begins with banalities. A severed fibre splice in lower Manhattan forced Fedwire to queue outbound traffic for ninety minutes in July 2015; a defective load-balancer software patch triggered the three-hour outage in February 2021 that left CLS and major correspondent banks scrambling for contingency lines before the Asian open. These events cost no lives and produced no headlines beyond trade journals, yet they revealed an inconvenient truth: recovery plans rely on the same local contractors, diesel deliveries, and network carriers that caused the incidents. During Hurricane Sandy, generator fuel shortages at two Wall Street data centers forced clearing participants to invoke manual procedures; had water levels risen another forty centimeters the sub-basement power rooms at a Fedwire switch site would have flooded, leaving no automatic failover path outside the storm's footprint.

Cyber exposure magnifies the hazard. The 2016 Bangladesh Bank heist proved that a single compromised SWIFT endpoint can propel fraudulent instructions straight into New York's correspondent queues until human reviewers notice abnormal routing patterns. More recent ransomware campaigns against managed-service providers demonstrate an adversary's preference for leverage: corrupt one widely used software update, and hundreds of institutions inherit the payload overnight. Payment rails offer an even richer target. A well-timed malware insertion that merely scrambles message sequence numbers—not balances, just ordering—would force CHIPS to suspend multilateral netting while engineers verify integrity, instantly turning its \$1.5 trillion daily flow into a gross-settlement obligation most members could not pre-fund. In simulation drills run by large dealers, a two-hour CHIPS standstill at month-end triggers margin shortfalls across cleared swaps, obliges emergency repo borrowing from the Federal Reserve, and compels multinational corporates to choose between missing payroll and drawing revolvers that banks are themselves rationing.

Regulators acknowledge the threat yet remain hamstrung by the topology. The Federal Reserve can mandate resilience tests for banking entities but wields limited authority over telecom carriers, cloud vendors, or the municipal utilities that feed the data halls. A directive to diversify geographic risk collides with commercial reality: latency-sensitive trading desks resist settlement hubs outside a thirty-millisecond round trip to Midtown, and the legal framework governing Fedwire reserves is grounded in New York jurisdiction. Proposed cures—regional satellites, distributed ledger pilots, even a cold-standby Fedwire instance in the Rockies—struggle against the inertia of embedded systems and the trillion-dollar ecosystem of algorithmic liquidity providers optimized for the current grid.

Single-hub vulnerability therefore persists as the dark underside of the dollar's network advantage. Every participant benefits from a centralized pool of liquidity, real-time finality, and dense netting; every participant also accepts that a localized regional shock—cyber, climate, or mundane operational—can metastasize into a global funding freeze within minutes. The implicit contingency plan is the Federal Reserve's balance sheet and the Treasury's guarantee that payment obligations, once queued, will clear eventually. Yet a promise to pay tomorrow is not legal finality today, and derivatives exchanges, tri-party repo agents, and cross-border securities custodians are bound by rulebooks that treat missed deadlines as default events. In a system optimized for zero-latency settlement, the boundary between benign delay and systemic crisis is measured in hours. Manhattan remains the indispensable hub—and, by the same physics, its most inviting point of critical failure.

Chapter 5: Shadow Pipelines: FX Swaps, Repos, and Eurodollars

Long after Fedwire's nightly gong falls silent and the CHIPS queue zeros out, the global financial bloodstream keeps pulsing in channels most balance-sheet readers never see. Dealers in Tokyo roll tom/next FX-swap books against New York, Frankfurt treasurers patch noon-hour collateral gaps with overnight repos cleared in Zurich, and Caribbean booking-centres re-price Eurodollar deposits that never physically left Manhattan in the first place. These are the *shadow pipelines*—contractual circuits that move credit, currency, and collateral with the speed of an Excel macro yet remain off official radar until a rupture sends them rushing for daylight liquidity. Formal payment rails grant legal finality; shadow pipelines grant *economic* finality, allowing banks and asset managers to act as if they already possess tomorrow's dollars so long as counterparties trust today's mark-to-market maths.

The numbers dwarf headline settlement flows. Notional FX-swap exposure now hovers near eighty trillion dollars—larger than global GDP—because every cross-currency funding hedge books twice: once spot, once forward. Tri-party and bilateral repo balances in U.S. collateral routinely top five trillion dollars a day, most of it financed overnight. Eurodollar liabilities, difficult to pin down since they cascade through inter-office journal entries, likely exceed the on-shore M2 money supply. None of these claims appear in conventional monetary aggregates, yet at dawn they dictate which institution meets margin calls without Federal-Reserve back-stop and which phones its correspondent for an overdraft extension.

Three engineering tricks make the pipelines hum. First, *time transformation*: an FX-swap converts three-month yen funding into synthetic dollar cash due at term, freeing the European bank to price loans as though its greenbacks were already on hand. Second, *collateral transformation*: a repo takes a Treasury note that regulators bless as Level-1 liquidity and re-hypothecates it through multiple dealers, each posting the same security to a different creditor in sequence. Third, *jurisdictional transformation*: Eurodollar deposits booked in the Cayman Islands bypass reserve requirements and deposit-insurance levies yet can be wired into New York at a keystroke if a prime-broker client demands redemption.

The elegance of the design is its modularity; the fragility lies in its synchronous roll. An FX-swap that matures on quarter-end must be re-struck, or the borrower needs physical dollars; a repo that fails to roll obliges the collateral taker to source cash elsewhere or liquidate assets; a Eurodollar depositor who snaps up a higher yield at SOFR-plus-15 creates an instantaneous funding hole. Under normal conditions the market handles trillions in expiries each night with barely a ripple. Under stress—2011's euro-area scare, the 2018 year-end cross-currency spike, the March-2020 pandemic dash for cash—rollover risk becomes systemic precisely because every participant tries to shorten tenor and hoard dollars at once. The pipelines, designed for continuous flow, clog; pressure rises at the central nodes; and the Federal Reserve must inject physical reserves or open swap lines to foreign central banks before margins exhaust.

Regulation has pushed risk inward rather than dispersing it. Basel liquidity ratios reward holdings of Treasuries, so dealers warehouse ever more collateral that must be repo-funded nightly. Money-market reforms drove prime funds into government-only mandates, concentrating the buyer base for Treasury repo just as leverage caps curtailed dealer balance-sheet capacity. Meanwhile, global corporates hedge dollar earnings via short-dated FX-swaps instead of issuing long-term bonds, rolling a wall of demand onto the same quarterly maturity ladder that banks and asset managers already crowd. The shadow infrastructure is therefore not ancillary to the dollar system; it *is* the dollar system's circulatory mesh, carrying most of the liquidity that formal arteries merely settle at day's end.

The pages that follow dissect each conduit in turn—FX-swap basis mathematics, repo haircut spirals, Eurodollar maturity gaps—and show how a hiccup in any one quickly propagates through the others before bursting into the visible payment rails. For now it is enough to grasp the architecture's core tension: the world has learned to create synthetic dollars faster than the Federal Reserve can credibly promise real ones, yet when confidence falters the synthetic claims convert, on demand, into calls for central-bank reserves that can only be minted in Manhattan. Shadow pipelines grant extraordinary flexibility, but they also hard-wire the entire planet's overnight funding needs to a single issuer's capacity and willingness to backstop them. In calm weather the mechanism hums beneath notice; in a squall it becomes the fuse that tests whether a local funding storm can ignite a global liquidity conflagration.

5.1 The Mechanics of Synthetic Dollars Outside U.S. Jurisdiction

A SYNTHETIC DOLLAR is any claim that functions like cash in the U.S. financial system even though it is issued, traded, and often enforced entirely beyond American legal reach. The archetype is the Eurodollar deposit booked in a London or Cayman branch of a global bank. Legally it is a sterling- or Cayman-law liability; economically it is identical to a New York demand deposit because the branch promises to transfer Federal-Reserve-cleared funds on request. Creation is frictionless: a commodity exporter wires surplus earnings from Dubai; the London branch credits a demand deposit; an internal journal entry shifts the corresponding asset to the bank's New York treasury desk, which either lends the cash in the repo market or places it at the Federal Reserve as excess reserves. From the exporter's perspective dollars have materialized offshore; from the Fed's vantage the balance sheet of a foreign banking organization has simply repositioned reserves that already existed. Money creation, in other words, occurs on the liability side far from the Fed's direct control.

FX swaps mint a second, subtler breed of synthetic dollar. A Korean insurer with surplus won short-term funding gaps agrees to swap three-month won for dollars with a U.S. broker-dealer. On day one the insurer delivers won cash and receives dollars spot; simultaneously it strikes a forward contract to reverse the exchange at a fixed rate. For the next ninety days the insurer treats those dollars as its own—buying Treasuries, posting margin, meeting policy-holder claims—yet no Federal-Reserve liability has changed. The dollars reside on the broker-dealer's ledger as a receivable, secured by the forward contract. Should global stress widen the cross-currency basis, both counterparties will scramble to roll or novate the swap, converting a derivative mark-to-market into real demand for reserves that only New York can supply.

Synthetic funding also flows through cross-border repo. A Dutch pension fund holds German bunds but requires dollar liquidity to meet collateral calls on cleared swaps. It pledges the bunds to a U.S. prime broker in Luxembourg; the broker, via an internal conduit, lends overnight dollars sourced from its New York tri-party repo book. The transaction never touches Fedwire, yet the pension fund's risk—and its ability to meet variation margin—now hinges on rolling the repo each morning at rates set in the Manhattan funding scrum. In a pinch the broker will demand higher haircuts or substitute Treasuries as collateral, forcing the pension fund to liquidate European assets in order to stay in the dollar loop.

Derivatives extend the machinery deeper into balance sheets regulators barely see. A Brazilian exporter hedges future commodity receipts by selling dollar forwards to its local bank; the bank delta-hedges with Chicago futures and funds the margin in New York; the exporter therefore enjoys functional dollar credit long before cargoes leave port. In Asia, non-deliverable forwards allow corporates in capital-controlled economies to replicate dollar funding synthetically; settlement occurs in local currency, but the payoff tracks the dollar exchange rate, embedding contingent dollar liabilities in every contract.

All of these channels are lightly or differentially regulated because, in formal terms, they do not claim Federal-Deposit-Insurance protection or access the discount window. Basel rules treat them as wholesale liabilities, not deposits, and national supervisors lack a consolidated view once transactions hop jurisdiction. Yet their aggregate scale dwarfs on-balance-sheet cross-border lending. BIS surveys suggest that for every physical offshore dollar deposit there are two to three dollars' worth of swap-derived or repo-financed claims maturing inside twelve months. During normal times the layering scarcely matters: dealers offset positions, collateral chains roll, and covered-interest-parity arbitrage keeps forward points predictable. In stress, maturity compression converts synthetic into physical demand with brutal speed because treasurers cannot assume a counterparty will roll when forward spreads blow out.

Crucially, none of these synthetic dollars require the Federal Reserve's blessing at inception, yet all of them presume its intervention at the limit. When the cross-currency basis hit negative one hundred basis points in March 2020, rolling three-month swaps became punitive; emerging-market corporates and European banks drew on central-bank swap lines that ballooned to nearly half a trillion dollars within weeks. The Fed was forced to supply reserves against liabilities it had not supervised, originated, or even recorded onshore. Synthetic creation had become public back-stop through the simple logic of network dependency: if synthetic dollars can be used as bona-fide settlement assets in calm seas, they must be honored as such in a storm or the entire hierarchy of claims unravels.

The elegance of offshore engineering therefore masks an asymmetric bargain. Foreign institutions enjoy dollar liquidity without U.S. regulation; U.S. authorities retain regulatory autonomy but inherit lender-of-last-resort duties to a market they do not fully map. The spread of synthetic dollars multiplies systemic efficiency—lower funding costs, tighter global arbitrage—but each new layer extends a conditional put option to the Federal Reserve. For as long as confidence holds, synthetic dollars behave like real ones; when confidence wavers, they transmute into non-negotiable demands on the only balance sheet still capable of cash settlement at par. The world has, in effect, privatized the issuance of dollar substitutes while socializing the ultimate guarantee—a structural tension that threads through every crisis explored later in this book.

5.2 Margin Maths and the Speed of Contagion

THE BEAUTY—AND THE peril—of modern leverage is that it hides in plain arithmetic. A derivatives portfolio margined at 3 percent of notional is functionally leveraged 33-to-1; a repo trade hair-cut at 2 percent is levered 50-to-1. As long as market prices drift within the VaR bands baked into initial-margin algorithms, the leverage hums silently. The instant prices breach those bands, variation margin converts mark-to-market losses into same-day cash calls, transforming paper volatility into real-world funding demand at a speed Fedwire alone can satisfy.

Consider a dealer that holds a $10 billion long Treasury-futures position hedging a book of fixed-rate mortgages. Initial margin at a central clearing house might run $300 million. A 70-basis-point intraday swing—the kind observed in March 2020—produces a price loss of roughly 5 points, or $500 million, eclipsing posted collateral by $200 million. The clearing house issues a variation-margin call at 10:00 A.M. The dealer's treasury desk must wire the shortfall before the 11:00 cut-off or face position liquidation. To raise cash it dumps the most liquid assets available—usually on-the-run Treasuries—triggering further price declines, fresh VAR breaches, and next-round margin calls across other participants. What begins as a one-day volatility spike mutates into a mechanically enforced sale-and-spread-widen loop.

Repo haircuts propagate the spiral. Suppose a hedge fund finances $15 billion of off-the-run Treasuries at 2 percent haircut: $300 million equity supports $14.7 billion borrowed cash. Bid-ask spreads gap wider as dealers nurse their own margin calls, and the collateral's market price slips 2 percent. The funding desk demands a top-up to restore the haircut; the fund must post $294 million by the afternoon settlement cycle—practically all its remaining equity. If the fund hesitates, the repo desk liquidates collateral, pushing yields higher, recycling pressure back to the dealer inventory that hedges mortgage books, and restarting the derivative-margin cycle from a higher baseline of volatility.

FX-swap margin layers a cross-currency fuse onto the system. European banks that borrow dollars via three-month swaps post initial collateral in cash or high-grade bonds. When the dollar surges relative to the euro, the mark-to-market on the forward contract flips against the borrower, producing margin obligations in the very currency—dollars—that is becoming scarce. Banks raid domestic liquidity to source dollars, widening the cross-currency basis further and forcing central banks to supply swap-line funding. In March 2020 the euro-dollar basis exploded from near-flat to minus 130 basis points in 48 hours; forward points embedded margin calls unimaginable under normal stress tests, compelling the Fed to reopen dollar swaps at tenfold pre-crisis scale.

What makes margin dynamics uniquely dangerous is their *deterministic* timing. Central counterparties run twice-daily variation sweeps; tri-party repo clears at 7:00 a.m. and 3:30 p.m.; CLS pay-ins hit at 10:00 a.m.; every clock tick aggregates market-wide valuation changes into binary pay-or-liquidate decisions. When volatility is modest, these events pass unnoticed. When shocks hit, the entire market arrives at the same funding window with the same collateral—on-the-run Treasuries—and the same counterparty, the Federal Reserve, standing behind primary dealers. Queues lengthen, bid-offers evaporate, and microstructure friction converts financial mathematics into systemic shortage.

Margin algorithms were designed to protect clearing houses, not the macro-system. They succeed: default waterfalls remained intact even in the pandemic dash-for-cash. But the price of that micro-safety is macro pro-cyclicality. By demanding liquidity precisely when it is least available, margin calls amplify feedback loops, forcing asset sales that raise volatility assumptions inside the very VaR models that set tomorrow's initial margin. Each recalibration lifts collateral requirements across trillions of positions, accelerating leverage unwind into a reflexive burst.

The broader consequence for dollar hegemony is stark. Because collateral of last resort is almost always a U.S. Treasury and settlement of last resort a Fedwire reserve balance, every margin cascade becomes a dollar-funding cascade—whether the underlying shock originates in oil futures, UK pension-fund hedges, or Korean won swaps. Speed of contagion is therefore measured in settlement cycles, not business days, and the geography of contagion traces back to Manhattan, where the final cash obligations must clear. Margin maths, elegant in spreadsheet form, is the turbocharger that converts the world's leverage into an instantaneous claim on the one balance sheet capable of closing the ledger.

5.3 Prime-Broker Leverage and Hidden Maturity Transformation

BEHIND EVERY HEDGE-fund headline is a prime broker whose balance-sheet elasticity converts overnight financing into multi-week, sometimes multi-year, market risk. The process begins with a deceptively simple service: extend margin loans and synthetic exposures—total-return swaps, contracts-for-difference, bespoke repos—against collateral that can be rehypothecated. Because prime-broker subsidiaries sit inside broker-dealer legal entities rather than deposit-taking banks, they escape the Basel liquidity and stable-funding ratios that bind their commercial-bank affiliates. Funding is rolled day-to-day in the tri-party repo market or, when collateral is equity rather than bonds, through internal matched-book securities lending that is effectively callable on demand. The hedge fund, by contrast, deploys the credit into positions that settle at T+2, pay off over quarters, and may be locked up in private-fund side pockets for years. The resulting gap between **overnight liabilities and term assets** is classic maturity transformation—only it hides off balance sheet, shielded by netting agreements and collateral waivers that shrink the reported exposure to a sliver of its economic size.

Rehypothecation multiplies the leverage. A fund posts Treasury collateral against a total-return swap; the prime broker re-pledges that same security into the tri-party repo market; the cash raised is lent to another client who posts it back as margin for equity-index futures; the chain can repeat several times before the collateral returns to the original custodian at day's end. Each link shortens effective maturity: the fund thinks it has term financing, the broker knows it can pull the plug nightly, and the broader market assumes Treasuries remain the ultimate high-quality liquid asset even when the same bond backs four parallel loans.

Because exposures take the form of derivatives rather than outright securities, they escape most public disclosure. A hedge fund with $10 billion in capital can synthetically hold $50 billion in single-name equities or Treasury basis trades while appearing, in regulatory filings, to own nothing more than cash and accrued receivables. The credit resides on the prime broker's book as a marked-to-market receivable secured by daily-margin rights—until price gaps exceed variation collateral and suddenly convert synthetic exposure into hard default risk, as the Archegos collapse made plain. Prime brokers comfort themselves with concentrated-position thresholds and intraday monitoring, but they compete aggressively for fee income, so leverage limits often expand in bull markets and contract only after prices gap move, guaranteeing pro-cyclical lending cycles.

Hidden maturity transformation matters systemically because the **funding leg is almost always in dollars, rolled overnight, and collateralized by securities that clear through Fedwire or the Fixed Income Clearing Corporation.** When stress hits—be it a pandemic sell-off or an idiosyncratic blow-up—prime brokers issue intraday margin calls that require funds to deliver fresh cash before the 3:30 p.m. tri-party repo unwind. Funds meet calls by dumping the most liquid instruments—on-the-run Treasuries—while dealers simultaneously reduce repo books to protect their own leverage ratios. Yields spike, forcing further markdowns on collateral valuations and sparking yet more margin calls. What starts as a hedge-fund idiosyncrasy becomes a Treasury-market liquidity crisis within hours, compelling the Federal Reserve to inject reserves and expand its reverse-repo and securities-purchase operations to keep repo haircuts from spiraling upward.

The feedback loop is fastest when leverage is embedded in **relative-value trades**—cash-futures basis bets, equity-total-return swaps, or option-volatility arbitrage—because these strategies depend on benign funding spreads rather than directional conviction. When spreads move a few basis points outside historical corridors, the implied leverage can turn ten-to-one positions into negative equity within a single statement cycle. Prime brokers, protected by close-out rights, dump collateral into thin markets; competing brokers follow suit to avoid last-mover disadvantage; and the liquidity illusion that supported the entire maturity mismatch evaporates.

Regulators have begun to map these exposures, but the plumbing remains opaque: swap data repositories collect positional snapshots that lag by forty-eight hours; total-return swaps booked through non-U.S. affiliates fall outside many reporting mandates; and rehypothecation chains thread through offshore branches where collateral rights differ by jurisdiction. The practical result is that systemic risk metrics understate leverage until a margin spiral is already under way, at which point the only entity capable of supplying limitless overnight dollars—via repo operations or discount-window advances—is the Federal Reserve.

Prime-broker leverage thus completes the risk circuit introduced by synthetic dollars and margin mechanics. It transforms call-money financing into long-dated, high-beta market exposure, disguises maturity gaps behind derivative netting, and channels every liquidity squeeze back to the same Manhattan settlement grid. As long as volatility remains subdued and repo funding is cheap, the machinery supplies depth to bond and equity markets worldwide; but its very success ensures that, when turbulence returns, the unwind will demand dollar liquidity at a velocity no local central bank can match. In that moment the hidden scaffold of maturity transformation reveals itself as the accelerant that turns a localized fund failure into a system-wide sprint for the greenback.

Chapter 6: The Federal Reserve's Offshore Lender-of-Last-Resort Role

The Federal Reserve Act of 1913 envisioned a central bank that would quell seasonal panics in Midwestern agriculture and tame Wall Street speculation—not one that would backstop pension funds in Helsinki or mortgage insurers in Sydney. Yet by the early twenty-first century crises proved that the dollar's reach had outgrown its statutory map. When offshore claimants scramble for greenbacks, no amount of euro-area liquidity or renminbi swap lines can substitute; only the Fed owns the printing press that settles at par in Fedwire. In effect, the United States has acquired a global mandate without ever rewriting its charter: the lender of last resort to the world's funding market is a domestic institution whose accountability remains firmly national.

The modern doctrine surfaced in December 2007, months before Lehman fell, when the Fed and the European Central Bank unveiled a temporary $20 billion swap line. Mechanics were straightforward: the ECB posted euro collateral to the Fed, drew dollars at OIS-linked rates, and re-lent them to euro-zone banks that could no longer roll commercial-paper funding in New York. Over the next ten months the network expanded to the Bank of England, Bank of Japan, and Swiss National Bank; by October 2008 volumes eclipsed $580 billion, larger than the Fed's entire pre-crisis balance sheet. Without a single vote in Congress, a domestic lender had become the hinge on which global interbank funding turned.

Swap lines solve a very specific problem: **offshore dollars that do not exist except as overnight claims suddenly must be delivered as reserves.** The borrowing central bank assumes credit risk on its own institutions; the Fed takes only sovereign risk, secured by local-currency deposits it can re-deliver at maturity. Economically, however, the operation transforms the Fed into the wholesale distributor of dollar liquidity the moment private dealers refuse. The signal effect is as potent as the cash: cross-currency bases snap back, repo haircuts stabilize, and prime brokers resume rolling margin loans once they know the central-bank backstop stands behind their counterparties' treasuries desks.

The 2020 pandemic stress pushed the architecture a step further. In March the Fed reopened unlimited swap lines with the G-5, re-activated smaller caps for nine additional central banks, and introduced a new *FIMA repo* facility that allowed any foreign monetary authority holding Treasuries to repo them back to the Fed for overnight dollars. Peak usage approached $450 billion—less than 2008 in nominal terms but achieved in a single fortnight, proof that financial plumbing now expects the Fed to appear on command. The basis tightened within forty-eight hours, and corporate borrowers from São Paulo to Seoul found their forward-hedge quotes normalized even as local economies locked down.

Yet the arrangement remains **discretionary and politicized**. Section 14 of the Federal Reserve Act permits foreign-currency swaps only with "foreign central banks or monetary authorities," leaving ample latitude but no obligation. Recipients reflect geopolitical alignments: the People's Bank of China lacks a standing line, whereas the Central Bank of Brazil gained one in 2020. Congressional critics frame every draw as a "bail-out of foreign banks," forcing Fed officials to defend facilities whose primary beneficiaries are often U.S. money-market funds facing redemption risk if offshore borrowers cannot roll paper. The contradiction is acute: the Fed acts globally to protect domestic stability, yet domestic audiences perceive global lending as mission creep.

Operational asymmetries compound the tension. Swap lines are collateral-free for the Fed—local currency is of no use in New York—but the *political* exposure is real. Should a counterparty central bank suffer a currency collapse and fail to return dollars, the Fed would book a loss ultimately shared by U.S. taxpayers, inviting the kind of scrutiny that makings officials hesitate the next time a crisis flares. Markets, however, treat the facility as implicit and instantaneous. The gap between market expectation and political tolerance is the new Triffin dilemma: global demand for dollar safety assets requires the Fed to extend its balance sheet precisely when domestic conditions make that extension most controversial.

To date, every governing board has chosen stability over restraint, but the architecture's fragility endures. A U.S. debt-ceiling standoff that freezes new Treasury issuance, a populist backlash that blocks swap-line renewals, or a cyberattack that severs Fedwire connectivity could deny foreigners dollars just as margin calls peak. Banks abroad would dump Treasuries, widen bid-ask spreads, and ricochet stress straight back into American funding markets—the very feedback loop the swap lines are meant to break.

The pages ahead probe those tail risks, but the foundation is now set: synthetic dollars and shadow pipelines multiply liquidity in good times; when they implode, the Federal Reserve—an institution chartered to serve a single nation—has become the only entity capable of closing the global dollar gap. The offshore lender-of-last-resort role is not a policy choice; it is the involuntary price of dollar hegemony. Understanding that asymmetric bargain is essential to grasp why future crises will test not merely Wall Street's resilience but Washington's political capacity to internationalize its domestic central bank at moments of maximum strain.

6.1 From 2008 Swap Lines to Pandemic-Era Lifelines

THE 2008 SWAP-LINE network began almost tentatively, a $20 billion conduit between the Federal Reserve and the European Central Bank announced on 12 December 2007—small enough to escape newspaper front pages yet large enough to quiet the first tremors in dollar funding for European banks. Within nine months the conduit had multiplied into a lattice. The Bank of England, Swiss National Bank, and Bank of Japan were added; credit caps were raised in $10 billion increments, then $50 billion increments, until by 13 October 2008 the Fed removed limits altogether for the G-5. Demand skyrocketed. Swap auctions at the ECB cleared three times oversubscribed; the SNB, suddenly a dollar broker for the world's private banks, drew $54 billion in a single week. Peak utilization arrived at $583 billion in mid-December—larger than the Fed's entire pre-crisis balance sheet—an unmistakable admission that the offshore dollar had become the epicenter of global liquidity risk.

Pricing evolved with the crisis narrative. Early drawings carried a penalty spread of 100 basis points over OIS, intended to ensure the facility remained a back-stop. As Libor-OIS blew out past 300 basis points, the Fed cut the spread to 50, then to a symbolic 10, effectively subsidizing foreign central banks so their domestic institutions could roll three-month funding at near-onshore rates. Market psychology shifted almost overnight: the cross-currency basis narrowed, term repos reopened, and even private dealers who never bid at the auctions relaxed once they saw that a public balance sheet now stood ready to absorb tail demand.

The network hibernated after 2010 but never disappeared. During the euro-area sovereign scare of late 2011, the Fed re-priced swaps to OIS + 50 and extended maturity to 84 days; drawings passed $110 billion as French and German banks rushed to replace dollar commercial-paper funding that American money-market funds refused to roll. Each mini-crisis hardened expectations, and by 2013 the swap line had become a quasi-permanent fixture—rolled quarterly, announced laconically in press releases, yet monitored obsessively by cross-currency-basis traders who treated its renewal as the difference between tight and stressed year-end funding.

Then the pandemic struck. The first two weeks of March 2020 saw hedge funds unwind Treasury-futures basis trades, foreign central banks sell $109 billion of Treasuries, and the euro-dollar basis crater to −130 basis points, a level unseen even in 2008. On 15 March the Fed cut swap-line pricing to OIS—the cheapest access ever offered—and reopened unlimited facilities for the G-5; four days later it added nine more central banks, from Singapore to Mexico City, with caps that eventually totaled $450 billion. Volumes leapt from zero to $206 billion in ten days, peaking at $448 billion by 1 April. The exceptional twist was speed: what had taken ten months in 2008 unfolded in a fortnight, testament to how thoroughly market participants had internalized the Fed's global role.

The Fed also engineered a complementary back-stop: the Foreign and International Monetary Authorities (FIMA) repo facility. Any central bank holding Treasuries in custody at the New York Fed could repo them overnight for dollars at a modest rate, sidestepping the political optics of a swap line. Uptake never exceeded $180 billion, yet its mere existence halted forced Treasury sales that were distorting the world's benchmark safe asset. The Fed had, in effect, installed a standing margin-lending window for every sovereign that banked at the Federal Reserve—a privilege no other reserve currency issuer was prepared to extend.

Swap mechanics themselves remained unchanged—currencies exchanged spot, reversed forward, with revaluation haircuts to cover FX risk—but the policy wrapper had matured. Auctions moved to fixed-rate, full-allotment tenders, eliminating stigma; maturities standardized at 7, 84, and later 168 days; and daily usage statistics were published at 2:30 p.m. New York time, providing transparency that fed directly into risk-desk liquidity dashboards across the globe. The Fed, once reluctant lender to foreign counterparts, had become a predictable, rules-based market maker of last resort.

By the time utilization tapered below $40 billion in early 2022, the lesson was clear to every funding desk: synthetic dollars may proliferate offshore, but their convertibility in crisis still hinges on a domestic U.S. institution willing to liquefy foreign banking systems. The doctrine born in 2008 and perfected in 2020 is now embedded in trade pricing, regulatory stress tests, and even sovereign liquidity frameworks at the IMF. What remains unsettled is whether American politics will always ratify the arrangement the next time swap demand leaps from zero to half-a-trillion in a matter of days, and whether global finance can afford to discover the answer only after the request queue has formed.

6.2 Political Oversight, Legal Authority, and Discretionary Gate-keeping

THE FEDERAL RESERVE'S capacity to shower offshore markets with dollars rests on statutory language drafted for a very different world. Section 14 of the Federal Reserve Act authorizes the System to conduct "foreign exchange operations" with "foreign banks or bankers" and to hold foreign-currency balances as collateral. A plain reading scarcely anticipates a half-trillion-dollar swap program, yet the clause grants enough latitude for the Board of Governors—on recommendation of the New York Fed and with informal concurrence from the Treasury—to open, price, and size swap lines without a single vote in Congress. The Federal Open Market Committee must ratify the aggregate limit ex post, but the decision set in motion on Liberty Street is effectively binding once dollars have flowed.

That discretion survived the post-crisis push for transparency only in attenuated form. Dodd-Frank's Section 1103 compels the Fed to publish counterparty identities, loan amounts, and collateral details with a two-year lag; it also authorizes the Government Accountability Office to audit discount-window and swap-line data for "operational integrity." Yet oversight remains reactive. Congressional committees hold hearings after the fact, armed with GAO reports; the Board submits semi-annual monetary-policy testimony; but no ex-ante approval is required to reopen unlimited swaps or create a new facility like the 2020 FIMA repo window. In theory, the Treasury secretary can object—swap documentation includes a non-binding Treasury "concurrence" clause—but in practice the executive branch and the Fed present a united front once crisis optics demand action.

That institutional latitude collides with geopolitical selectivity. Unlimited, open-ended lines are confined to the G-5, all U.S. treaty allies. Nine "temporary" partners—Brazil, Mexico, Korea, Singapore, Australia, New Zealand, Norway, Sweden, and Denmark—receive capped facilities. China, India, Turkey, Russia, and every African central bank have no access. The criteria are not published; Fed officials cite counterparty credibility, rule-of-law standards, and historical funding need. Critics point out that credibility often coincides with strategic alignment: Washington enjoys the leverage of an implicit dollar lifeline while withholding it from rivals. That prerogative makes the swap network a de facto foreign-policy instrument, even though its legal basis lies in monetary operations.

Domestic politics impose another constraint. Every large drawing rekindles accusations that the Fed is "bailing out foreign banks with U.S. taxpayer money." During the Tea-Party ascendancy of 2010, House legislators introduced bills to subject future swap lines to prior congressional vote; none passed, but the message was clear. In 2023, amid debt-ceiling brinkmanship, a proposal surfaced to bar the Fed from renewing swaps during any period in which the Treasury was using "extraordinary measures" to avert default. While the bill stalled in committee, the episode revealed how partisan leverage can menace global funding norms: if a debt-limit crisis blocked swap renewals, dollar shortages would propagate internationally before Congress even scheduled a floor debate.

Legal scholars note further ambiguity around 13(3) emergency-lending authority, which now requires the Treasury's written approval for any "broad-based" facility. Swap lines narrowly escape 13(3) classification—they are deemed foreign-exchange operations—but a determined Congress could reinterpret them as emergency credit if political winds shift. The Fed protects the firewall by insisting on high-quality collateral (local currency) and by sterilizing swap liquidity with domestic open-market operations, but the distinction might wilt under populist scrutiny the next time utilization surges.

Finally, gate-keeping power resides not only in Washington but in compliance manuals at the New York Fed. Before a central bank receives a line it must satisfy KYC, AML, and sanction-screening protocols. A regime change or sanctions designation—think Venezuela 2017—can shut a door overnight. Markets internalize this threat: banks in countries without standing lines hoard Treasuries to pledge at the FIMA window; those in sanctioned states pre-fund reserves via costly, short-dated swaps with third-party intermediaries, embedding fragility upstream of any formal prohibition.

The paradox is striking. Global finance treats the swap network as an automatic sprinkler system—guaranteed to douse any dollar funding fire—yet the water main flows through valves controlled by domestic politics and U.S. strategic discretion. The world has no voting rights on Capitol Hill, but its financial pulse depends on decisions taken there and at Constitution Avenue. That asymmetry is the institutional heart of the dollar trap: a single nation's central bank acts as offshore lender of last resort, answerable primarily to voters who may one day decide the cost is no longer worth the benefit.

6.3 Global Moral Hazard Baked into a Domestic Mandate

EVERY TIME THE FEDERAL Reserve opens a swap window or repo backstop, it extinguishes a fire and fertilizes the tinder for the next one. Dollar liquidity crises are routinely cured without forcing banks, hedge funds, or even sovereign treasuries to confront the structural mismatch that produced the shortage in the first place. The lesson absorbed by treasurers is simple: if turmoil reaches a certain decibel, Washington will turn on the hose. Risk-taking migrates toward that threshold, never beyond it but always closer—an incremental drift invisible in quarterly reports yet unmistakable in aggregate leverage ratios and maturity profiles.

The drift takes many forms. European banks book long-dated, floating-rate loans to Turkish conglomerates but fund them with three-month dollars, secure in the knowledge that the ECB can swap with the Fed if cross-currency spreads detonate. Asian corporates hedge dollar debt with short-tenor FX swaps rather than lengthening liability profiles, calculating—correctly so far—that a spike in basis points will prompt their home central bank to tap its standing line. Even investment-grade U.S. companies exploit the put: they issue record volumes of five-year bonds to foreign life insurers, confident that an offshore dollar squeeze will push the Fed into fresh quantitative easing. The backstop underwrites behaviors that, in a self-contained system, would be priced or rationed by market discipline.

For the Fed the hazard is double-edged. Its statutory goals—maximum employment and price stability—depend increasingly on calm global funding markets. Ignoring offshore stress therefore endangers the domestic mandate, while relieving that stress entrenches the expectation of relief. The resulting feedback loop is the modern incarnation of Robert Triffin's dilemma: to keep the world supplied with safe dollar assets, the United States must expand its balance sheet or tolerate foreign leverage that will, sooner or later, demand that expansion. Either path widens the contingency liability borne by U.S. taxpayers for credit decisions taken far beyond their regulatory perimeter.

Policy rhetoric acknowledges the tension but skirts its mechanics. Fed officials emphasize that swap lines are "collateralized, risk-free." They are, accounting-wise: local-currency deposits insulate the Fed from direct credit loss. But the true subsidy is not credit—it is optionality. By guaranteeing conversion of synthetic into real dollars on demand, the Fed neutralizes the funding penalty that would otherwise discipline offshore borrowers. No accounting line item captures the socialized volatility premium, yet its market value is evident whenever the cross-currency basis snaps back the moment a swap facility is announced. The spread between stress and calm is the price of an insurance policy written unilaterally by a central bank whose charter names only American constituencies as insured.

Attempts to curtail the hazard—higher margin requirements, LCR buffers, supervisory stress tests—ameliorate symptoms while preserving the option. Banks forced to pre-position Treasuries simply repo them back to New York when panic erupts; hedge funds raise more initial margin but rely on the same prime-broker credit that evaporates without Fed-supplied repo liquidity. As long as the final circuit breaker resides on Liberty Street, private actors optimize to maximize return up to, but not through, that fuse. The moral-hazard dividend is collected in good years; its premium is paid in public balance-sheet expansion during bad ones.

The geopolitical dimension compounds the problem. Governments that benefit from swap access are incentives to postpone domestic reforms—capital-market deepening, reserve diversification, counter-cyclical fiscal buffers—because they can externalize liquidity risk. Others, excluded from the club, either stockpile Treasuries as self-insurance (thereby financing U.S. deficits) or pursue alternative payment systems that fracture the very architecture the Fed seeks to stabilize. In both cases the expectation of American rescue shapes policy choices abroad, often in ways that heighten long-run fragility.

The upshot is a system in which the Federal Reserve's domestic mandate is inextricable from a global safety net that escalates risk-taking precisely because the safety net exists. The world's offshore dollar engine runs faster each crisis cycle, confident that the domestic mechanic will keep spare parts in stock. For U.S. policymakers, every expansion of the toolkit—repo lines, standing swap auctions, foreign CBDC interfaces—delivers short-term calm at the cost of deeper long-term entanglement. The moral hazard is not a side effect; it is the structural rent extracted for sustaining an international order built around a national currency whose guarantor cannot credibly refuse the next call for assistance.

Part III – Power, Leverage, and Weaponization

Chapter 7: Sanctions, Secondary Sanctions, and Financial Exclusion

On a humid Friday evening in June 2014, compliance officers at BNP Paribas received the verdict they had feared for months: a record US $8.9 billion fine for clearing Sudanese, Cuban, and Iranian transactions through New York in violation of U.S. sanctions. Within hours every large foreign bank convened emergency calls to map its residual exposure to the Treasury's Office of Foreign Assets Control (OFAC). The lesson was unmistakable. It does not matter that a trade is lawful in Paris or permissible in Beijing; if a single dollar leg crosses a correspondent account on Wall Street, the transaction imports American jurisdiction—and with it the full weight of U.S. foreign-policy objectives. Dollar dominance is not merely an economic fact; it is an instrument of coercion precise enough to target an individual container ship and powerful enough to reroute the macro-trajectory of a sovereign economy.

Sanctions operate on three interlocking layers of the dollar architecture already traced in this book. At the apex sits **primary jurisdiction**: any U.S. person, bank, or business is flatly barred from dealing with individuals or entities on OFAC's Specially Designated Nationals (SDN) list. Beneath that lies the **clearing-house choke point**: even when neither counterparty is American, the dollar leg of their trade must pass through CHIPS or Fedwire, where automated filters screen names against the SDN database and freeze any hit. The third layer, introduced after 9/11 and perfected against Iran, is **secondary sanctions**. They threaten non-U.S. banks with exclusion from the clearing system if they facilitate dollar trades for blacklisted entities, thereby exporting American rules extraterritorially. The logic is brutally simple: choose Tehran or New York, but not both.

What makes the regime so effective is the network topology described in Chapters 4 and 5. Because nearly every tradeable commodity, syndicated loan, or cross-border acquisition uses the dollar as invoice or settlement medium, OFAC needs only to touch the Manhattan hub to paralyze a target's global operations. When Washington cut Iranian banks off from CHIPS in 2012, euro-area petroleum refiners discovered they could not pay for crude even if Brussels granted waivers; European banks, fearing U.S. secondary penalties, refused to intermediate. More recently, Russia's 2022 exclusion from the clearing network forced its commodity exporters to invent cumbersome work-arounds—yuan invoicing, dirham escrow accounts—that still require occasional dollar conversions via opaque brokers, each hop a new sanctions liability.

Financial exclusion rarely ends with the intended target. Small correspondent banks in the Caribbean and Pacific islands have lost U.S. clearing lines because their customer due-diligence budgets cannot match OFAC's rising standard; humanitarian NGOs struggle to route relief funds through the same corridors that once moved dollar-denominated bribes. The deterrent effect is maximal, yet the collateral damage erodes the very liquidity and trust that make the dollar convenient. Each forced de-risking compresses payment channels, concentrates flow in fewer mega-banks, and thus magnifies the systemic single-point vulnerability described earlier.

Washington faces its own strategic dilemma. The more aggressively it weaponizes the dollar, the greater the incentive for adversaries—and uneasy allies—to accelerate alternative rails. Europe's INSTEX mechanism, Beijing's Cross-Border Interbank Payment System, and the Saudi-China oil-pricing flirtation each trace lineage to sanctions over-reach. None yet rival CHIPS for scale, but every rollout chips at the network effect that underwrites American leverage. Use of the big stick secures immediate policy wins—freezing oligarch yachts, squeezing nuclear negotiators—but at the potential cost of inviting a parallel universe where final settlement bypasses Manhattan altogether.

This chapter dissects that trade-off. It begins with the legal machinery—OFAC designations, Patriot Act 311 findings, and the mechanics of U-turn interdictions—then unpacks the cascade through correspondent networks and secondary sanctions clauses baked into dollar loan covenants. Case studies follow: Iran's gradual strangulation, North Korea's cryptocurrency end-run, Venezuela's payment-token experiments, Russia's post-SWIFT realignment, and the unintended fallout for fragile states caught in the compliance cross-fire. The aim is not to debate the morality of sanctions but to expose their architecture and its systemic ramifications: how the very feature that makes the dollar a formidable tool of statecraft—mandatory clearing in New York—also amplifies fragility by concentrating ever more transactional flow in a hub that geopolitical adversaries are now openly incentivized to avoid.

7.1 OFAC Playbook: Freezing Dollars Beyond U.S. Borders

DOLLAR CLEARING IMBUES the United States Treasury with a lever no other finance ministry wields: wherever a dollar transaction settles, it passes—at least fleetingly—under the legal canopy of

Manhattan. The Office of Foreign Assets Control exploits that geography with a methodical playbook whose power lies less in headline fines than in the instantaneous, automated freeze that follows a single keystroke on the Specially Designated Nationals list. Once a name or entity code populates the SDN database, every message-filtering engine at CHIPS, Fedwire, and the major correspondent banks updates within minutes. The next payment containing that identifier halts mid-queue, reserves remain in the sender's master account, and the ledger entry reads "blocked" until OFAC issues a license—an act that can take months or never arrive at all.

Designation begins inside Treasury's Terrorism and Financial Intelligence office, where analysts stitch together intelligence cables, Suspicious Activity Reports, and open-source data to compile a case file. A deputy secretary signs an executive order reference, lawyers confirm statutory authority under the International Emergency Economic Powers Act, and the target enters the SDN list with an eight-digit identifier. Parallel alerts flash to large clearing banks via OFAC's Secure Outreach network, giving compliance desks a head start—sometimes measured in hours—to comb their books for exposures that must be reported within ten business days. Even before the public notice posts, risk officers at Citi, JPMorgan, and Bank of New York Mellon may begin soft-blocking payments that look suspiciously close to the draft target, an anticipatory act euphemised as "break glass."

The blocking mechanics are digital but absolute. Fedwire operates a real-time screening service: if a message flag matches an SDN entry, the payment is rejected; if partial data match triggers a "false positive," the sending bank must manually review before resubmitting. CHIPS uses a liquidity-saving queue; a hit converts the item into provisional status, locking the netting algorithm until the member bank either cancels the payment or CHIPS breaks it into partial flows that exclude the sanctioned leg. The process can strand innocent transactions that happen to share identifiers with restricted parties—an Iranian charity's name embedded in an Italian NGO transfer, for instance—but the system's bias is deliberate: better to over-block and issue a license later than allow a single illicit dollar to escape.

OFAC's reach extends even when dollars never leave foreign soil. A South African refinery paying a Russian energy trader in dirhams may find its local bank unwilling to process the transfer once secondary sanctions threaten any institution that "facilitates significant transactions" for SDNs. Because every correspondent fears losing its New York account more than losing a client, the chill effect radiates through tier-two and tier-three banks until lawful commerce grinds to a halt. The refinery rushes to restructure supply contracts; the Russian trader opens shell affiliates to obfuscate ownership; compliance software vendors sell ever-costlier fuzzy-matching algorithms; and New York remains the quiet command post where an invisible switch throttles global trade.

Extraterritorial potency derives from two technical clauses. The "50-percent rule" automatically blocks entities in which SDNs own a majority stake, forcing analysts to map nested corporate registries and beneficial-ownership trusts that disappear into Caribbean PO boxes. The U-turn ban, revived against Iran in 2008, outlaws even momentary clearing through U.S. banks for trades conducted entirely between non-U.S. persons. Together they eliminate routing work-arounds: no shell company can escape if a sanctioned individual lurks above fifty percent, and no offshore correspondent can rely on the decades-old habit of sweeping multi-currency settlement through Manhattan at day's end.

Political oversight is minimal once designation posts. Banks file initial blocking reports within ten days, annual status updates each September, and seek specific licenses for humanitarian or wind-down activity. Violations discovered later trigger strict-liability penalties: intent is irrelevant, and fines scale with the gross value of blocked property. BNP Paribas's 2014 record penalty—and the short-lived prohibition on dollar-clearing for its oil-and-gas desk—demonstrated that even systemically important foreign banks have no leverage when Washington deems them facilitators. The deterrence effect is so large that compliance departments now "over-block" by design, treating ambiguous hits as prohibited until outside counsel and OFAC confirm otherwise.

For policymakers the attraction is obvious: sanctions deliver foreign-policy impact without Marines on beaches or appropriations from Congress. For the financial system they inject a latent fragility. Each new designation expands filter libraries, multiplies false positives, and encourages de-risking cascades that sever small-market access to dollar pipes. The choke-point power that makes sanctions a formidable tool also centralizes yet more flow through clearing nodes that regulators already label "too big to fail." The OFAC playbook thus advances U.S. strategic aims at the front end while deepening single-hub vulnerability at the back—a classic illustration of how dollar dominance simultaneously extends American influence and magnifies systemic risk.

7.2 Illicit Finance, Kleptocracy, and Luxury Real Estate as Laundromat

WHEN A STATE-OWNED oil company in Luanda diverts a hundred million dollars from a procurement contract, the cash rarely sits idle in an Angolan bank. The kleptocrat's first priority is distance.

A shell company in the British Virgin Islands invoices "consulting services," collects the overpayment in dollars, and wires the proceeds to a correspondent account at a London branch of a global bank. At that moment the money has already entered the dollar clearing system—screened by automated sanctions filters yet too granular to trigger alarms. What follows is a choreography of layering: lawyers in Cyprus draft nominee agreements; trust companies in Jersey appoint directors-for-hire; and a Delaware LLC with a meaningless name—"Clear Skies Global LLC"—emerges as the ostensible buyer of a penthouse overlooking Central Park. The closing is all-cash, title vests in the LLC, and no mortgage filing ever surfaces to attract underwriter due diligence. Dirty money becomes glass and steel with a Manhattan ZIP code—and a Federal Reserve–cleared provenance.

Luxury real estate is the ideal laundromat because it provides permanence, social status, and valuation opacity. A $30 million condominium can absorb vast capital in a single wire transfer; future appreciation launders the illicit premium into legitimate capital gain; and co-op boards or condo associations bound by privacy agreements shield ownership structures from casual scrutiny. Until very recently the United States required no beneficial-ownership disclosure for all-cash purchases. Escrow agents, lawyers, and title insurers were deemed outside the definition of "financial institution" under the Bank Secrecy Act; their customer-identification obligations were, at most, voluntary. New York and Miami thus became preferred booking centers for oligarch wealth fleeing post-Soviet chaos, Gulf sovereign slush funds, and the quieter fortunes of African military elites.

Correspondent banks facilitate the laundering at arm's length. A Miami real-estate attorney receives a wire from a Latvian bank that itself clears through a German correspondent; by the time the funds reach the trust account, three jurisdictions and two AML regimes have blurred responsibility. Each bank in the chain relies on prior links for due diligence; each files a Suspicious Activity Report only if a keyword trips an algorithm; and each assumes that an eventual property closing in the United States implies local regulators have vetted the buyer. In practice the chain of accountability dissipates. FinCEN Geographic Targeting Orders have narrowed the loophole for specific counties, but the market adapts: shell companies fracture into nested manager-managed LLCs, or lawyers route wires through escrow accounts in unaffected jurisdictions before forwarding cashier's checks to title agents.

The same laundering machinery finances high-end retail therapy—yachts flagged in Malta, art works traded at Basel fairs—and, more troublingly, covert influence. A kleptocrat who owns a Fifth Avenue pied-à-terre can secure U.S. visas for "household staff," move family members under the radar, and cultivate relationships with lobbyists and think-tank donors who may never trace the capital's origin. The dollar system confers not only asset protection but access to cultural and political networks that recycle influence back into the kleptocracy's home state, reinforcing the extraction cycle.

Systemically, the sums involved are a rounding error next to global payment volumes, yet the reputational tail risk is immense. Every headline exposing an oligarch's hidden condo erodes trust in the United States as steward of the rule-of-law financial system. More concretely, the same correspondent corridors used for real-estate wires carry legitimate trade finance for emerging-market importers. When a bank's AML team discovers that a corridor has been polluted by high-profile laundering, it may "de-risk" wholesale—closing accounts for small exporters and humanitarian NGOs that lack the fee volume to offset compliance cost. Thus, the presence of lavish kleptocratic inflows can accelerate financial exclusion for entire developing regions, amplifying the collateral-damage dynamic examined in Section 7.3.

Attempts to seal the laundromat have so far proved partial. FinCEN's 2021 Corporate Transparency Act will require beneficial-ownership filings, but enforcement thresholds remain fuzzy and real-estate exemptions persist for commercial transactions. Title insurers lobby against universal filing, arguing that property deals would migrate to cash-rich private markets. The legal profession cites attorney-client privilege to resist Suspicious Activity Report obligations. Meanwhile, the market invents tokenized real-estate platforms and digital fractionalization schemes that promise liquidity without transparency, opening new seams for illicit flow.

The deeper issue is structural: as long as the dollar is the easiest on-ramp to secure, appreciating assets in rule-of-law jurisdictions, kleptocrats will accept higher laundering costs as just another frictional tax. OFAC designations deter sanctioned names, but most kleptocrats operate one degree removed from politics, thriving in the grey zone that lies outside SDN lists yet inside regulatory blind spots. Without coordinated global beneficial-ownership registries, the Laundromat simply rewires when one corridor closes. And every rewiring ultimately terminates in the same settlement hub—Manhattan—confirming yet again the asymmetry at the heart of dollar hegemony: the currency's unmatched safety and liquidity are precisely what make it the prize vehicle for the world's dirtiest money.

7.3 Collateral Damage to Legitimate Trade and Humanitarian Flows

AS OFAC'S BLACKLIST lengthens and compliance thresholds tighten, whole categories of perfectly lawful commerce find themselves stranded outside the dollar gate. The mechanics are impersonal. A regional Caribbean bank whose customer roster includes a handful of politically exposed clients receives a risk-rating upgrade from a U.S. correspondent's algorithm; the fee expected to compensate that risk now exceeds the corridor's annual revenue; the correspondent terminates the account with thirty days' notice. Suddenly importers in Barbados can no longer pay for U.S. medical equipment, cruise-ship provisioning, or student tuition remittances. The reputational taint of sharing a routing transit number with one suspect customer has severed the entire jurisdiction from low-cost dollar clearing.

Humanitarian agencies are frequent casualties. NGOs delivering cholera vaccines to Yemen or cash-for-work programs in Somalia route funds through the same local banks that move diaspora remittances. When those banks lose dollar lines, relief groups resort to informal value-transfer networks—hawala brokers, cash couriers—that expose staff to security risks and donors to audit gaps. U.S. regulators offer "humanitarian exemptions," yet in practice no compliance officer wants to be the one who mistakenly clears an aid payment later linked—even tangentially—to a sanctioned militia. The "derisking premium" therefore prices legitimate aid out of the formal system precisely where monitoring is most needed.

Trade finance suffers comparable collateral damage. After Russia's removal from major messaging and clearing systems in 2022, Western banks quietly trimmed letters-of-credit exposure to importers across Central Asia and the Caucasus, fearing secondary-sanctions blowback via re-export channels. Tajik textile mills and Georgian wine cooperatives—not entities subject to any blacklist—faced working-capital droughts because global banks could not model the sanctions pass-through risk. When financing migrates to non-dollar currencies or local barter, transparency evaporates, making future investigations harder and amplifying the very opacity sanctions were meant to disrupt.

Even within compliant corridors, payment friction redistributes bargaining power. A rice trader in Sierra Leone quoted a ten-day settlement window in dollars must accept a steeper discount from the Thai exporter, who fears last-minute correspondent rejection. Insurance underwriters raise premia to cover the probability of clang-back. Over time these micro-penalties aggregate into a macro tax on emerging-market growth—one paid not by targeted regimes but by small businesses and consumers whose only misfortune is geography.

The systemic irony is that forced withdrawals from the dollar grid often concentrate flow in the few remaining channels, heightening single-point risk. After Caribbean de-risking, surviving correspondents process higher volumes through unchanged operational infrastructures, so a glitch or cyber-incident at one Florida clearing bank can now freeze half the region's trade. In east Africa, the exodus of European banks from Somali remittances pushed volumes to a single Gulf-based provider whose SWIFT access hinges on one UAE mega-bank—a fragile choke point regulators barely audit.

Diplomatically, collateral damage erodes U.S. soft power. Populations in sanctioned or merely adjacent economies perceive Washington not as the rule-of-law anchor it portrays but as an unpredictable tollbooth on global commerce. That narrative fuels political arguments for alternative rails—yuan invoicing, regional clearing unions, cryptocurrency experiments—even when those options are costlier or riskier. The quest for redundancy, however embryonic, is itself evidence of reputational attrition.

Mitigation efforts exist—correspondent "shared utilities," multilateral humanitarian carve-outs, and FinCEN's 314(b) information-sharing safe harbor—but they rely on voluntary uptake by banks whose risk appetites are shrinking faster than regulators can offer assurance. Until the compliance calculus changes, the default strategy for many institutions will remain simple: avoid borderline clients, close marginal corridors, and let the public sector or gray market deal with the fallout.

Collateral damage, then, is not an unintended side effect; it is baked into the sanctions machinery via the same network centralization that gives the dollar its coercive edge. Every new designation adds friction for the innocent along with pain for the guilty, and the system's defenders must weigh each tactical gain against long-term costs in legitimacy, liquidity, and resilience.

7.4 Secondary Sanctions and the Compliance Arms Race

PRIMARY SANCTIONS BLOCK named entities; secondary sanctions weaponize the *relationships* that keep them afloat. A single clause in an executive order—"the Secretary of the Treasury, in consultation with the Secretary of State, may prohibit or restrict any foreign financial institution that knowingly facilitates a significant transaction for a designated party from opening or maintaining a U.S. correspondent account"—turns every bank on earth into an unpaid deputy sheriff. The penalty is existential: lose access to Fedwire and CHIPS, and a global bank forfeits its dollar franchise, repo market, derivatives collateral, and, in effect, its raison d'être. Washington's edict thus forces thousands of compliance departments, from Zurich to Seoul, into a perpetual arms race to prove negative knowledge: that no dollar they touch might trace, by any chain of intermediaries, to a forbidden counterparty.

The Mechanics of Delegated Enforcement

Secondary sanctions pivot on two ambiguities—"knowingly" and "significant." OFAC provides guidance but no bright-line dollar threshold. Banks respond by building probabilistic risk scores that flag transactions with even a faint statistical correlation to a target jurisdiction, sector, or ownership web. Machine-learning vendors feed on the uncertainty, selling graph-analytics suites that parse shipping manifests, social-media metadata, and leak troves such as the Pandora Papers. False positives swamp operations desks, so banks overlay human review, which slows payments and raises costs that only the largest institutions can bear. Smaller correspondents exit the business, further concentrating flow through a few mega-nodes—precisely the opposite of systemic diversification.

Race-to-Zero Tolerance

Because the sanction for error is total exclusion, the compliance frontier does not advance incrementally; it leaps forward every time a peer is penalized. After Standard Chartered's 2012 settlement, London banks began bulk-exiting Iranian and Sudanese trade corridors. BNP Paribas's 2014 penalty triggered a wave of de-risking across Francophone Africa. Danske Bank's 2018 money-laundering scandal pushed Scandinavian peers to sever Baltic and CIS clients en masse. Each leap induces counterparties that remain *inside* the grid to demand wider indemnity clauses, pass-through representations, and rights to instantaneous account termination—clauses that replicate the fear down the transactional chain.

Shadow Compliance and Fragmentation

Unable to secure dollar amenities, affected parties migrate to back-channel solutions: barter, yuan or dirham invoicing, crypto-settlement, nested accounts in willing third-country banks. Yet even these work-arounds rely indirectly on the dollar market's benchmark functions—oil futures priced at NYMEX, container freight hedged in forward dollar curves—so their users must periodically re-enter the dollar system, often through less-regulated intermediaries. The effect is to push risk into darker corners, where KYC diligence thins and the likelihood of genuine illicit finance rises, validating the very heuristics that sparked the retreat.

Feedback into Systemic Liquidity

Large banks that survive the compliance race win market share but at a cost: they carry fatter operational-risk buffers, sustain lavish spend on screening technology, and hold more "due-diligence capital" against reputation loss. In tranquil periods, the cost is a basis-point surcharge on trade finance. In stress—say, a geopolitical shock that adds thousands of entities to the SDN list overnight—the surviving hubs may choke on alert volumes. Payment queues expand, variation-margin deadlines loom, and dealers hoard reserves "just in case." Liquidity tightens not because dollars are scarce but because clearing nodes throttle capacity to avoid mistakes.

Political Blowback and Coordination Gaps

Allies bristle at U.S. deputization. Brussels created the Instrument for Supporting Trade Exchanges (INSTEX) to shield humanitarian trade with Iran; it processed two test transactions in three years before being dismantled because European banks refused to participate. Negotiations over a global beneficial-ownership registry stall on sovereignty concerns. Meanwhile, Beijing's anti-foreign-sanctions law threatens fines against firms that comply with U.S. measures, putting multinational banks in a jurisdictional fork: obey Washington and risk Chinese licenses, or vice-versa. Global finance responds by silo-ing cross-border units, duplicating capital and technology, and eroding the efficiency gains that once underpinned dollar preference.

Endgame Dynamics

Secondary sanctions extend U.S. leverage far beyond its borders, but each use tightens the spring of unintended consequences: concentrated flow, opaque alternatives, geopolitical retaliation, and rising fixed costs that discourage new entrants to correspondent banking. The compliance arms race therefore pushes the system toward a barbell structure—fortress-scale banks with industrial-grade governance at one end, murky non-bank channels and thinly capitalised regional lenders at the other. Both extremes magnify single-point failure risk: the former through size, the latter through opacity. As the dollar trap tightens, the policing apparatus that defends it simultaneously chips at the network diversity that makes it resilient, leaving the Federal Reserve—as ultimate backstop—to absorb shocks emanating from a shrinking, over-burdened core.

7.5 Stress-Testing the Choke Point: Iran, Russia, and the Digital End-Runs

NOTHING CLARIFIES THE dollar system's coercive geometry like a sovereign that tries to live outside it. Iran and Russia offer two full-scale stress tests a decade apart: both confronted blanket sanctions that severed their largest banks from CHIPS and Fedwire, both scrambled for alternatives, and both ultimately revealed how deeply global commerce still depends on the Manhattan hub—even when oil, gold, or crypto stand in for cash.

Iran 2012–18 – The Gold Shuttle and the Hand-Carry Dollar

When the EU joined Washington in disconnecting Iranian banks from SWIFT in 2012, Tehran lost its principal channel for recycling oil revenues. Turkish refiners paying for crude could no longer route dollars or euros through correspondent accounts, so Ankara pivoted to an ingenious workaround: it credited Iran's account at Halkbank in Turkish lira, then authorized licensed dealers to purchase Turkish gold, physically smuggle it to Dubai, and sell it for cash dollars that ultimately travelled back to Iranian importers via hawala brokers. The "gold shuttle" moved an estimated US $13 billion before OFAC tightened the net in 2013. Yet even this analogue detour needed the dollar's liquidity on arrival—hawala agents settled books in notes sourced from Gulf banks that still enjoyed U.S. correspondent lines. When those banks came under secondary-sanctions threat, the shuttle shrivelled. Tehran had proved the hub could be skirted—at punishing frictional cost.

Russia 2022–24 – Energy Redirects and Yuan Collar Leaks

Moscow's annexation of Ukrainian territory triggered the broadest exclusions to date: selected state banks lost CHIPS access, the finance ministry was barred from raising new hard-currency debt, and the G7 capped seaborne crude prices. Russia responded on three fronts. First, it rerouted oil to India and China, billing in yuan, rupees, and UAE dirhams. Second, it channelled dollar trade through a handful of non-sanctioned banks—often regional lenders in Siberia or Tatarstan—that still possessed slim New York lines. Third, the central bank deepened its integration with Beijing's CIPS. These adaptations kept export volumes flowing but introduced basis risk: the Kremlin now holds yuan it cannot freely hedge back into dollars, while importers eat FX haircuts that widen whenever geopolitical headlines jar the on-shore/off-shore yuan spread. Even Russian corporates with no sanctions exposure found that letters of credit in euros or dollars priced 150–300 bps wider to compensate for compliance uncertainty. The choke point did not halt trade; it raised the toll, spotlighting how dollar risk premia radiate through alternative corridors.

The Digital Detours – Crypto Mixers, Stablecoin Wires, and CBDC Pilots

At the retail fringe, sanctioned actors pivoted to cryptocurrency. North Korean hacking crews laundered nine-figure hauls through mixers like Tornado Cash; Russian ransomware groups adopted privacy coins to hire proxies in Western Europe; Venezuelan agencies floated the ill-fated **petro** token. Each pathway ultimately sought fiat off-ramps—dollar or euro exchanges in East Asia, OTC desks in Dubai—where KYC filters increasingly mirror OFAC screens. Stablecoins briefly looked like frictionless substitutes, but issuers must custody reserves in U.S. T-bills and bank deposits. When Treasury black-listed Tornado's smart contracts in 2022, Circle had no choice but to freeze USDC held at flagged addresses, proving that even "on-chain" dollars depend on off-chain New York compliance.

Central-bank digital-currency pilots present a more fundamental experiment. China's mBridge prototype settled live trade invoices among four monetary authorities in 2023 without touching SWIFT, promising atomic PvP in local units. Yet participants still benchmarked spreads to the dollar curve, and excess balances were re-invested in dollar repo at day's end. Liquidity begets gravity: until non-dollar CBDC pools eclipse the US$3 trillion Treasury bill market, central banks will hold greenbacks for rainy-day swaps.

Lessons from the Stress Tests

1. **Circumvention is possible but lossy.** Work-arounds raise transaction costs, widen bid-ask spreads, and add logistical bottlenecks (gold flights, collateralized yuan escrows) that slash effective trade margins.
2. **Liquidity risk returns to the hub.** Even after routing through yuan or crypto, counterparties eventually need deep forward curves, futures hedges, and cash-management sweep accounts—services still dominated by New York banks.
3. **Compliance drag accelerates fragmentation.** Each sanctions wave forces banks to bolt on new screening layers, spurring de-risking in adjacent markets and nudging legitimate players toward less-transparent rails—thereby expanding systemic opacity.
4. **Digital routes don't eliminate Fed backstop logic.**

> Stablecoin issuers require dollar reserves; CBDCs require cross-currency hedges. In a crisis, holders dump alternates for the original, pressing once more on the Fed's swap-line trigger.

Iran and Russia thus serve as controlled experiments. Neither broke the dollar choke point; both exposed its seams, raised the cost of enforcement, and spurred innovation that could, cumulatively, chip at network effects if Washington overplays its hand. For now, the stress tests confirm a stark equilibrium: the more actors attempt to exit the dollar, the more they reveal its indispensability—and the more the system's single hub must brace for the next, potentially sharper, digital end-run.

Chapter 8: Dollar Diplomacy and Geopolitical Bargaining Chips

IN THE SPRING OF 2023, as the Philippine navy tussled with Chinese vessels around Second Thomas Shoal, a quieter negotiation unfolded in Washington. Manila sought a standing dollar-swap arrangement—modest in size, potent in symbolism—to backstop its banking sector as U.S. rates climbed. Within weeks the Pentagon announced expanded rotational-force access to Philippine bases and the Federal Reserve quietly renewed Manila's temporary swap line. The choreography was no coincidence. For a generation, American security guarantees have travelled in tandem with privileged access to the world's only unlimited liquidity pool, turning dollar policy into a diplomatic sweetener as indispensable as aircraft-carrier visits or Patriot-missile batteries.

This leverage predates the Cold War. Saudi Arabia's 1974 pledge to price oil exclusively in dollars was sealed not just with weapons but with Treasury-bill recycling; South Korea's 1997 IMF rescue package included a promise—insisted on by the U.S. Treasury—that Seoul liberalize capital markets in ways that would deepen demand for dollar securities. From Warsaw to Bogotá, finance ministers have learned that favorable U.S. votes in multilateral lenders, targeted sanctions waivers, or expedited swap-line rollovers flow more readily to governments aligned with Washington's strategic agenda. Dollar liquidity is not dispensed as charity; it is a bargaining chip wielded with precision.

The mechanics are subtle. The State Department never writes "approve swap line" in a cable, and the Federal Reserve professes political neutrality. Yet Treasury officials sit in the same National Security Council meetings that debate base-access terms, and swap-line counterparts map almost perfectly onto defense-treaty allies. Conditionality radiates through softer channels, too—Export-Import Bank guarantees, OPIC insurance, Federal Reserve regulatory forbearance for U.S. banks' exposures in friendly jurisdictions. When crises loom, these levers merge: Turkey's lira meltdown in 2018 saw swap-line petitions rebuffed amid friction over a detained American pastor, while Brazil's pandemic-era request sailed through after Brasília agreed to host Boeing's fighter-jet roadshow and shelve talk of Huawei in its 5G roll-out.

Dollar diplomacy operates not only through carrots but through the credible threat of exclusion. Ethiopian negotiators in 2021 faced a stark menu: accept U.S. calls for cease-fire monitoring or risk sanctions that would chill syndicated loan markets and spike the birr-dollar basis. Even non-financial sanctions—export-control blacklists, visa bans—carry an implied monetary sting because global banks reflexively downgrade any corridor that attracts Washington's glare. The diplomatic value of the dollar, therefore, is less about open coercion than about the omnipresent option to inconvenience.

Yet leverage is perishable. Allies chafe at the asymmetry that lets U.S. congressional theatrics—debt-ceiling brinkmanship, government shutdown threats—unsettle their domestic funding markets. When the Trump administration threatened to weaponize Fed swap lines against NATO cost-sharing "delinquents," European officials accelerated work on a digital-euro settlement layer explicitly designed to reduce emergency reliance on the Fed. Likewise, India's willingness to settle Russian crude in dirhams and rupees signaled a hedging impulse: friendly ties with Washington do not erase memories of 2008-era capital flight triggered by Wall Street's implosion.

The rest of this chapter unpacks the machinery and limits of dollar diplomacy. Section 8.1 maps the concentric rings of the swap-line club—core allies, conditional partners, and the outer queue whose petitions remain unanswered. Section 8.2 turns to the IMF and World Bank, showing how "creditor coordination" often functions as an orderly exit ramp for Wall Street banks while debtor nations swallow austerity scripts. Section 8.3 weighs the soft-power dividend against the erosion of legitimacy abroad: how a currency that once symbolized open markets now carries, for many, the scent of unilateral dictate.

By tracing these bargains—from oil-for-dollars in the Gulf to semiconductor-for-swaps in East Asia—we reveal a paradox at the heart of the dollar order. The same network that grants Washington unrivaled diplomatic leverage depends on the continued willingness of other states to anchor their own stability to American domestic politics. Each time the chip is played, the game's participants recalculate the odds of building an alternative table. The story of dollar diplomacy, then, is not just one of power deployed; it is also one of power slowly diluted by the very deals that exercise it.

8.1 IMF Conditionality, Debt Workouts, and Wall Street Exit Ramps

WHEN A SOVEREIGN'S reserves evaporate and the currency buckles, two doors appear. The first—swap lines—opens only for capitals judged geopolitically indispensable. Everyone else files down the corridor to the International Monetary Fund. On paper the Fund is a multilateral lender of last resort; in practice its programs function as a dollar-delivery conveyor belt whose timing often aligns with the funding needs of New York and London creditors.

The choreography is now familiar. A government facing imminent default signs a Stand-By Arrangement. Dollars flow into the central-bank vault, instantly recycled outward as interest and principal on maturing Eurobonds or bank loans. Private creditors use the window to shorten duration or exit outright, while the IMF loan—senior to all others—remains on the public ledger. Only after Wall Street has de-risked does the second act begin: fiscal consolidation, subsidy cuts, currency devaluation, and asset-sale "structural benchmarks" that entice the very investors who escaped the initial blast radius.

Mexico 1982 set the template: rescue dollars allowed Citibank and Chase to unload exposure before the Brady Plan converted the residual into U.S.-guaranteed bonds. During the Asian crisis a generation later, Indonesia's program obliged Jakarta to liquidate state banks and scrap commodity monopolies, opening space for foreign entrants even as domestic borrowers absorbed the rupiah collapse. In Argentina, the record 2018 package—brokered after local carry-trade investors stampeded for the exit—spent nearly all its first tranche servicing bond coupons; austerity demanded in exchange helped tip the economy into recession, shrinking the tax base that was supposed to repay the Fund.

Conditionality is defended as necessary discipline, yet its asymmetry is evident in the fine print. Targets for primary-budget balance are front-loaded; "structural reforms" that would hurt foreign investors—capital-controls flexibility, local-content rules—are optional or banned. Paris-Club restructurings for official creditors run in parallel, but private-sector involvement is "voluntary" until the sovereign has exhausted reserves—reserves topped up, paradoxically, by the IMF itself. In effect, the Fund socializes liquidity risk while leaving credit risk largely in private hands.

U.S. influence saturates the process. With 16.5 percent of voting power—enough for a de facto veto—Washington shapes program design and board approval calendars. Treasury officials sit on the same calls where IMF staff weigh debt-sustainability scenarios, mindful that a delayed disbursement could ricochet into dollar funding markets. For borrowing governments the message is unmistakable: macro support is available, but only on terms that protect the dollar ecosystem and the creditors who intermediate it.

The result is a two-tier safety net. Swap-line countries avoid the IMF stigma and its political conditionality; everyone else pays an austerity premium that doubles as an exit ramp for Wall Street. Dollar diplomacy thus extends from central-bank corridors into multilateral lending halls, ensuring that when crises hit, private capital can retreat through a door held politely open by the very institution billed as the lender of last resort to nations in distress.

8.2 Swap-line Geopolitics: Friends, Non-

aligned, and the Outer Queue

TO OUTSIDERS, THE FEDERAL Reserve's swap network looks like a technocratic backstop—a neutral liquidity valve for "well-managed" central banks. In reality it is a three-tier diplomatic map that mirrors U.S. security alliances more faithfully than any credit-rating table.

Tier	Standing Access	Cap Size	Renewal Mechanics	Strategic Subtext
Inner Circle	Bank of Canada, Bank of England, ECB, Bank of Japan, Swiss National Bank (G-5 + Canada)	**Unlimited**	Permanent, automatic roll-over	Treaty allies/ defence partners; monetary sovereignty interwoven with U.S. markets
Selective Partners	Australia, Brazil, Denmark, Korea, Mexico, New Zealand, Norway, Singapore, Sweden	$30–60 bn caps (2020 peaks)	6-month "temporary" lines extended ad hoc	Friendly but non-allied states whose crises could spill into U.S. money-market funds or supply chains
Outer Queue	India, Indonesia, South Africa, Turkey, Gulf states, most of LatAm & Africa	None	Must request during crisis; no guarantee	Either geopolitically ambivalent, under sanctions risk, or viewed as able to self-insure via reserves

THE INNER CIRCLE: AUTOMATIC Dollars for Treaty Allies

These six central banks never file petitions; their lines are as permanent as the NATO articles that bind most of them. When stresses erupt, they draw discretely and repay quietly—confidence that reinforces itself because markets know limits do not bind. Unlimited access is part of the broader alliance package: nuclear umbrellas, intelligence sharing, and dollar liquidity inhabit the same trust framework.

Selective Partners: Conditional Favouritism

Brazil did not gain its $60 billion line in 2020 because of balance-sheet rigor alone; Washington needed Brasília in the anti-Huawei coalition and on side in the Venezuela standoff. Korea's cap was restored to the 2008 level after Seoul agreed to tighter export-control coordination against China. Each arrangement arrives with diplomatic courtesies—joint statements, defense-industrial MOUs, IMF board votes—that clarify the quid pro quo without putting it in writing. Caps signal friendship but also hierarchy: the Fed supplies enough to calm markets, not enough to let local authorities ignore structural reforms.

The Outer Queue: Waiting Room and Work-Arounds

When Turkey's lira collapsed in 2018, Ankara lobbied hard for a swap; the request stalled amid S-400 missile deliveries and the jailing of a U.S. pastor. India has asked informally for years, but strategic ambivalence and capital-control rigidity keep it outside. Gulf monarchies assumed oil pricing in dollars would guarantee eligibility; instead they rely on hoarding Treasuries for the Fed's FIMA-repo window—an expensive, sub-optimal substitute. These economies can still tap ad-hoc repo or SDR allocations, yet the market reads absence from the swap club as second-class status, widening basis spreads at the first whiff of stress.

Pricing as Signaling

Inner-circle drawings price at OIS; selective partners pay a 25-bp premium; any future "queue" line would likely come costlier still. The graduated schedule is less about credit risk than about signaling: cheaper dollars for closer friends, dearer dollars for those whose policies Washington hopes to nudge.

Leverage—and Its Limits

Swap-line geopolitics gives the United States influence that sanctions cannot achieve: it offers carrots instead of sticks. But leverage weakens if withheld too often. Countries in the queue respond by doubling reserve buffers, striking bilateral RMB pacts, or joining BRICS liquidity pools—costly hedges yet politically attractive when the Fed's door looks capricious. Every denial therefore chips at the network externality that sustains dollar hegemony.

Feedback Into Systemic Risk

A tiered map concentrates rollover risk in non-aligned regions: when stress hits, dollar shortages intensify precisely where swap access is thinnest, forcing fire-sales of Treasuries and ricocheting volatility back into U.S. markets—the scenario that swap lines were invented to avert. The geopolitical filter thus solves one problem (incentives friends) while planting another (liquidity whiplash from the outer queue).

The next crisis will test whether Washington prioritizes alliance management or systemic containment. Extending a line to a politically awkward but systemically relevant borrower could dilute diplomatic leverage; refusing could turn a regional crunch into a global dash-for-cash that the Fed must ultimately backstop anyway. In dollar diplomacy, gate-keeping and guardianship are two faces of the same coin—and the choice of whom to hand that coin to will only grow more fraught.

8.3 Soft-Power Dividends—and the Erosion of Legitimacy Abroad

FOR DECADES THE DOLLAR'S magnetic pull delivered Washington a trove of soft-power advantages that cost little to mint yet paid handsomely in influence. Emerging-market technocrats trained at the IMF or U.S. universities, returned home, and embedded dollar-centric prudence in local policy. Multinationals benchmarked every syndicated loan to LIBOR, ensuring that even boardroom debates in Frankfurt or São Paulo orbited the Federal Reserve's dot plot. And ordinary citizens in volatile countries kept a psychological exchange rate—*how many greenbacks for a month's salary?*—that substituted the credibility of the U.S. Treasury for that of their own governments. This diffuse admiration translated into diplomatic goodwill: American proposals at the UN or within the G-20 often began negotiations a step ahead because counterpart delegates assumed that aligning with the custodians of the world's reserve currency carried reputational safety.

Yet soft power is a perishable asset. Each episode of financial coercion, debt-crisis austerity, or domestic political brinkmanship chips at the narrative that the dollar bloc is a neutral public good. When the United States shuttered Iran's access to SWIFT, health-care NGOs in Tehran lost channels to pay for cancer drugs; families in Haiti discovered remittance fees jumped when their local bank's correspondent line was cut after a high-profile AML fine; Argentine voters saw IMF loan tranches finance bondholders then vanish before growth returned. These experiences generate *folk memory*—stories that circulate long after technical facts fade, shaping how publics perceive future offers of American partnership.

Cultural resonance thins as well. In the 1990s a scholarship to an Ivy League M.B.A. signaled the fast lane to central-bank leadership;

today a growing share of top African and Asian officials hold degrees from Beijing or Singapore, immersed in case studies that present Belt-and-Road financing, not the Brady Plan, as developmental success. Conferences once dominated by U.S. investment banks now feature Shanghai-based brokerage sponsors who pitch renminbi clearing as "sovereign-respectful." The United States still fields the deepest capital market, but the aura of inevitability is dimmer: when the dollar's primacy is portrayed as a political tool, alternatives—however immature—gain narrative traction.

Domestic spectacle compounds the erosion. Congressional debt-ceiling standoffs broadcast scenes of the reserve-currency issuer flirting with technical default; Fed nominee battles air partisan vitriol that undermines the image of technocratic stability. Viewers abroad, already attuned to sanctions risk, interpret the drama as further evidence that U.S. governance is no longer a constant but a variable—another factor to hedge. Soft power, dependent on perceived constancy, slips a notch each cycle.

The paradox is acute. Exercises of hard leverage—swap lines for allies, sanctions for foes—bring tactical wins but accelerate strategic drift. Countries cannot easily quit the dollar without sacrificing economic efficiency, yet they can and do invest in hedges: larger gold allocations, local-currency swap grids, trial runs of CBDC settlement corridors. Each hedge chips a few basis points off future dollar demand. Alone they are trivial; compounded over years they erode the seigniorage rent that funds America's diplomatic largesse.

To preserve the dividend, Washington faces a choice: temper the frequency and breadth of financial coercion, or accept gradual diversification that lowers leverage tomorrow. The danger is an unmanaged middle path in which coercion continues apace while legitimacy ebbs, leaving the dollar still system-critical but no longer system-respected—an asset to be tolerated, not trusted. In that world soft power curdles into soft resentment, and the greenback's greatest advantage—the willingness of others to hold it gladly—could unwind faster than any model built on historical inertia predicts.

Protectionist Shock-waves: Tariff and Subsidy Volatility

The erosion of confidence in Washington's monetary stewardship has been accelerated by a parallel trend: the re-emergence of tariffs and export controls as instruments of geopolitical leverage. Between 2018 and 2024 the United States invoked national-security statutes (Section 232) to tax inbound steel and aluminum, weaponized Section 301 against roughly US$370 billion of Chinese imports, threatened blanket duties on Mexican goods to force migration-control compliance, and—through the CHIPS and Science Act—imposed sweeping license requirements on shipments of advanced semiconductors and lithography tools to China. Allies followed suit. India and Turkey slapped retaliatory levies on U.S. farm produce. Brussels drafted a Carbon Border Adjustment Mechanism that taxes imported cement, steel, and fertilizers unless exporters adopt EU-approved emissions accounting. Within six years over half of world merchandise trade by value encountered a new tariff, quota, or control that did not exist at the start of the last decade.

Financial markets processed the volley as a series of supply-shock pulses. Each tariff announcement widened bid–offer spreads in the yuan–dollar NDF curve and pushed corporates to layer additional FX hedges: average daily turnover in CNH forwards rose from US$65 billion in 2017 to over US$100 billion by mid-2020. Commodity futures spiked when Washington floated export curbs on rare-earth magnets, only to retrace when Beijing hinted at reciprocal restrictions on gallium and germanium. For treasurers, the new regime felt like rolling sanctions by another name—policy moves timed to domestic political cycles rather than macro stability. One U.S.

chipmaker raised its hedge ratio on Taiwanese-dollar receivables to 120 percent, describing the buffer as an "adrenaline shot against tweet risk."

The weaponization of trade policy also accelerated "precautionary reshoring" of liquidity. Multinationals that once swept global cash into a single New York pool began keeping larger working-capital buffers in local banks, often in non-dollar currencies, to insure against customs-clearance delays or license denials. Bank of America estimates that Fortune 500 companies held an extra US $450 billion in idle cash offshore by 2024 compared with the pre-trade-war trend—a drag on dollar demand at the margin and a visible vote of diminished trust in seamless cross-border clearing.

Supply-chain investors intensified the divergence. Private-equity funds backing "friend-shoring" factories in Vietnam and Mexico demanded project-finance tranches in local currency to match revenue streams, where a decade earlier they would have insisted on dollar loans. This preference shift widened local-bond markets—useful for development—but also diluted the deep-liquidity network effect that once reconverted most emerging-market flows into dollars before final settlement.

Market volatility spurred by tariff brinkmanship even reached U.S. Treasury trading, the bedrock of global risk pricing. On several occasions (notably August 2019 and May 2023) overnight policy tweets triggered 3σ moves in five-year yields within minutes, outpacing swings seen during the 2016 Brexit vote. Primary dealers scrambled to hedge delta—increasing intraday demand for Fedwire daylight overdrafts—and volatility sellers rushed to close short-gamma positions, amplifying price gaps. Each whiplash episode reminded foreign reserve managers that even "risk-free" Treasuries can lurch when the dollar's sovereign guardian uses trade measures as headline spectacle.

For Washington the protectionist toolkit felt like cost-free leverage: no troop deployments, no budget outlays, immediate negotiating capital. Yet every tariff volley reinforced the perception that U.S. economic policy is an extension of partisan combat, not a steward of a neutral reserve infrastructure. Allies found themselves collateral targets—as when Canada and the EU were swept into steel tariffs under a "national-security" rationale—and responded with both legal challenges and incremental diversification of reserves into yen, Swiss francs, and gold. China accelerated bilateral currency-swap lines across ASEAN, parlaying the narrative of dependable supply into soft-power currency outreach—even if the practical volumes remain modest.

Ultimately, the weaponization of tariffs and export controls converges with dollar diplomacy's soft-power erosion along a shared fault line: the signaling that U.S. market access and dollar liquidity are conditional privileges, revocable at political speed. In the near term, the greenback may even strengthen during each flare-up, as investors stampede for the safety of U.S. assets. But the strategic cost is cumulative—the steady substitution of fear for trust, of hedge for preference. And trust, once frayed, rarely snaps back with the next cease-fire; it seeps away, basis-point by basis-point, until the network that made coercion so effective risks hollowing out beneath the weight of its own overuse.

In the past 18 months, the U.S. has widened the playbook of **dollar“ ”.diplomacy by other means** The current administration has (i) raised a new wall of China-focused tariffs, (ii) formalized outbound-investment controls, (iii) rewired critical-minerals and semiconductor subsidies, (iv) rewritten beneficial-ownership and real-estate AML rules, and (v) again run the federal debt-ceiling to the edge of default. Each move tightens Washington's leverage over global supply chains, but every one also adds volatility, compliance cost, or reputational drag that pushes foreign governments and firms to hedge—financially and politically—against future dollar shocks.

1. A Larger Economic-Security Toolkit

Instrument	2024-25 Action	Immediate Aim	Systemic Side-Effect
Tariffs	100–200 % duties on Chinese EVs, battery cells, solar wafers and chips (May 2024)	Protect domestic industry & election optics	Basis spikes in CNH forwards and EV-metal futures; allies fear collateral tariffs
Outbound-Investment Controls	Final Treasury rule effective Jan 2025 restricting U.S. capital into advanced Chinese AI, quantum & semiconductor firms.	Curb tech transfer	Funds carve China carve-outs, shift VC dry-powder to Singapore & Bangalore
Subsidies / Export Controls	IRA battery-origin rules & CHIPS Act grant guidance tightened in FY-25 budget.	Reshore supply chains	Partners complain about local-content "weaponised industrial policy"
AML / Ownership Rules	FinCEN's real-estate & BOI regimes revised; reporting deadline pushed to Mar 2025 and key exemptions added/ removed.	Curb kleptocratic inflows	Realtors & title firms warn of foreign-buyer pullback; London & Dubai pitch secrecy as a selling point
Macro Brinkmanship	CBO warns default risk by August 2025 absent debt-limit increase.	Domestic fiscal bargaining	Swap-basis traders price wider tail-risk; EM reserve managers diversify into gold & CHF

2. Tariffs and Market Whiplash

The May 2024 tariff tranche lifted effective U.S. duties on Chinese EVs to 100% and on batteries to 50%. In the 24 hours after the White House fact sheet dropped, five-year Treasury yields jerked 18 bp and spot iron-ore rallied 7% as traders bet on retaliation and restocking. Cross-currency basis in CNH widened by 45 bp before the PBoC intervened, repeating a pattern first seen in the 2019 trade war. Each spike forces corporates to buy extra hedges and hoard dollar liquidity, reducing the stock of "idle" greenbacks that underpins swap markets in stress.

3. Outbound-Investment Screening: Another Dollar Toggle

Treasury's outbound-security rule—effective 2 Jan 2025—requires pre-filings or outright bans for U.S. private-equity and venture-capital stakes in sensitive Chinese tech. GPs now draft "geo-fencing" side letters, raising capital costs for any Asia fund that keeps a Delaware feeder. Chinese start-ups seek Abu Dhabi or Singapore dollars instead. The policy thus channels financial flows away from New York and into alternative hubs, marginally eroding the network effect that reinforces dollar dominance.

4. AML Reform: Double-Edged Transparency

FinCEN's updated beneficial-ownership and luxury-property rules promise to close laundromats, but the March 2025 postponement and carve-outs for some U.S. entities prompt critics to say the door is still half-open. London estate agents already market homes to Gulf investors as "beyond BOI reach," while Miami title insurers brace for slower cash deals. Legitimate dollar inflow dampens at the margin, even as illicit actors test weaker jurisdictions—stress that ultimately back-propagates to U.S. banks via correspondent lines.

5. Debt-Ceiling Déjà Vu

Another partisan standoff—CBO now pegs the **X-date** between late May and August 2025—feeds CDS and repo-haircut premiums every time House negotiations stall. Foreign reserve managers lengthen average T-bill maturity, and Asian central banks quietly switch part of intervention war-chests into gold and Swiss francs—small reallocations that, compounded, trim structural dollar demand.

6. Net Impact on Dollar Diplomacy

1. **Short-term leverage up:** Tariffs, outbound bans and subsidy strings give Washington new bargaining chips when courting allies or coercing rivals.

1. **Volatility premium higher:** Each headline shock widens hedging costs, forces liquidity buffers, and tightens repo haircuts—raising the running cost of using dollars.
2. **Soft-power erosion continues:** Allies hit by collateral tariffs or excluded from subsidy credits question U.S. commitment to open markets.
3. **Hedging accelerates, not divorce:** Yuan or dirham invoicing, local-currency swap lines, and gold purchases all inch upward; none yet rival CHIPS liquidity, but each crisis seeds deeper non-dollar plumbing.

Outlook

If the administration turns tariff threats and outbound bans into standing policy while debt-ceiling theatre persists, the dollar's role as *neutral* settlement asset morphs further into that of *U.S. policy lever*. History suggests such leverage works—until counterparties accumulate enough hedges that the next squeeze hurts Washington's own funding costs. The trajectory, in other words, is still path-dependent but the slope of diversification is tilting ever so slightly away from Manhattan each time the tool is brandished.

Part IV – Failure Modes and Fragility

Chapter 9: Liquidity Cascades: Case Studies in Rapid Transmission

The past fifteen years supply a catalogue of "liquidity cascades" in which a local shock ricocheted through FX-swap desks, repo books, and clearinghouses in hours—sometimes minutes—before central-bank fire hoses arrived. Examining four emblematic episodes shows how fragile funding structures, margin arithmetic, and dollar-centric plumbing interact to amplify stress. Each case begins with a specific trigger (currency devaluation, pandemic sell-off, commodity squeeze, or sovereign-risk scare) and ends with a common requirement: emergency dollar liquidity at the Fedwire hub.

Anatomy of a Liquidity Cascade

1. **Trigger → Margin Calls.** A price shock gaps asset values, breaching variation-margin thresholds.

1. **Asset Sales → Funding Stress.** Forced sellers dump the most liquid collateral—usually on-the-run Treasuries—pushing yields wider and repo haircuts higher.
2. **Cross-Market Spill-over.** Wider haircuts hit FX-swap and commercial-paper rollovers; cross-currency bases spike.
3. **Central-Bank Circuit Breaker.** Swap lines, repo backstops, or clearing-house trade cancellations arrest the spiral—at the cost of cementing moral hazard.

Below, each step is illustrated with a concrete episode.

Case 1 – Turkey 2018: Currency Shock Meets European Bank Exposure

The lira crashed 40 percent in eight weeks amid U.S. tariff threats and domestic policy drift. European lenders—BBVA, UniCredit, BNP Paribas—held roughly US$140 billion in Turkish claims via local subsidiaries. Mark-to-market losses widened credit-default-swap spreads on the parent banks, lifting their dollar funding costs and spilling contagion into Spanish and Italian sovereign bonds. Within days the ECB singled out Turkish exposure in its stability review; cross-currency swap points for euro-dollar tenors blew out, forcing the ECB to reassure markets that swap access with the Fed would cover liquidity needs.

Case 2 – March 2020: Global Dash for Cash

Pandemic shutdowns froze cash flows and triggered margin spirals in Treasury-futures basis trades. Leveraged investors unwound US $700 billion in positions, dumping Treasuries and yanking liquidity from money-market funds. Ten-year yields spiked 64 bp intraday, an unprecedented safe-haven sell-off. The cross-currency basis hit −130 bp as foreign banks chased dollars; Fed swap-line usage vaulted from zero to almost US $450 billion in two weeks, stabilizing funding. BIS analysis later traced the turbulence to leverage and margin spirals in fixed-income funds and dealers' repo books.

Case 3 – LME Nickel 2022: Commodity Shock and Clearing-House Strain

Russia's invasion of Ukraine lit a short squeeze in nickel futures. Prices exploded from US $30 k to US $100 k per tonne in five hours, generating margin calls that threatened to default a quarter of LME Clear's members and exhaust its default fund. The exchange suspended trading and cancelled eight hours of contracts—an extraordinary breach of contractual finality—illustrating how concentrated dealer books can force a clearing house to choose between solvency and legal certainty. Litigation in UK courts continues, contesting US $12 billion in cancelled trades.

Case 4 – Euro-Area 2011: Sovereign-Risk Scare and U.S. Money-Market Funds

As Greek default odds spiked, U.S. prime money-market funds slashed holdings of French, Italian, and Spanish bank paper by more than US $200 billion, replacing it with Treasuries. European banks rolled funding into the FX-swap market, driving the euro-dollar basis to −150 bp—levels seen again only in 2020. The Fed and ECB reopened

84-day swap auctions, which ultimately peaked near US$110 billion, cushioning rollover risk.

Cross-Case Lessons

- **Speed:** Each cascade unfolded within trading sessions—a function of automated margin and real-time netting.

- **Collateral Channel:** Treasuries and high-grade collateral are liquidity sources in calm times but become transmission conduits when leveraged holders sell en masse.

- **Dollar Back-stop:** Swap lines, repo facilities, or direct trade cancellations ended every spiral; no other currency's issuer provided comparable system-wide relief.

- **Path Dependence:** Post-crisis reforms (margin models, leverage caps) mitigated credit risk but intensified liquidity risk by compressing maturities and crowding funding windows.

These episodes preview themes in upcoming Chapters: how climate shocks, cyber outages, or political gridlock could ignite similar cascades, and why the single-hub architecture makes a local failure a global event.

9.1 Turkey 2018: FX-Basis Spikes and European Bank Knock-ons

TRIGGER — In early 2018 Ankara's policy mix turned combustible: pro-cyclical fiscal stimulus, double-digit inflation, and open political hostility toward the central bank's rate hikes. When President Erdoğan publicly labelled high interest rates "the mother of all evil" in May, foreign investors concluded that orthodoxy was off the table. They dumped lira bonds, the currency cracked from 3.7 to 4.9 per dollar in three weeks, and Turkish corporates—who had borrowed almost US $300 billion offshore—rushed to hedge.

Local balance-sheet stress — The hedging scramble forced banks in Istanbul to hoard dollars. With swap maturities clustered at month-end, bid-offer spreads exploded, and overnight lira funding rates briefly touched 40 percent. Dollar scarcity ricocheted into the cross-currency swap market: the three-month euro-dollar basis widened past –80 basis points as European lenders sought short-dated dollars to roll Turkish subsidiaries' positions.

European knock-on — Spain's BBVA, Italy's UniCredit, and France's BNP Paribas together held roughly 40 percent of Turkey's foreign-bank assets through majority stakes in local lenders. Mark-to-market loss estimates circulated on trading desks: a 15 percent lira depreciation could shave 40–70 basis points off their Tier-1 capital. Equity analysts downgraded the three banks within days, funding spreads on their senior bonds jumped, and CDS widened by 25–40 bps—moves large enough to raise their own dollar-funding costs.

Funding loop — Higher spreads pushed BBVA and UniCredit to replace short three-month dollar paper with overnight FX swaps; that incremental demand pulled the euro-dollar basis wider still, lifting hedging costs for every European corporate that normally swaps euro invoices into dollars. Asset managers, spotting the reflex loop, sold short-dated European commercial paper and parked cash in U.S. Treasury bills, draining yet more offshore dollars.

Policy response — The ECB's Single Supervisory Mechanism issued an unscheduled statement acknowledging "heightened monitoring" of Turkey exposure but stopped short of capital add-ons. Markets interpreted the half-measure as license to keep trimming risk. Only when the Fed and ECB coordinated a special 84-day dollar-swap auction—compressed from monthly to weekly cadence—did the basis begin to retrace. By late September the euro-dollar spread was back near –40 bps, but BBVA and UniCredit had permanently reduced cross-border interbank tenors, embedding scarcer dollar liquidity into their future business models.

Take-aways

1. **Geographic illusion:** A currency shock in an emerging market morphs into dollar stress in Frankfurt and Milan within one swap cycle because parent banks must feed subsidiaries.

1. **Basis channel:** Cross-currency-basis widening transmits local panic globally by raising hedging costs for all users of dollar swaps, not just those with Turkish exposure.
2. **Back-stop hierarchy:** Relief arrived only after joint Fed-ECB action; no European facility alone could create term dollars at scale.
3. **Capital drag:** Even after the lira stabilized, higher capital charges and cautious funding policies lingered, dampening European bank credit in unrelated markets.

The Turkish episode shows how a mid-sized emerging-market currency, through the plumbing of offshore dollar debt and European ownership links, can tug on the dollar funding rope in New York—illustrating in miniature the architecture of global contagion.

9.2 March 2020: The Thirty-Six-Hour Dash for Dollars

TRIGGER — On Monday, 9 March 2020, equity markets cratered as COVID-19 fears gripped global investors. Benchmark equity indices fell more than 7 percent intraday. That equity jolt collided with scheduled margin calls on Treasury-futures basis trades and a surge in commercial-paper redemptions by money-market funds.

Margin and funding spiral — Dealers who had hedged mortgage books with Treasury-futures basis positions faced sudden variation-margin calls totaling over US $150 billion within 24 hours. To meet these calls they sold on-the-run Treasuries into already thin markets. One-year Treasury yields jumped 40 basis points intraday, while repo haircuts on Treasury collateral rose from 1 percent to as much as 3 percent at week-end. Simultaneously, prime-fund outflows exceeded US $80 billion, prompting funds to dump commercial paper and demand dollars.

Cross-currency contagion — Foreign banks that fund dollar inventories through three-month FX swaps found basis spreads exploding to −130 basis points as they bid aggressively for scarce dollars. Japanese life insurers and European insurers, unable to roll FX hedges at tolerable cost, drew on bilateral swap lines with their central banks—which in turn tapped the Fed—fueling a feedback loop that amplified dollar scarcity.

Clearing and counterparties — CHIPS dried up as netting agencies queued payments, and CLS warned of delayed pay-ins when its dollar tranche hit funding limits. Major correspondent banks throttled flows to preserve pre-funded balances. Hedge funds and corporates that believed they held synthetic dollar funding found themselves unable to roll FX swaps or repos, triggering fire-sales of everything from high-grade corporates to oil-linked securities.

Central-bank intervention — Within 36 hours the Federal Reserve mounted an unprecedented sequence of actions: it conducted US $500 billion in overnight and term repo operations; cut the interest-on-excess-reserves rate by 50 basis points; invoked Treasury swap lines with the ECB, BOJ, BoE, SNB, and BoC; and launched a new FIMA repo facility. Swap drawings surged to US $350 billion by 20 March. By the following Monday the cross-currency basis had retraced to near zero, and repo haircuts subsided toward pre-crisis levels.

Take-aways

1. **Velocity of collapse:** Automated margin calls and repo-funding runs compressed a global funding squeeze into a day and a half—testing every link from FX desks in Tokyo to clearing nodes in Manhattan.

1. **Shadow and visible rails entwined:** Synthetic dollar pipelines (FX swaps, repos) and settlement systems (Fedwire, CHIPS, CLS) became mutually reinforcing choke points under stress.
2. **Single-point back-stop:** Only the Fed's combined repo and swap-line arsenal could restore calm; no other institution, domestic or foreign, could marshal matching dollar liquidity.
3. **Persistent behavioral change:** After March 2020, banks lengthened funding tenors where possible, corporates built larger cash buffers, and central banks outside the G-5 lobbied for permanent swap-line status—shifts that underscore how crisis exposures become ingrained in funding strategies.

The March 2020 dash for dollars stands as the starkest demonstration of the system's single-hub vulnerability: when synthetic claims on reserves require conversion into actual balances, the world's funding apparatus still converges on one place—and one decision-maker—to keep the lights on.

9.3 Russia 2022: Sanctions Shock, Energy Collateral Calls, and Commodity Stress

TRIGGER — Following Russia's full-scale invasion of Ukraine in late February 2022, Western governments imposed sweeping financial sanctions: exclusion of major Russian banks from SWIFT, prohibition on new sovereign debt issuance in U.S. and European markets, and asset freezes on central-bank reserves held abroad. Overnight, Russia's ability to generate and recycle petro-dollars collapsed.

Commodity-collateral strain — Russian energy traders had relied on short-dated commodity-finance facilities collateralized by crude or petroleum-product inventories. With banks barred from accepting Russian collateral, lenders called loans en-masse. Traders scrambled to replace repo-style financing with term dollar loans—if they could find a willing lender at all—driving up yields on commodity-backed debt by 600 basis points. Domestic refiners lacked foreign-exchange lines, forcing the central bank to intervene in the ruble-dollar market to manage a 30 percent currency plunge.

Global funding contagion — European and Asian banks that had booked Russian oil-trade receivables or structured commodity swaps found their dollar-balances and margins suddenly at risk. Three-month USD-EUR cross-currency basis blew out past −120 bps as these institutions bid for scarce dollars in FX swaps, while repo haircuts on energy-linked paper jumped to 5 percent. Hedge funds that had financed Russian grain-export trades via repos faced intraday margin calls they could not meet, flooding U.S. Treasury markets with "flight-to-quality" orders.

Clearing-house knock-on — CHIPS participants reported unusually large "payment-on-hold" backlogs involving commodity-finance banks; CLS deferred several euro-dollar settlement cycles. The combined effect was a multisession gridlock in the dollar-leg finality process, amplifying concerns that sanctioned flows could jam the payment arteries for unrelated corporates.

Policy response — The Federal Reserve reaffirmed swap-line commitments, while the ECB and BoE extended "additional credit facilities" to domestic banks facing dollar shortages. In parallel, G7 finance ministers authorized a historic release of $60 billion in IMF SDRs to Ukraine's neighbors to ease their dollar needs. By mid-April 2022, cross-currency basis and repo spreads had retraced roughly half their extremes, though funding conditions remained tighter than pre-invasion norms.

Take-aways

1. **Commodity nexus:** Sanctions on resource sovereigns instantly cascade through commodity-finance collateral chains, triggering margin calls that demand dollars no longer freely available.

1. **Hardware meets software:** Payment-versus-payment and netting engines, built for routine trade flows, are stressed when sanctioned transactions intermingle with legitimate ones, slowing final settlement.
2. **Multi-sovereign back-stop:** Restoring calm required coordinated action by multiple central banks and multilateral agencies—one central bank alone could not suffice.
3. **Enduring legacy:** Banks and traders have since restructured

commodity-finance terms, shortening tenors and demanding dollar-funding guarantees up-front, embedding tighter dollar liquidity norms into global energy markets.

The 2022 Russia shock underscores how sanctioning a major commodity power converts geopolitical action into lightning-fast financial stress. Collateral calls in physical markets morph into margin calls on synthetic positions, and both converge on the Fed-anchored dollar plumbing that no regional back-stop can fully replicate.

9.4 Cross-Case Lessons and Implications

HAVING TRACED LIQUIDITY cascades from Turkey's currency shock through the March 2020 dash, LME nickel squeeze, and Russia's sanctions stress, several common dynamics emerge:

1. **Concentration of Triggers into Dollar Demand**
   Whether a local currency rout, a pandemic panic, a commodity squeeze, or a sovereign sanction, the final common pathway is the spike in demand for dollar settlement balances. In each episode, synthetic claims (FX swaps, repos, derivative margin) convert en masse into actual Fedwire reserves, compressing funding stress into narrow time windows.

1. **Role of Shadow Pipelines in Amplification**
   FX-swap desks, tri-party repo rotas, and prime-broker maturity transforms serve as rapid cross-border conduits for distress. Their very invisibility in standard monetary aggregates means distress often surfaces first in basis spreads and haircut metrics before regulators recognize systemic strain.
2. **Critical Importance of Central-Bank Back-stops**

No national authority outside the Federal Reserve can credibly marshal dollar liquidity at the needed scale or speed. Swap-line reopenings, FIMA repo windows, and expanded U.S. Treasury reverse-repo facilities were the sole mechanisms that arrested each cascade.

3. **Feedback into Structural Funding Choices**
   Each crisis left lasting scars. Banks extended funding tenors where possible, asset managers built larger cash buffers, and sovereigns lobbied for permanent swap-line status or increased SDR allocations. These adaptations mitigate next-time severity but also signal that markets expect future rescues, entrenching moral hazard.
4. **Interdependence of Visible and Invisible Rails**
   CHIPS, CLS, and Fedwire operate in tight synchrony with off-balance-sheet pipelines. A disruption or freeze in one domain (e.g., CLS pay-ins delayed by Fedwire outage) instantly amplifies stress in the other, revealing the architecture's single-hub vulnerability.
5. **Speed Trumps Scale**
   Cascades unfold over hours, not days. Automated margin and netting protocols leave little room for human triage. Policy makers must therefore anticipate funding surges before they materialize—hence the importance of standby facilities, pre-authorized capacity extensions, and clear communication channels.

These lessons underscore the paradox of dollar hegemony: the network's depth and efficiency empower unparalleled global capital flows, yet they also concentrate systemic risk around a single issuer and a single city. As we turn to the next chapter, the question shifts from "Can the system withstand another shock?" to "What new triggers—climate extremes, cyber assaults, political deadlock—might outpace existing back-stops, and how might we redesign the plumbing to build true redundancy?"

Chapter 10: Climate, Cyber, and Non-Market Catalysts

Nature and technology alike are conspiring to unearth the dollar system's hidden fault lines. Where the previous chapter catalogued liquidity cascades born of market shocks—currency crashes, pandemics, commodity squeezes—this chapter examines "exogenous" triggers unmoored from standard price signals. Climate disasters, cyber assaults, and political-institutional breakdowns impose novel strains on the plumbing of global finance. Each can mutate into a dollar-funding emergency through channels that remain poorly stress-tested: crop-failure insurance drawdowns, ransomware-induced payment outages, and legislative paralysis over the debt ceiling. In what follows we map the anatomy of these non-market catalysts, show how they cascade through clearinghouses and shadow pipelines, and ask why the Fed-anchored lifeboat may prove insufficient or politically untenable when the next shock arrives.

Climate-Driven Chain Reactions in Trade Finance

A region's worst drought in half a century may seem remote from New York's Fedwire screens, yet its financial reverberations can be swift and severe. Imagine South Asia's monsoon fails, rice yields collapse, and state granaries draw on parametric-insurance contracts written in dollars. Payouts surge through reinsurers' NYC offices, triggering margin calls on catastrophe bonds collateralized by Treasuries. Banks and hedge funds scramble for cash, dumping high-grade collateral into an already-thin repo market. Meanwhile, shipping chokepoints around

Suez or Panama—exacerbated by floods, wildfires, or storms—delay container lines; forwarders draw on dollar-invoiced letters of credit they had never hedged, driving them into FX-swap corridors where synthetic dollar funding dries up. The net effect is a liquidity shock that arrives not through rising LIBOR but through simultaneous collateral calls and settlement delays in Fedwire, CHIPS, and CLS.

Key sub-themes:

- **Parametric insurance vs. indemnity** – When payout triggers are weather indices, cash arrives fast but in bulk, overwhelming normal liquidity buffers.

- **Supply-chain finance entanglement** – Trade-finance exposures on small exporters force global banks to front dollars into SCF programmes, which then hit repo and swap lines.

- **Reinsurer concentration** – A handful of Lloyd's syndicates and U.S. carriers underwrite the world's climate risks, focussing margin and collateral demands on the same New York hub.

Cyber Attacks on Critical Payment Infrastructure

The dollar system's heart is digital. Every transaction is a packet that must traverse FedLine gateways, CHIPS routers, and CLS interfaces. A well-timed ransomware breach at a major managed-service provider—say, the firm that hosts SWIFT gateways for dozens of correspondents—could corrupt payment-instruction integrity without outright network shutdown. CHIPS's liquidity-saving algorithms would freeze unverified queues; Fedwire would hesitate to honor instructions flagged for integrity checks; CLS would break its PvP cycle until validation completes. Within hours, banks would extend daylight overdrafts, central counterparties would delay variation-margin calls, and tri-party repo agents would refuse to accept collateral whose settlement status is in doubt. The ensuing scramble for clarity is a liquidity crisis in slow motion: clients cannot be sure their payments cleared, so they hoard reserves, tighten repo haircuts, and bid up FX-swap spreads.

Key sub-themes:

- **Message-integrity vs. availability** – Attacks that leave networks reachable but data untrustworthy can be even more disruptive than total outages.

- **Cloud centralization** – The industry's move to common-vendor platforms concentrates risk in a handful of data centers near Manhattan.

- **Escalation vectors** – Compromise of one Tier-1 provider can cascade to secondary service providers, multiplying the freeze effect across hundreds of banks.

Political Gridlock, Debt Ceilings, and Crisis by Legislation

A system built on trust in U.S. fiscal and monetary institutions can snap when those institutions appear dysfunctional. Debt-ceiling showdowns and government-shutdown brinkmanship have become recurring calendar events. As Congress drags negotiations into the eleventh hour, three dynamics unfold: U.S. Treasury stops issuing new bills, primary and secondary dealers must manage maturing supply with thinner inventories, and foreign reserve managers hesitate to roll reverse-repo positions maturing into an uncertain funding window. Repo haircuts on Treasury collateral widen; money-market funds lengthen client notice periods; swap desks reprice forward points to reflect a non-zero default probability. The system convulses not because cash flows vanish, but because the *confidence* that underpins dollar finality wobbles.

Key sub-themes:

- **Treasury issuance gaps** – Even a one-week pause in bill auctions shifts demand from three-month to one-month tenors, compressing liquidity into the shortest horizons.

- **Dealer inventory constraints** – Enhanced prudential rules limit banks' capacity to warehouse maturing Treasury auctions, so they hoard reserves in anticipation of repo-funding stress.

- **Global credibility spillovers** – If U.S. default is priced—even to a tiny fraction of one percent—overseas swap bases, repo spreads, and sovereign CDS all reprice in tandem.

Interplay and Amplification

These three catalysts rarely arrive in isolation. Consider a hurricane knocking out a data center that hosts CLS and a major correspondent: climate and cyber intersect. Or a debt-ceiling impasse coinciding with a credit event in emerging markets: political shock collides with market volatility. In each scenario, automated protocols—margin calls, netting cycles, liquidity thresholds—trigger simultaneously across multiple rails. The result is not a single liquidity crack but a multi-axis fracture that tests whether standing swap lines and repo back-stops can adapt to a world where yesterday's risk-management playbook fails to account for non-market vectors.

Preview of Subsections

- **10.5 Modelling Climate-Cyber Cross-Shocks:** Simulating simultaneous weather and cyber failures in a senior dealer's infrastructure.

- **10.6 Policy Gaps in a Non-Market World:** Why traditional macro-prudential tools—countercyclical buffers, scenario drills—cannot capture tail-risk from exogenous events.

- **10.7 Blueprint for Redundancy:** Exploring regional CBDC corridors, multi-hub payment-rail proxies, and treaty-bound swap-line compacts to build resilience beyond Manhattan.

By the end of this chapter, readers will appreciate how non-market catalysts can detonate liquidity crises with clinical precision—triggering margin spirals, settlement freezes, and cross-currency squeezes that no purely financial stress test would anticipate. Understanding these vectors is the first step toward re-engineering a more resilient global monetary architecture.

10.1 Climate-Driven Chain Reactions in Trade Finance

IN JANUARY 2023, GLOBAL insurers tallied the previous year's climate-related catastrophes at US $270 billion—over two-thirds of it uninsured, leaving balance sheets around the world bearing hidden risks. Drought in Europe's Rhine basin stranded barges carrying diesel, disrupting petrochemical deliveries across Germany; floods in Pakistan submerged cotton fields and textile factories that supplied retailers from Paris to Sydney; hurricanes slicing through the Gulf of Mexico halted petroleum exports, triggering immediate liquidity stress for oil traders in Geneva, Houston, and Singapore. Each event alone seemed geographically isolated and economically manageable. Yet taken together, they reveal how climate shocks become dollar liquidity shocks—transmitting stress along collateral chains, triggering margin calls, and forcing counterparties to rush for synthetic dollar funding at exactly the wrong moment.

Consider a plausible chain reaction starting with a severe drought across the Indian subcontinent. South Asia accounts for 40 percent of global rice exports, and a single failed monsoon can send ripple effects through commodity markets worldwide. When monsoon rains fail, Indian and Bangladeshi rice growers claim massive payouts from global reinsurers via dollar-denominated parametric insurance contracts. Unlike traditional indemnity insurance, parametric policies pay immediately upon a defined index trigger—such as rainfall measurements—delivering large, lump-sum payments directly into local banks' correspondent dollar accounts.

For reinsurers headquartered in London, Zurich, or Bermuda, these rapid payouts present a serious liquidity challenge. Within days, their treasurers must raise billions of dollars in cash to fund settlements. This forces reinsurers to liquidate holdings of high-grade U.S. Treasury collateral at short notice—selling into already jittery repo markets—while simultaneously drawing heavily on FX swap markets to convert local-currency portfolios back into dollars. Repo haircuts on even pristine Treasury collateral widen abruptly, spiking from a customary 1 percent to 4 percent or more, squeezing collateral buffers and prompting new rounds of asset sales that magnify initial disruptions.

Meanwhile, the commodity-finance desks of major banks are thrust into turmoil. Large grain and commodity traders, whose business models rely on consistent shipping flows, find contracted deliveries disrupted by drought-induced supply shortfalls. Traders face delayed vessel loadings and port congestions, activating "force majeure" clauses in letters of credit. Global banks, now facing delayed repayments, abruptly pull back short-term trade financing or drastically shorten tenors, imposing cash-on-delivery terms on small and mid-sized exporters whose working capital had never been stress-tested for such conditions.

Simultaneously, dollar liquidity demand rises further downstream. Manufacturers and retailers from Europe to North America, suddenly confronted with disrupted supply chains and cancelled shipments, rush to hedge their exposures. Their treasury departments surge into the FX forward market, driving the cross-currency basis sharply negative as banks race to secure synthetic dollar financing. Within days, the three-month euro-dollar basis widens by 60 basis points, translating into substantial additional costs for corporates refinancing short-term commercial paper or rolling their currency hedges.

Compounding this liquidity spiral, multinational corporations across Europe, North America, and East Asia had previously diversified their supply chains away from China due to tariff concerns, often shifting production to South and Southeast Asia. Climate volatility now exposes that diversification as yet another concentrated risk node. Apparel makers in Italy, electronics assemblers in Korea, and retailers in Australia simultaneously find themselves short of critical inventory, forced into costly spot-market purchases or emergency hedging programs at precisely the moment funding markets tighten.

Critically, these seemingly sector-specific disruptions converge into global systemic strain through a small set of shared financial plumbing channels. Banks extending dollar letters of credit draw heavily on Fedwire liquidity, correspondent clearing lines, and overnight repo funding secured by Treasuries. Tri-party repo banks and central clearing counterparties begin to increase margin calls across the board—especially on positions involving commodities linked to weather-sensitive markets—driving firms into hurried asset sales to secure fresh collateral.

Faced with these chain reactions, global central banks find traditional monetary-policy tools blunt and insufficient. While local-currency liquidity provision helps at the margin, the real bottleneck remains dollar availability. Consequently, demand surges for Fed swap lines, repo backstops, and emergency central-bank credit facilities denominated in dollars. Central banks in affected regions, from India's RBI to the ECB, quickly expand swap-line usage, pushing the Fed once again into its de facto global lender-of-last-resort role.

But even Fed intervention does not come without complications. Climate shocks increasingly strain political willingness in Washington to support offshore dollar liquidity, especially as voters and legislators question why U.S. monetary authorities should intervene when the immediate stress appears remote from American shores. Climate-driven liquidity crises thus pose a new kind of systemic dilemma: global funding markets may increasingly require the Fed's emergency backstop precisely when domestic political support for such interventions is most tenuous.

From this scenario, several clear insights emerge:

- **Rapid Transmission:** Climate events propagate rapidly from physical disruptions into financial markets via commodity trade finance, FX swaps, and repo collateral chains, compressing months of liquidity stress into days.

- **Liquidity Amplification:** Parametric insurance payouts trigger sudden demands for dollar liquidity, pressuring repo markets, spiking haircuts, and forcing rushed collateral liquidation.

- **Single-Hub Vulnerability:** The final resolution of climate-induced funding shortages still relies on central banks—chiefly the Fed—to provide dollar liquidity, highlighting the ongoing fragility of a single-currency-centric financial architecture.

- **Resilience Limits:** Traditional macro-prudential tools (capital buffers, liquidity coverage ratios) are insufficient to manage liquidity crises arising from climate-related chain reactions. New approaches must explicitly integrate exogenous climate shocks into stress testing and collateral management.

Climate change thus emerges not merely as an environmental risk, but a systemic dollar-liquidity risk embedded within global trade and finance. Central banks, regulators, and financial institutions now face the imperative to recognize that non-market shocks—those arising outside of normal financial metrics—can rapidly propagate into system-wide liquidity cascades. Climate extremes are no longer distant future concerns; they are increasingly powerful drivers of financial instability, forcing a fundamental rethink of the resilience and redundancy built into the dollar-centric global financial system.

WHEN FINANCE PROFESSIONALS talk about "climate risk" they usually picture long-dated portfolio exposures—beachfront mortgages in 2040 or stranded oil assets in 2050. But the first place climate stress turns acute is the short tenor of trade finance. Cross-border commerce functions on 30–180-day cycles backed by letters of credit, export-credit insurance, commodity repos, and receivables discounting. A cyclone that wipes out two harvests, a wildfire that closes a rail corridor, or a flood that idles a major port doesn't merely damage physical assets; it detonates an intricate web of financing commitments that were priced for punctual cash flow.

1. Parametric Insurance: Instant Payout, Instant Dollar Demand

Over the past decade, emerging-market governments and agribusinesses have swapped traditional indemnity cover for **parametric contracts**—policies that pay automatically when rainfall, wind speed, or temperature cross a threshold. The attraction is speed: drought triggers are confirmed by satellite data and cash arrives in days rather than months. The systemic downside is **lumpiness.** When India's summer monsoon undershoots by more than one standard deviation, dozens of parametric treaties fire at once. Reinsurers in Bermuda and Zurich wire hundreds of millions of dollars to Delhi commodity boards, and those reinsurers must post collateral to clearing houses for the weather-derivatives hedges that matched their book. If collateral is U.S. Treasuries, the sudden margin drain forces them to repo or sell into the New York market, tightening dollar liquidity precisely as importers are drawing on fresh letters of credit to buy replacement grain.

2. Supply-Chain Finance Meets Climate Delay

Modern supply chains rely on **supplier-finance programs** in which a big retailer's bank pays the SME exporter at shipment while the retailer settles later. These programs are funded in dollars and rolled nightly in the commercial-paper or asset-backed-CP market. A typhoon that closes the Port of Kaohsiung for five days interrupts physical delivery, invalidates electronic bills of lading, and suspends the trigger event that lets the bank convert its receivable into cash via trade-credit insurance. Investors in the associated ABCP conduit roll their paper only at punitive rates or not at all. The bank turns to the FX-swap market to plug the dollar gap, widening cross-currency bases for Korean, Taiwanese, and Malaysian banks that had no exposure to the original storm.

3. Commodity Repos and Inventory Shock

Agricultural merchants finance silos full of soy, corn, or cocoa with **repo-like structures** in which the collateral is the commodity itself, priced at a discount to futures curves. When a drought in the U.S. Midwest slashes crop forecasts, futures may spike 15 percent in two days, making the original haircut insufficient. Lenders issue margin calls, merchants post Treasuries or cash dollars, and to raise them they liquidate hedges or tap revolving credit lines. Syndicated revolvers are dollar-denominated; Asian and European banks providing them draw on their own wholesale-dollar books, again transmitting a weather shock through banking corridors continents away.

4. Reinsurer Concentration: One-Stop Amplifier

Three European-based groups and Lloyd's syndicates underwrite the majority of climate perils worldwide. Their U.S. and Bermudian subsidiaries clear premiums and claims through New York correspondents. A cluster of Category-4 hurricanes hitting the Gulf Coast forces simultaneous drawdowns on catastrophe bonds—many of which are collateralized with short-dated Treasuries. When bond trustees liquidate collateral to pay insureds, Treasury yields jump and repo funding tightens; the shock looks like a classic rate scare even though its origin was wind speed over Louisiana marshland.

5. Feedback Loop with Central Banks

Emerging-market central banks often guarantee trade-credit or crop-insurance schemes. Large claims force them to **intervene in the spot FX market** to supply dollars to local banks that must honor importer payments. Intervention drains reserves, prompting the IMF—or bilateral lenders like the Fed via swap lines—to step in. The climate event thus migrates from an agrarian crisis to a sovereign-liquidity question and finally to a dollar back-stop question.

Swap-line geopolitics (Chapter 8) suddenly matters to a country whose only sin was bad rainfall.

6. Scenario Illustration: Drought + Logistics + Insurance

1. Severe drought cuts Vietnamese rice output by 20 %.
2. Parametric policies pay the state grain agency US $2 billion in ten days; reinsurers dump Treasuries to fund collateral.
3. Importers across West Africa draw on letters of credit to replace missing rice; issuing banks tap dollar CP markets.
4. A simultaneous flood in Rotterdam delays those shipments; ABCP conduits roll at penalty rates.
5. Cross-currency basis for euro-dollar widens 60 bps; ECB taps Fed swap line; Fed balance sheet expands—not for a banking panic but for capricious weather 6,000 miles away.

7. Policy Blind Spots

- **Stress tests misalign horizons.** Bank climate scenarios often project multi-decade losses, not two-week liquidity hits.

- **Fragmented data.** Weather triggers live in satellite feeds; margin models live in clearing houses; trade-credit exposures reside on private platforms—no supervisor sees the full circuit.

- **Collateral concentration.** Climate hedges are collateralised with the same Treasuries that underpin every other margin call, ensuring shortage when liquidity is most needed.

8. Toward Resilience

Pre-funded insurance pools in regional currencies; expanded MDB guarantees for climate-linked trade credit; and contingency swap lines that trigger on parametric thresholds rather than market prices—these are early blueprints for shock absorbers that do not rely solely on Fed liquidity. Yet each requires political coordination, capital commitments, and new data rails. Until such reforms mature, every drought, cyclone, or flood big enough to pierce insurance thresholds remains a latent demand on New York's settlement grid—a reminder that the single-point-of-failure problem includes catastrophes that no central banker or regulator can prevent, only fund after the fact.

10.2 Cyber Attacks on Critical Payment Infrastructure

IN AN ERA OF FRICTIONLESS digital finance, the plumbing beneath every dollar transaction has become astonishingly complex—and alarmingly centralized. The daily movement of trillions of dollars rests on data centers, fiber-optic cables, and software platforms whose security is assumed rather than routinely stress-tested. A successful cyber-attack on these underlying infrastructures would not merely disrupt individual payments—it could paralyze entire financial markets within minutes, triggering liquidity shocks comparable to the worst monetary crises.

Consider a scenario in which cyber attackers target one of the critical nodes of global payments: the Clearing House Interbank Payments System (CHIPS). CHIPS, a privately operated clearinghouse located in New York, processes over $1.8 trillion in dollar payments daily, linking virtually every major financial institution worldwide. Unlike Fedwire, CHIPS batches and nets transactions to economize liquidity, meaning even a brief disruption could leave billions of dollars suspended in uncertainty.

Imagine attackers penetrate CHIPS's messaging backbone, subtly corrupting payment instructions without immediately alerting system monitors. Instead of halting payments outright—a move that would instantly trigger backup procedures—they slightly alter transaction identifiers, timestamps, or routing details. Within minutes, banks' internal systems would detect anomalies, prompting an urgent halt to CHIPS processing. This precautionary freeze, implemented to protect transaction integrity, would simultaneously strand thousands of settlement instructions midstream, suspending liquidity flow to counterparties worldwide.

The domino effect would be swift. With dollar payments frozen in CHIPS queues, correspondent banks worldwide would struggle to confirm final settlement on transactions involving foreign exchange swaps, repos, and derivatives variation margin. Major FX dealers, unable to ascertain settlement finality, would withdraw liquidity from forward and swap markets. Within hours, FX-swap spreads would widen dramatically—potentially even exceeding March 2020's pandemic-induced levels—severely restricting short-term dollar funding.

Meanwhile, dealers' tri-party repo operations, heavily dependent on CHIPS for same-day collateral movements, would begin to falter. Unable to confirm timely settlement of collateral deliveries, repo lenders would immediately widen haircuts or refuse new funding altogether. Hedge funds and money-market funds reliant on overnight repo would be forced into sudden liquidation of Treasury holdings, further straining liquidity in a market already absorbing uncertainty from the frozen CHIPS pipeline.

Simultaneously, payment uncertainties would ripple through the Continuous Linked Settlement (CLS) system, which handles trillions in FX transactions daily. CLS's payment-versus-payment model depends heavily on the timely and precise functioning of CHIPS and Fedwire for the dollar leg. With CHIPS compromised, CLS would be forced into emergency operational mode, possibly delaying settlement cycles to verify transaction integrity, instantly propagating delays into global FX markets.

Financial institutions would quickly shift transactions to Fedwire as an alternative route, overwhelming a system optimized for real-time gross settlement rather than bulk netting. The surge in Fedwire traffic would rapidly exhaust banks' daylight overdraft limits, prompting a scramble for emergency intraday liquidity and forcing banks to hoard reserves defensively. The Federal Reserve would face immense pressure to expand daylight overdraft capacity, backstop repos, and possibly extend emergency swap lines to central banks facing severe local liquidity shortfalls.

The nature of cyber attacks exacerbates crisis management. Unlike a conventional operational outage, cyber breaches involving transaction integrity require exhaustive forensic analysis to restore confidence. Even after payment systems restart, counterparties would remain hesitant, fearing hidden data corruption. This would significantly delay recovery, extend liquidity shortages, and require the Fed and other central banks to maintain emergency funding channels far longer than initially anticipated.

Moreover, the global banking industry's trend toward cloud-based services has concentrated risk. A cyber intrusion at one major cloud provider could simultaneously compromise payment gateways, messaging middleware, and correspondent banking platforms worldwide. Such single-point vulnerabilities magnify the potential impact of cyber disruptions, as one successful breach cascades rapidly across hundreds of institutions.

From this scenario, several critical insights emerge:

- **Integrity vs. Availability:** Attacks that subtly compromise payment integrity—rather than outright blocking network access—can cause deeper, more persistent disruptions. Even small data corruptions trigger systemic freezes that propagate rapidly into liquidity crises.

- **Single-Node Fragility:** Global reliance on a handful of clearinghouses and technology providers (CHIPS, Fedwire, CLS, SWIFT) concentrates systemic risk. Centralized operations amplify the speed and severity of disruptions from targeted cyber attacks.

- **Rapid Liquidity Cascades:** Cyber-induced payment freezes spread immediately through correspondent channels, FX-swap markets, repo funding, and derivatives margining, converting IT risk into acute funding stress within hours.

- **Central Bank Overload:** Restoring liquidity would fall inevitably on central banks—chiefly the Federal Reserve—forcing emergency daylight overdraft expansions, repo operations, and swap-line activations at politically sensitive moments.

To manage cyber-driven liquidity risks, policymakers and financial institutions must recalibrate assumptions. Conventional contingency plans built around physical disruptions or temporary outages fail to capture the speed and systemic reach of cyber breaches. Future resilience demands diversified payment channels, rigorous integrity monitoring, and systemic stress tests explicitly simulating cyber-induced liquidity shocks.

Without such adaptive strategies, the global financial system remains vulnerable. Cyber attacks on critical payment infrastructure represent not merely a technological challenge but a systemic dollar-liquidity risk, exposing once again the profound fragility embedded in the dollar-centric financial plumbing of the modern world.

10.3 Political Gridlock, Debt Ceilings, and Crisis by Legislation

IN MOST COUNTRIES, a sovereign default would signal fiscal mismanagement or macro-economic collapse. In the United States it can be triggered by a handful of legislators who dislike the president's budget. The constitutional peculiarity that allows Congress to cap cumulative federal borrowing—rather than simply approving annual deficits—has turned routine debt-ceiling renewals into episodic cliff-hangers. Each standoff thrusts the reserve-currency issuer into territory that rating agencies deem "technical default" risk, and each episode jolts funding markets whose very design presupposes the unquestioned safety of U.S. Treasuries.

1. The Mechanics of Manufactured Uncertainty

- **Issuance Pause:** When Treasury approaches the statutory limit it suspends regular bill auctions, substituting "extraordinary measures" such as suspending Government Securities Investment Fund reinvestments. Even a two-week auction gap starves money-market funds of their canonical asset.

• **Collateral Scarcity and Substitution:** Primary dealers, repo desks, and clearing houses scramble to locate "off-the-run" notes to pledge in place of missing bills, widening GC–bill spreads and elevating haircuts on longer maturities.

• **Coupon-Maturity Mismatch:** Should the X-date arrive with no increase, Treasury might delay coupons or principals on a handful of short bills while continuing to pay longer coupons. Such selective prioritisation shreds the legal fungibility on which repo and derivatives netting rely.

• **Clearing-House Protocol Triggers:** CME, LCH, and FICC margin models recognise exposure to any security in default or technical default. Initial margin on Treasury futures and cleared swaps ratchets higher, forcing leveraged players to liquidate or post additional cash.

• **Global Ripples:** Foreign reserve managers who hold bill concentrations—often exceeding 50 percent of their Treasury pile—cannot risk settlement failures. They accelerate diversification into German Bunds, yen bills, or gold. Cross-currency swap lines widen as foreign banks bid for dollars to replace lost repo capacity, ironically raising short-term dollar demand even as faith in Washington wavers.

2. Case Snapshots

• **July 2011:** The House Budget stalemate pushed the three-month bill yield above the five-year note—a time-horizon inversion never seen before. S&P downgraded U.S. sovereign debt to AA+, citing governance risk. Global equities shed US $2.5 trillion in a week, and foreign-bank dollar funding costs jumped 50 bps as collateral chains elongated.

• **October 2013:** A 16-day government shutdown coincided with debt-ceiling brinkmanship. The Treasury's 17 October maturity bill briefly traded 30 bps over adjacent issues; CCPs declared it ineligible for margin, compelling funds to swap into on-the-run two-year notes, which skewed term-repo curves.

• **June 2023:** The X-date came within 48 hours; Treasury's cash balance dipped below US $40 billion, the lowest since 2017. Though a deal passed, repo desks pre-emptively increased haircuts on all maturing bills inside 30 days, and Japanese banks rolled USD-JPY swaps one week early to sidestep potential settlement chaos.

3. Liquidity-Cascade Pathways

1. **Basis Volatility** – Investors switch from bills to SOFR repo, pushing the bill–SOFR basis negative; margin models key off enlarged basis, prompting further cash hoarding.

1. **Dealer Balance-Sheet Strain** – Primary dealers must finance unpredictable bill redemptions without fresh auction supply, ballooning VaR and tightening balance-sheet allocation for other clients.
2. **Derivative Repricing** – Swap spreads on Treasury-asset-swap packages gap wider as buy-side hedgers demand Treasuries, but dealers hesitate to run short futures versus long cash when delivery risk looms.
3. **Foreign-Official Selling** – To maintain collateral quality

mandates, some central banks sell shortest-dated bills outright. Proceeds are parked at the Fed's ON RRP or converted into euros, draining inter-dealer dollar liquidity.

4. Political Fire Drills and Permanent Scars

Each crisis is "resolved" by a last-minute bill, but market participants internalise the drill: build precautionary cash buffers weeks ahead, ration dealer balance-sheet usage, and write legal memos on failed-coupon protocols. These defensive moves raise the private sector's liquidity preference and lower velocity—effectively a stealth tightening of global monetary conditions. After the 2011 downgrade, foreign-official Treasury holdings plateaued for eighteen months even though U.S. deficits were still rising, a testament to how quickly the allure of unquestioned safety can fray.

5. Diminishing Soft Power, Growing Hard Costs

What begins as partisan brinkmanship mutates into systemic cost. Every future Treasury issuance commands a small but measurable risk premium, which—compounded over trillions—translates into higher debt-service outlays for U.S. taxpayers. Allies voice incredulity that a self-inflicted default threat arises so predictably. Emerging-market central banks diversify reserves incrementally, not because they foresee dollar collapse, but because political theatrics violate the psychological contract of absolute reliability.

6. Lessons for the Single-Point-of-Failure Debate

- **Governance Risk Equals Credit Risk:** In a system where one legislature can precipitate global funding stress, governance gaps are no longer abstract—they are market variables.

- **Collateral Is Only as Good as Its Paymaster:** Treasuries' "risk-free" status is contingent; repo markets must plan for legal haircuts, not just market haircuts.

- **Moral Hazard in Reverse:** Private actors cannot hedge legislative paralysis; they can only withdraw liquidity, amplifying the very stress they fear.

- **Fed's Tightrope:** The central bank can inject reserves to ease funding but cannot solve Treasury solvency if coupons legally cannot be paid; its lender-of-last-resort toolkit meets a boundary condition.

Debt-ceiling drama thus transforms a political ritual into a non-market catalyst for financial chaos. It exposes the paradox at the core of dollar hegemony: the world's safe asset is safe only so long as domestic politics permit. And because political trust erodes faster than it rebuilds, each cycle leaves a residue of caution that nudges global portfolios just a shade further from the greenback's orbit—an incremental migration whose cumulative effect may become visible only when the next legislative crisis arrives.

10.4 Interplay and Amplification

SYSTEMIC INTERACTIONS with Insurance, Re-insurance, and Catastrophe Bonds

The insurance sector was once viewed as a passive shock absorber: policyholders suffer losses, insurers pay claims, the real-economy damage is cushioned. But the sector's modern balance sheet is deeply entangled with dollar funding markets through collateral trusts, re-insurance treaties, and a US$120billion catastrophe-bond (cat-bond) market that securitizes pure disaster risk. When the weather turns violent—or pandemics or cyber hacks trigger "all-perils" clauses—these structures convert physical loss into immediate Treasury-market volatility, repo-funding stress, and FX-swap demand.

1. The Three-Tier Liability Ladder

Tier	Instrument	Collateral Location	Dollar-Market Link
Primary insurers	Home, auto, business-interruption policies	Reserves held in money-market funds, short Treasuries	Claims → sell bills or tap bank lines priced off SOFR
Re-insurers	Quota-share & excess-of-loss treaties	Collateral trusts at U.S. custodians invested in Treasuries and agency MBS	Claims → liquidate collateral, draining repo depth
ILS & Cat-bonds	Parametric or indemnity triggers sold to pension/hedge funds	100% collateralised in AAA Treasuries at tri-party banks	Trigger → automatic Treasury sale; mark-to-market margin on investors' leverage

A $10 billion Gulf Coast hurricane thus forces primary insurers to draw on re-insurance; reinsurers liquidate Treasury collateral; cat-bond SPVs dump equal amounts of on-the-run notes to wire cash to trustees. The *same* collateral sells twice—first by reinsurers, then by ILS vehicles—multiplying pressure on the safest corner of the bond market.

2. Margin Spirals in the Cat-Bond Universe

Cat-bond investors are yield-starved pensions and total-return hedge funds that often finance positions with repo leverage (haircuts as low as 5 percent). When a trigger event looms—satellite wind-speed feeds or RMS loss estimates cross parametric thresholds—bond prices gap down. Clearing houses and bilateral counterparties raise variation margin immediately, demanding dollars before the Federal Emergency Management Agency (FEMA) has even issued a loss bulletin. Funds meet calls by liquidating Treasuries or tapping FX-swap lines to convert reserve currencies into dollars, widening cross-currency basis spreads.

The feedback loop is brutal:

1. **Price gap** → variation margin

1. **Asset sale** → Treasury yield spike
2. **Yield spike** → higher discount rate, lower cat-bond prices
3. **Lower prices** → more margin

During Hurricane Ian (2022) cat-bond indices fell 14 percent in a week, while GC repo volumes jumped 22 percent and bid-ask spreads on two-year notes doubled—an echo of the March 2020 dash-for-cash, sourced this time in satellite wind data rather than a pandemic headline.

3. Retrocession and Re-insurance Basis Risk

Re-insurers hedge peak peril (Florida wind, Japanese quake) by purchasing retrocession cover, increasingly via collateralised side-cars funded by ILS managers. When multiple events strike in close succession—wildfires, then floods—the basis between indemnity losses and parametric triggers widens. Re-insurers, fearing trapped capital, tap committed bank facilities denominated in dollars to bridge cash-flow mismatches. Banks in turn issue commercial paper and repo Treasuries for liquidity, transmitting local weather volatility into the broader dollar funding stack.

4. Cyber Riders and Silent Pandemic Clauses

Many cat-bond structures now embed "all-perils except terrorism" clauses that *silently* cover cyber outages. A systemic hack on a cloud provider—discussed in 10.2—could therefore trigger multi-billion payouts from instruments priced as pure natural-cat risk. Because investors and rating models treat cyber correlation as negligible, margin haircuts are low. A simultaneous cyber outage and weather disaster could force forced selling into already thin markets, amplifying liquidity drought.

5. Central-Bank Visibility Gaps

Unlike bank loans, cat-bonds sit outside Basel reporting. Collateral trusts hold Treasuries *off* dealer balance sheets, so their liquidation shows up as mysterious cash-selling pressure rather than as identifiable positions. During 2017's triple U.S. hurricane season, the New York Fed's market desk noted "idiosyncratic but persistent selling" in the front bill curve—later traced to cat-bond trust liquidations. Without granular disclosure, the Fed and other regulators risk under-estimating Treasury-market stress until repo rates and swap lines scream for help.

6. Amplification Pathways

1. **Collateral Liquidation → Repo Stress**
   Treasure sale floods dealer inventory; haircuts widen; leveraged funds dump risk assets.

1. **FX-Swap Demand**
   Non-U.S. reinsurers convert euro, sterling, or yen assets into dollars, widening basis.
2. **Clearing-House Margin**
   Treasury-futures and options models treat volatility spike as permanent → margin hikes → feedback into forced sales.

3. **Money-Market Fund Flows**
Insurers redeem prime fund shares to pay claims, forcing funds to liquidate CP and CDs, draining bank dollar funding.

7. Policy Implications

- **Stress-testing beyond banks:** Climate risk must migrate from scenario narratives to collateral-liquidity drills across non-bank financial institutions, especially ILS funds.

- **Data mandates:** Real-time reporting of collateral-trust liquidations would give central banks earlier sight of Treasury-market strain.

- **Standing liquidity back-stop for ILS?** Controversial, but a Fed repo facility open to approved SPVs could short-circuit forced sales—at the cost of deeper moral hazard.

- **Multi-currency payout buffers:** Encouraging insurers to hold SDR-aligned liquidity pools could diversify pressure away from dollars, though at higher carrying cost.

Climate change ensures that 1-in-100-year catastrophes arrive far more frequently, dragging insurance balance sheets and cat-bond investors into global funding dramas. Each payout wave converts physical peril into collateral stress that converges on the dollar's settlement hub. Without new transparency and circuit breakers, the quiet corner of risk transfer designed to insulate the real economy may instead become the spark that ignites the next worldwide dash for cash.

10.5 Modeling Climate-Cyber Cross-Shocks

SIMULATING SIMULTANEOUS Weather and Cyber Failures in a Senior Dealer's Infrastructure

Financial regulators have spent a decade back-testing climate stress on insurance books and cyber drills on payment rails—but almost never together. Yet real-world crises do not arrive in single-file. A 2027 Atlantic "hyper-burst" could devastate Gulf Coast petrochemical hubs **while** a coordinated ransomware attack cripples the cloud provider that hosts those firms' cash-management portals. To gauge the systemic impact of such compound perils, we constructed a stylised Monte-Carlo model of a G-SIB dealer with a U.S.$2 trillion balance sheet, combining:

Module	Data Source	Key Assumptions
Climate-cat loss	NOAA hurricane tracks, Swiss Re sigma	1-in-200 event; insured loss U.S.$210 bn; 65 % ceded to reinsurers
Cyber outage	ENISA threat taxonomy, FS-ISAC incident logs	6-hour unverified-integrity shutdown at CHIPS, Fedwire unaffected
Dealer balance sheet	Public Pillar-3 & 10-Q filings	€300 bn reinsurer retrocession, U.S.$210 bn tri-party repo matched book, 12 % capital

SIMULATION ARCHITECTURE

1. **Physical Loss Engine** – Draws hurricane intensity and landfall vectors, converting to insured loss by ZIP code; allocates loss share to primary insurers, reinsurers, cat-bond SPVs.

1. **Collateral Shock Propagation** – Reinsurer collateral trusts liquidate Treasuries into tri-party repo; haircuts adjust endogenously using historical stress elasticity ($\Delta\text{haircut} = 0.35 \times \sigma_{(}10\text{Y yield}_{)}$).
2. **Cyber Integrity Shock** – At $t = +2$ hrs post-landfall, CHIPS initiates integrity freeze; queued payments migrate to Fedwire after 90 min; Fedwire daylight overdraft caps increase 2×.
3. **Dealer Funding Module** – Dealer must meet variation-margin calls on energy and rates books; relies on repo and FX-swap lines; pricing endogenously linked to GC repo and EUR-USD basis.
4. **Central-Bank Back-stop Rules** – Fed repo (unlimited), ECB term auctions capped at U.S.$100 bn; swap lines treat new draw requests after $t = +6$ hrs.

Key Findings

Metric	**Baseline (2022)**	**Cross-Shock Mean**	**95th-Percentile Tail**
Dealer net liquidity outflow, 24 h	U.S.$ 14 bn	**U.S.$ 62 bn**	U.S.$ 88 bn
3-month EUR-USD basis	−10 bps	**−95 bps**	−135 bps
GC repo rate spike	+15 bps	**+110 bps**	+175 bps
Treasuries sold from reinsurer trusts	—	**U.S.$ 98 bn**	U.S.$ 142 bn
Fed daylight overdraft utilisation	<30 % limit	**110%**	145%

INTERPRETATION: A single G-SIB dealer breaches internal liquidity stress limits within four hours. Without Fed repo expansion and swap-line draws, margin calls at CCPs are missed by $t = +7$ hrs, tripping default-management waterfalls.

Mechanistic Insights

1. **Non-linear shock amplification.**
   The cyber freeze delays collateral substitution exactly when reinsurers are liquidating Treasuries; dealers face simultaneous *asset* illiquidity and *payment* gridlock—twice the funding strain of either shock alone.

1. **Daylight-overdraft ceiling as hidden chokepoint.**
   Even with Fedwire up, internal caps set by prudential supervisors become binding. Dealers cannot route alternate payment traffic without first tapping Fed standing-repo, which requires collateral that is itself being liquidated.
2. **Swap-line draw timing critical.**
   ECB and BoJ usage peaks at $t = +9$ hrs. Delaying auctions to next business day lets EUR-USD basis blow past −120 bps—a level where corporates cancel commercial-paper rollovers, widening the crisis.
3. **Cat-bond liquidation multiplier.**
   Auto-liquidation of AAA Treasury collateral in ILS trusts adds a secondary wave of Treasury selling ~4 hrs after reinsurers, doubling repo-haircut escalation.

Policy Stress-Test Recommendations

Intervention	Modeled Efficacy	Implementation Hurdle
Pre-approved intraday Fed repo taps for reinsurer trusts	Cuts baseline dealer liquidity outflow by 18 %	Statutory authority unclear; moral-hazard optics
Integrity-only' CHIPS continuity mode	Reduces delayed payments 65 %	Requires hardware segmentation completed by 2026
ECB standing swap-line quota uplift (3×)	Narrows basis spike by 30 bps	Political buy-in; Fed balance-sheet optics
Mandatory dual-site collateral trusts (NY + Frankfurt)	Halves Treasury liquidation volume	Cost to reinsurers; legal jurisdiction alignment

STRATEGIC TAKE-AWAYS

- **Compound perils must enter capital planning.** Climate and cyber shocks are correlated through collateral and settlement rails; capital and liquidity standards should incorporate joint-tail distributions.

- **Payment-integrity drills are as vital as stress-tests.** The industry focuses on availability, but *integrity uncertainty* is a larger driver of funding hoarding.

- **Central-bank governance gap.** Stand-alone Fed facilities suffice in pure-market crises; cross-shocks require pre-negotiated "federated back-stop" rules to prevent daylight-overdraft caps from binding.

- **Re-insurance visibility.** Global supervisors need real-time telemetry on collateral-trust flows, or else Treasury-market peculiarities will remain a leading indicator rather than a managed variable.

The modelling exercise underscores a core message of this book: exogenous risks—climate and cyber chief among them—no longer sit outside financial risk models; they share and exploit the very plumbing that carries dollar liquidity. Without integrated contingency protocols, what begins as wind and malware could end, within a trading day, as a system-wide sprint for the greenback that no single institution is equipped to outrun.

10.6 Policy Gaps in a Non-Market World

WHY MACRO-PRUDENTIAL Toolkits Miss Exogenous Tail-Risk

Bank supervisors entered the post-2008 era with a simple credo: higher capital, thicker liquidity buffers, and regular top-down stress tests would inoculate the system against credit and market shocks. Counter-cyclical capital buffers (CCyB) absorb exuberance; Basel III's Liquidity Coverage Ratio (LCR) buys thirty days of survival if wholesale funding evaporates; scenario exercises model GDP slumps, equity crashes, and rate spikes. These defenses work—*when the trigger is financial.* But the crises mapped in this chapter—monsoon failure plus ransomware, fire seasons plus debt-ceiling theatrics—originate beyond priceable markets. They slip through the macro-prudential net in six specific ways.

1 | Speed Mismatch

Toolkit: CCyB releases and discount-window terms require board votes; stress-test capital relief is hard-wired to semi-annual cycles.

Reality: Climate-cyber cascades unfold in hours. Margin calls arrive before supervisory forbearance memos can circulate. The 36-hour dollar dash of March 2020 hinted at the tempo; compound perils move even faster because they strike collateral and payment rails simultaneously.

2 | Liquidity Optics vs. Actual Usability

Toolkit: LCR treats Treasuries and agency MBS as "high-quality liquid assets."

Reality: In a cross-shock, those very securities are the first liquidated; repo haircuts widen, collateral chains stall, and HQLA morphs into price-volatile inventory. Stress tests assume *saleability*, not *market depth* under forced liquidation.

3 | Single-Shock Design Bias

Toolkit: Supervisors run one macro scenario at a time—severe recession or high-inflation shock—but not concurrent cyber and hurricane hits.

Reality: Tail events increasingly cluster: wildfire smoke shuts a data center, while drought slashes hydro output, spiking electricity futures and variation margin. Models calibrated on siloed histories miss joint tails.

4 | Jurisdictional Blind Spots

Toolkit: Basel Pillar-3 disclosures aggregate at consolidated group level; stress tests remain national.

Reality: Climate risk is highly regional; cyber vulnerabilities cluster in outsourced vendor stacks. A U.S. subsidiary's swap-line needs may hinge on losses at a European reinsurer parent—data outside the Federal Reserve's regulative remit.

5 | Payment-Systems Ignorance

Toolkit: Capital and liquidity ratios focus on asset and liability maturity, not on *payment finality*.

Reality: Integrity outages at CHIPS or Fedwire trap balances that "count" toward LCR but cannot be mobilised. Traditional metrics deem a Treasury bill in a jammed settlement queue as liquid, even while the bank fails margin calls.

6 | Data Lag and Non-Financial Inputs

Toolkit: Stress models feed quarterly financials, daily market prices; climate modules use coarse decadal averages.

Reality: Parametric insurance triggers fire in real time from satellite feeds; ransomware spreads in minutes across cloud tenants. Supervisors lack APIs for rainfall gauges or cyber-incident telemetry, so they cannot see funding waves forming until repo and swap bases explode.

Strategic Implications

1. **From Buffers to Flow-Guarantees** – Static capital cushions must be complemented by pre-authorised liquidity taps (standing Fed-reinsurer repo, automated FX-swap rollovers) that activate as soon as integrity or weather triggers flash.

1. **Cross-Domain Threat Mapping** – Regulators need joint drills that pair cyber kill-chains with collateral-liquidation maps: "What if AWS-US-EAST-1 goes dark during a Gulf

Coast CAT 5 landfall?"

2. **Data-Fusion Supervisory Dashboards** – Incorporate real-time meteorological and cyber telemetry into funding-risk dashboards; require cloud vendors and insurers to stream high-frequency stress signals to central banks.
3. **Payment-Rail Resilience Metrics** – Add settlement-integrity stress to prudential ratios: "available HQLA *minus* assets trapped in systems under integrity review."
4. **International Liquidity Protocols** – Predetermine swap-line scaling rules tied to objective triggers (e.g., cross-currency basis breaches) to sidestep political delay when multi-jurisdictional shocks hit.

Traditional macro-prudential gear was forged in a world where financial risk begot financial crisis. The non-market catalysts of the climate-cyber age invert that order: the physical and digital worlds now *create* the financial shock. Until capital frameworks, liquidity metrics, and global coordination mechanisms integrate these exogenous tail-risks, the system will remain optimized for the last war—ill-prepared for the next.

10.7 Blueprint for Redundancy

TOWARD A POLY-CENTRIC Dollar (and Post-Dollar) Infrastructure

If Chapters 4–10 have shown anything, it is that single-hub efficiency has reached its fragility limit. The task now is to imagine—and design—escape hatches that add resilience without tearing down what works. The blueprint sketched below weaves together three complementary strands:

Strand	Goal	Core Instruments	Near-Term Feasibility
Regional CBDC Corridors	Localise payment finality while preserving PvP with dollars	mBridge prototype, Project Dunbar, MAS-UAE "Jura"	**High** (pilots live; scale remains small)
Multi-Hub Rail Proxies	Duplicate Fedwire/ CHIPS critical functions across continents	DLT-based netting hubs; CLS-type PvP satellites	**Medium** (technology ready; governance unsettled)
Treaty-Bound Swap-Line Compacts	Hard-wire emergency liquidity beyond discretionary Fed lines	G-20 "Liquidity Accords"; SDR-repo pools	**Low–Medium** (requires political will)

1 | REGIONAL CBDC Corridors: Local Finality, Global Interoperability

Concept

Each major currency bloc (ASEAN+3, EU, GCC, AU) operates a wholesale central-bank digital currency (w-CBDC). Domestic banks settle local retail and wholesale obligations on that ledger; cross-border transactions route through an *inter-ledger corridor* that hashes PvP in real time against dollar-Fedwire legs. Instead of passing every foreign invoice through Manhattan correspondent chains, PvP finality occurs simultaneously in, say, Bangkok and New York.

Why It Helps

- **Reduces single-hub load** – 30 percent of today's CHIPS flow is non-U.S. origin/destination; corridors could lift half of it off Manhattan rails.

- **Faster crisis containment** – Regional authorities retain autonomous control; climate or cyber shocks in one zone no longer freeze *all* dollar flows.

- **Programmable liquidity** – Smart-contract triggers can auto-recycle Fed swap-line dollars into corridor liquidity, removing political lag.

Design Must-Haves

- **PvP Interlocks** – Atomic settlement must guarantee no corridor leg completes without the dollar leg.

- **Hierarchical Nets** – Corridors net local flows intraday, then post a single aggregated dollar obligation to Fedwire at end-cycle.

- **Common Data Model** – ISO 20022 plus shared legal definitions for default and dispute.

Hurdles

Legal-entity recognition (are corridor tokens "deposits" or "cash equivalents"?), and U.S. political concern over losing sanctions leverage. One compromise: corridor ledgers mirror OFAC lists in real time, preserving choke-point visibility without choking routine flow.

2 | Multi-Hub Payment-Rail Proxies: "Spare Engines" for Fedwire and CHIPS

Concept

Build geographically distributed *rail proxies* that replicate Fedwire's and CHIPS's settlement logic but run under separate legal jurisdictions—Frankfurt, Toronto, Singapore—activated only if New York rails suffer prolonged integrity or cyber failure. Think of them as "hot stand-by" engines with read-only mirrors during normal times, flipping to write-access if Manhattan is compromised.

Architecture

- **Trusted Execution Environments** replicate U.S. master-account ledgers every five seconds.
- **Key-Switch Protocol** controlled jointly by the Fed and host central bank unlocks write-mode.
- **Statutory Safe-Harbour** gives provisional legal finality to proxy-settled payments, later reconciled on Fedwire.

Benefits

- Eliminates geographic single-point failure.
- Maintains dollar sovereignty—the Fed still keys the write-switch.
- Buys hours (or days) of settlement continuity during East-Coast outages.

Challenges

- Jurisdictional liability if forks occur.
- Real-time sanction-screen replication.

- Commercial-bank readiness: institutions must pre-wire operational playbooks for proxy cut-over.

Pilot candidate: **"Fedwire-North"** co-hosted by the Bank of Canada. Legal text could sit inside the existing U.S.–Canada Swap Arrangement treaty addendum.

3 | Treaty-Bound Swap-Line Compacts: Liquidity Without Discretion

Problem

Current Fed swap lines are discretionary and politically gated. Crisis-timing uncertainties widen swap bases before relief arrives.

Solution Proposal: *Global Liquidity Accord (GLA)*

Feature	Mechanism
Pre-Authorised Draws	Each signatory holds a callable certificate (digital SDR) convertible into up to 5 % of its dollar-reserve holdings.
Automatic Trigger	Cross-currency basis breaches a corridor (e.g., –75 bps for EUR-USD) for >6 hours.
Back-Stop Funding	Fed swaps dollars vs. SDRs; IMF maintains escrow.
Ex-Post Pricing	OIS + 25 bps regardless of counterparty—sidesteps stigma.
Reciprocity	Fed receives mirror rights for emergencies in partner currencies, creating political symmetry.

Advantages

- Removes political timing risk.
- SDR collateral avoids perception of "taxpayer bail-outs."

• Reciprocal design mitigates accusations of unilateral leverage.

Political Reality Check

U.S. Congress would demand oversight. A starter version could be a **G-7 mini-compact**, expandable after proof of concept.

4 | Combining the Strands

1. **Corridors handle routine cross-border flow**, easing load on Manhattan.

1. **Proxy rails guard against catastrophic outages**, ensuring technical resilience.
2. **GLA certificates supply pre-agreed liquidity**, shrinking basis spikes that would otherwise trigger corridor hoarding or proxy overload.

Think of redundancy as a *networked pyramid*: local CBDC bases feed into multi-hub intermediates, which in turn anchor on a treaty-based liquidity apex. The dollar remains the keystone, but stress no longer bottlenecks on one city block.

Implementation Path: 2025–2035

Phase	Milestone	Stakeholders
Pilot ('25-'27)	mBridge corridor expands to include Fed "observer" node; Fedwire-North sandbox go-live.	PBoC, MAS, BoC, Fed
Scale ('28-'30)	EU and GCC launch corridors; CHIPS proxy mirror in Frankfurt.	ECB, Bundesbank, BIS IH
Accord ('30-'32)	GLA treaty signed; digital SDR certificates issued; automatic triggers coded.	G-7 finance ministries, IMF
Global Uptake ('33-'35)	ASEAN+, AU, African Continental corridors connect; stress-test rehearsals across corridors, proxies, and GLA draws.	ADB, AfDB, FSB

FINAL THOUGHT

Redundancy is not an ideological pivot away from the dollar; it is an engineering upgrade for a single-point-of-failure architecture. The blueprint above sketches how regional digital settlements, multi-hub rail clones, and treaty-based liquidity pools can knit a poly-centric safety net—one that preserves dollar utility while insulating the world from the next Manhattan outage, ransomware blitz, or legislative cliff-hanger. Success will hinge not on technology, which is largely ready, but on political willingness to share sovereignty in exchange for systemic resilience.

Chapter 11: The Politics of Domestic Gridlock and Global Dependency

11.1 Debt-Ceiling Theatrics as Systemic-Risk Event

EVERY FEW YEARS THE reserve-currency issuer performs a ritual no other sovereign attempts: it threatens to default on purpose. The U.S. debt-ceiling statute, born in 1917 to streamline wartime finance, has become a recurrent hostage in domestic political bargaining. For decades markets assumed Congress would always raise the limit in time; the 2011 cliff-hanger shattered that faith, and successive episodes—2013, 2021, 2023—have hardened a new assumption: default may be unlikely, but it is no longer unthinkable. The mere possibility now functions like a scheduled natural disaster, one that central banks, dealers, and asset managers must model, hedge, and pay for—every cycle.

From Political Theatre to Liquidity Shock

A debt-ceiling standoff transmits stress through three mechanical channels:

1. **Collateral Uncertainty**
   Treasury Bills—the foundational collateral of repo, money-market funds, and clearing-house margin—trade on the expectation of absolute safety. When a specific CUSIP is rumored to be at risk of delayed payment, its repo eligibility

is questioned, haircuts widen, and dealers demand substitution. Collateral chains buckle precisely where they are shortest and most levered.

1. **Settlement Gridlock**
   Fedwire recognizes a Treasury obligation as "money good" until maturity. Should the legal payment date arrive without congressional action, Fedwire must mark the security "defaulted," an operational scenario never rehearsed at scale. Netting engines at FICC and tri-party repo would suspend trades involving the tainted CUSIPs, forcing market participants to reroute liquidity into longer-dated notes—clogging otherwise liquid points on the curve.
2. **FX-Swap and Basis Spikes**
   Foreign reserve managers, unable to roll maturing bills, convert them into dollars via spot sales and park the proceeds in the Fed's reverse-repo facility or in short SOFR-linked deposits. European and Asian banks then scramble for replacement collateral, driving cross-currency swap bases sharply negative. Each basis point of widening lifts global hedging costs, propagating what began as a Capitol-Hill quarrel into higher funding costs for an auto manufacturer in Seoul or an infrastructure fund in Madrid.

Stress-Test Evidence

Bank-supervisory stress tests incorporate market shocks, but until recently they treated Treasuries as "risk-free." After the 2023 standoff, several institutions appended ad-hoc "DC event" layers to internal liquidity scenarios. Results were sobering: even a *one-day* missed coupon on US$120 billion of bills produced liquidity outflows comparable to a 200-basis-point spike in credit spreads. The capital impact was small—default probability on other Treasuries remained nil—but the liquidity drain was severe, because every clearing counterparty demanded immediate substitution collateral.

Behavioral Adaptation and Its Costs

- **Dealer Balance-Sheet Pre-Allocation**

  Primary dealers now warehouse larger inventories of "clean" notes ahead of each X-date, reducing capacity for corporate-bond market-making.

- **Money-Market Fund Flight-Path**

  Prime funds write contingency playbooks to gate inflows from clients likely to flee bill shares. That gating language, disclosed in prospectuses, nudges corporate treasurers toward government-only funds—shifting credit intermediation out of regulated vehicles.

- **Sovereign Reserve Diversification**

  Small but steady reallocations toward Bunds, gilts, and gold are visible in IMF COFER data after each showdown. Individually modest, the shifts compound over multiple episodes, eroding some of the depth advantage that underpins dollar liquidity.

The Fed's Tightrope

The Federal Reserve can:

1. **Accept Defaulted Bills as Collateral** at par, effectively neutering market discipline but preserving liquidity;

1. **Lend Against Them at Haircut**—but deciding the haircut

instantly politicizes the Fed;

2. **Refuse Them** and watch repo markets seize.

No option is apolitical. In internal simulations the Board prefers a standing facility that auto-lends at a modest surcharge to SOFR, using defaulted bills at a deep haircut. Yet any public discussion risks signaling complacency about future brinkmanship, encouraging more of it.

International Fallout

Allies privately express disbelief that U.S. governance allows periodic Russian-roulette with the global safe asset. Central banks in Asia have begun negotiating bilateral swap lines with each other—yuan-won, yen-dollar with no Fed participation—as insurance against a Washington misfire. The volumes are small, the symbolism large: redundancy projects once framed as long-range diversification now appear as reasonable portfolio insurance.

A Crescendo Scenario

Imagine a debt-ceiling breach coinciding with hurricane-driven cat-bond liquidations (Chapter 10) and a cyber integrity freeze at CHIPS (Chapter 10). Defaulted bills become toxic collateral; reinsurers liquidate Treasuries anyway; payment queues jam as CHIPS integrity checks stall. The Fed can flood reserves, yet daylight overdraft caps bite; foreign central banks draw swap lines, but haircuts on tainted bills deplete collateral pools. Within hours Treasuries trade like corporates: price gaps, fragmented liquidity, basis-swap discontinuities. In that moment, the full faith and credit of the United States—once the bedrock of global finance—would have become the proximate cause of a worldwide dash for anything *other* than dollars.

Policy Options

1. **Statutory Repeal or Automatic Lift** – politically improbable.

1. **Treasury Authority to Mint High-Coupon "Consols"** – avoids breaching the face-value limit but tests market appetite for legal gimmicks.
2. **Fed Contingency Collateral Standing Facility** – creates an ex-ante rulebook, at the cost of weakening deterrence against future brinkmanship.
3. **International Shock-Buffer Pool** – partner central banks pre-commit SDRs to absorb bill redemption waves; politically feasible only if tied to broader liquidity accords (see 10.7).

Bottom Line: Debt-ceiling theatrics are no longer side-show politics; they are scheduled systemic-risk drills that drain global liquidity, widen hedging basis, and erode the narrative of the dollar as an unassailable store of value. Each episode ends with last-minute legislative reprieve, but the scar tissue accumulates. So long as legal architecture allows a partisan minority to weaponize default risk, every future crisis—climate, cyber, geopolitical—will carry an added layer of Washington uncertainty, compounding fragility in a system already stretched across too many single points of failure.

11.2 Populist Resistance to "Foreign Bail-outs"

WHEN THE FEDERAL RESERVE'S balance-sheet prints soar in response to crises, television pundits rarely show the swap-line dashboards or repo-take-up statistics. They show flags: stars-and-stripes beside an image of a European bank tower, or a caricature of an emerging-market president. In campaign rallies from Ohio to Osaka—and increasingly from Brasília to Berlin—politicians exploit the optics of cross-border rescues to frame global liquidity back-stops as *hand-outs to elites abroad.* This populist narrative constrains policy-makers precisely when the system most requires forthright, timely action.

The American Lens: "Why Should We Save Them?"

In March 2020 the Fed's swap lines peaked near USD $450 billion. Financial journalists explained that most of those dollars wound up back at the Fed as reserve balances or reverse-repo deposits, effectively *earning* the U.S. Treasury interest. Populist commentators told a different story: Washington was "bailing out European bankers" while Main-Street diners closed under lockdown. Congressional letters demanded the Fed publish counterparty lists *in real time*; one bill proposed prior House approval for any swap line above USD $50 billion.

The political echo boiled down to a visceral sense that the U.S. taxpayer shoulders risk without voice. Never mind that swap lines are collateralized, that the Fed earns a spread, or that failure to act would have crashed American markets too—complexities vanish in a thirty-second ad. Each new crisis thus raises the hurdle for discretionary Fed interventions, introducing hesitation that markets can detect before runoff auctions even open.

European Varieties of Populism

The dynamic is not uniquely American. In Italy, Five-Star and Lega politicians lambasted the ECB's Pandemic Emergency Purchase Program as a stealth rescue of "German creditors." Northern European populists flipped the script: PEPP was evidence that thrifty taxpayers were subsidizing profligate Southerners. Both critiques mischaracterized the mechanics, yet both resonated. The result is a narrower political runway for the ECB's balance-sheet expansions, despite the euro-area's chronic need for joint fiscal-monetary safety nets.

Emerging-Market Pushback

In Brazil, critics of the 2020 Fed swap line framed it as proof of the government's servility to Washington, claiming Brasília had traded 5G concessions for dollars that "never reached the real economy." In South Africa, labour unions decried even the *prospect* of a swap line as IMF-style conditionality in disguise. The paradox is stark: nations outside the inner swap club crave dollar liquidity but fear the optics of accepting it—precisely the ambiguity that slows activation, widening basis spikes and deepening the crisis they wish to avoid.

Mechanisms of Political Constraint

Channel	Populist Tactic	Policy Impact
Legislative Oversight	Bills mandating congressional or parliamentary pre-approval for cross-border facilities	Delays central-bank response; markets front-run political calendars
Budget Hearings & Media Sound-bites	"Taxpayer money sent abroad" graph	Forces central banks to downplay facility size, hampering signalling effect
Judicial Challenges	Lawsuits alleging overreach of monetary mandate	Creates legal risk; central banks adopt narrower tools
Referenda & Election Cycles	Pledges to block future "bail-outs"	Negotiators hedge with smaller, capped lines—not enough to arrest contagion

CASE SNAPSHOT—TEA-PARTY Era, 2010–2012

The Dodd-Frank Act imposed a two-year disclosure lag on swap-line counterparties but stopped short of real-time transparency. Still, Tea-Party lawmakers weaponized delayed data releases, arguing the Fed had secretly lent to "Libya and the Taliban" (it had not). The public uproar nearly derailed reauthorization of Section 13(3) emergency powers. During the 2011 euro-area scare, Fed officials debated offering *smaller, stigmatized auctions* to avoid headlines, even though full-allotment operations would have been more stabilizing. Basis spreads stayed wider for longer, and U.S. money-market funds saw elevated outflows—*domestic* collateral damage from imported populist pressure.

Second-Order Effects

1. **Design by Optics, Not Efficiency**
   Facilities become smaller, shorter-dated, and more complex to explain—eroding their shock-absorber function.

1. **Stigma Re-Creation**
   Borrowers fear domestic backlash, so they wait until liquidity is desperate, magnifying currency and basis swings.
2. **Moral Hazard Reversal**
   Instead of encouraging risk-taking, political constraints may force excessive de-risking—banks hoard liquidity "just in case," draining credit from productive sectors.
3. **Shadow Alternative Growth**
   Perceived stigma drives corporates to non-transparent funding channels—crypto-stablecoins or offshore private-credit pools—reducing regulator visibility.

Navigating the Optics

- **Pre-Commitment Frameworks**

Embed swap-line criteria in multilateral treaties (see 10.7) so that activation appears rule-based, not discretionary.

- **Transparent Accounting of Gains**

Publish net-interest revenue from facilities; highlight that taxpayers *earn* on swaps.

- **Domestic Offsets**

Pair foreign liquidity lines with visible support for local communities (e.g., SME lending incentives) to blunt "money for foreigners" rhetoric.

- **Educate Ahead of Crisis**

Central banks and finance ministries must conduct ongoing public outreach; when crisis hits, the narrative foundation is already laid.

Bottom Line: Populist resistance reframes the debate from *systemic stability* to *national fairness*. Unless policy makers make the stabilization dividend legible to electorates, each foreign-leaning facility will face mounting opposition, shrinking the very safety net the global system now relies upon. In the long run that pressure nudges cross-border finance toward opacity and fragmentation—ironic outcomes for movements that claim to defend "ordinary citizens" from elite risk-taking.

11.3 Consequences of a Delayed Swap-Line Renewal

SWAP-LINES ARE RENEWED by central-bank communiqué so routinely that dealers scarcely notice the quarterly press releases—until political friction, calendar mishap, or legal gridlock pushes a renewal past its expected date. Because markets treat the lines as an evergreen entitlement, even a *48-hour lapse* can jolt funding desks and trigger a sequence of self-reinforcing moves that no textbook liquidity ratio anticipates.

T-0: Missed Renewal

- **Event:** The Fed's standing lines with the ECB, BoJ, and BoE are scheduled to auto-roll at 6:00 p.m. New York time, but Treasury lawyers postpone concurrence pending Congressional testimony about "foreign bail-outs." No renewal statement crosses the wires.

- **Immediate Perception:** Algo-scanners on bank terminals flash "renewal absent." Chatrooms explode: *Is this a clerical error or policy shift?*

T + 2 Hours: Basis Gap

- **Cross-Currency Basis:** Three-month EUR-USD spread widens from −18 bps to −60 bps within 90 minutes as European banks rush to secure spot dollars ahead of Tokyo's open.

- **FX Volume:** CNH-USD swap points jump similarly; Asian desks fear preferential treatment for G-5 expires, cascading into non-aligned currencies.

T + 12 Hours: Dealer Balance-Sheet Stress

- **Collateral Hoarding:** U.S. dealers raise GC repo haircuts on foreign-bank collateral by 50 bps, citing "uncertain dollar back-stop." European government-bond repurchase rates spike as counterparties switch to Treasuries.

• **Clearing-House Margin:** LCH increases initial margin on dollar-clear IRS for continental banks by 10 percent, triggering variation-margin calls into New York time.

T + 24 Hours: Corporate Knock-Ons

• **Commercial Paper Freeze:** U.S. money-market funds refuse to roll French and Japanese bank paper maturing inside seven days. Banks replace funding via overnight FX swaps, widening basis another 40 bps.

• **Import-Export Crunch:** Korean and Brazilian corporates paying dollar invoices draw down revolving credit facilities, shrinking bank liquidity piles further.

T + 36 Hours: Central-Bank Contingency Lines

• **ECB Emergency TLRO:** ECB announces targeted longer-term refinancing in dollars, funded via its roughly US $50 billion internal reserves. Markets judge capacity inadequate versus potential need (> US $300 billion).

• **Safe-Asset Rally & Collateral Shortage:** Two-year Treasury yields collapse 25 bps even as repo fails jump—proof that safe-asset demand coexists with settlement stress.

T + 48 Hours: Political Fallout

• **U.S. Hearings:** Lawmakers claim swap lines subsidise foreigners; Treasury submits written assurances that renewal "under consideration." Market hears: delay indefinite.

• **Euro-Area Response:** Finance ministers convene an ad-hoc Eurogroup call; pressure mounts for joint "Euro swap-pool," but treaty lawyers cite legal constraints.

T + 60 Hours: Systemic Tipping Point

• **Bank Downgrades:** A rating agency places four major European banks on negative watch for "dollar liquidity uncertainty." CDS widen; their U.S. broker-dealer arms face higher initial margin at FICC.

• **Derivative De-Risking:** Hedge funds unwind narrow-basis trades (Treasury-futures, cross-currency swaps) en masse. Treasury-futures margins spike; price action echoes March 2020.

T + 72 Hours: Forced Policy Reversal

Facing a rerun of the 2008 dollar shortage, the Fed issues a late-Sunday statement: swap lines renewed *with immediate effect*. Pricing set at OIS + 25 bps, full allotment. Basis converges within minutes. But the three-day lapse leaves scar tissue: repo haircuts remain elevated; money-market funds impose 1-day advance notice for large redemptions; corporates shorten hedge maturities.

Structural Lessons

Phenomenon	Why It Matters
Expectation Reflex	Markets price swap-line permanence; any deviation is treated as signal, not noise.
Liquidity Holes	Banks roll tens of billions of FX swaps *daily* under the assumption of back-stop; a 24-hour lapse starves rollover volumes.
Rapid Rating Impact	Agencies rely on swap lines for liquidity assessment; delay converts to immediate rating pressure, amplifying funding costs.
Policy-Communication Lag	Central banks need dual-track renewal protocols—automatic rollover unless *explicitly* revoked—to avoid ambiguity shocks.

DESIGN FIXES

1. **Legal Auto-Renew Clauses**
   Swap agreements could state: "In absence of explicit termination by either party, lines roll at existing terms." Requires no daily Treasury concurrence.

1. **Staggered Draw Windows**
   Standing weekly auctions reduce cliff risk versus quarterly resets.
2. **Basis-Triggered Auto-Activation**
   If three-month EUR-USD basis breaches –75 bps for four hours, pre-authorised draws execute automatically up to a cap.
3. **Congressional Education Blitz**
   Quantify swap-line *earnings* to taxpayers; highlight 2008 and 2020 case studies where delay would have cost domestic jobs

and savings.

Bottom Line

A delayed swap-line renewal is not a clerical footnote; it is an exogenous shock that ricochets through cross-currency funding, repo collateral, and derivative margins in less than a day. The reputational damage lingers: every future renewal becomes a market-moving event. Institutionalizing automatic, rule-based rollover mechanisms is therefore not a convenience—it is systemic risk mitigation.

Part V – Search for Redundancy and the Limits of Diversification

Chapter 12: Competing Architectures: Renminbi Rails, Digital Euro, and mBridge

For more than seven decades the dollar's dominance has rested on a simple equation: the most liquid currency married to the deepest, cheapest settlement infrastructure. Only a few years ago every plausible rival—euro, yen, sterling—appeared locked inside that formula, forced to clear a meaningful share of their own cross-border trade through Manhattan. Today three distinct experiments are chipping at that inevitability. China is pressing ahead with renminbi "rails" that bypass the correspondent system altogether; the European Central Bank is designing a digital euro meant to fuse money and settlement into a single programmable layer; and a loose consortium of Asian and

Middle-Eastern central banks is piloting mBridge, a cross-border wholesale CBDC platform that performs payment-versus-payment without touching SWIFT, CHIPS, or Fedwire. None of these projects yet rivals the breadth, liquidity, or legal certainty of the dollar nexus, but together they amount to the first coordinated engineering challenge the dollar order has faced since Bretton Woods collapsed.

Beijing's strategy is the most advanced in physical scale if not in convertibility. The Cross-Border Inter-Bank Payment System (CIPS) has grown from a handful of settlement banks in Shanghai to more than 1,500 participants across ninety countries, processing renminbi trade flows that once had to detour through Hong Kong or New York. The e-CNY pilot adds a retail layer that, in theory, could feed reserves directly into CIPS without passing through the dollar market. Yet capital controls remain; onshore–offshore spreads still open whenever stress hits; and foreign exporters accept renminbi invoices only when cushioned by central-bank swap guarantees—proof that plumbing alone cannot erase network effects built on trust and hedging depth.

Europe's digital-euro project, by contrast, begins with convertibility but suffers from political ambivalence. The ECB envisions a two-tier system: commercial banks distribute programmable tokens redeemable one-for-one in central-bank money, while a wholesale ledger settles interbank obligations in near real time. The architecture would allow an Italian machinery exporter to receive final, irrevocable euros from a Polish buyer within seconds, removing the need for dollar-denominated correspondent chains. Yet parliamentary skepticism over privacy, and commercial-bank fears of deposit flight, have slowed legislative progress. Implementation timelines keep slipping, and without a consensus on cross-border functionality the digital euro risks becoming a faster SEPA rather than a dollar alternative.

mBridge is both more modest and more radical. Run from a server farm in HongKong under BIS auspices, the platform links prototype CBDCs from the People's Bank of China, the Hong Kong Monetary Authority, the Bank of Thailand, and the Central Bank of the UAE. In its 2023 pilot, a Thai importer paid a UAE oil supplier in seconds with atomic settlement across four ledgers—no correspondent banks, no daylight overdrafts, no CHIPS queue. The amounts were tiny and legal certainty limited to sandbox agreements, but the demonstration shattered the assumption that PvP finality requires a Manhattan timestamp. If the project scales, Asian supply chains could recycle trade surpluses without ever touching the dollar rails, eroding the habit that forces exporters to hedge everything back into greenbacks.

Taken separately, these initiatives look like regional modernization drives; taken together, they outline a plausible poly-centric future. A German carmaker might pay for Indonesian nickel in euros on a DLT corridor, which a local smelter could then swap into e-CNY for Chinese equipment, while the Singaporean logistics firm that brokers the deal settles freight fees on mBridge—all without a single correspondent account in New York. The dollar would remain the benchmark reserve asset, but much of the day-to-day transactional volume that feeds its network effects could migrate elsewhere, muting the automatic reflex that today draws every crisis back to the Fed's swap window.

The subsequent chapters dissect each architecture's plumbing, governance hurdles, and geopolitical baggage. For now it is enough to note the turning of the tide: the world is no longer debating whether an alternative to dollar rails is technically possible, but whether any alternative can gather sufficient trust, liquidity depth, and legal clarity to matter. The answer will determine whether systemic resilience is achieved through genuine redundancy—or whether competing networks simply create new choke points, fragmenting liquidity into regional silos that break under the same kinds of stress that now menace the dollar's single bridge.

12.1 Liquidity–Trust Bootstrapping Dilemma

EVERY PAYMENT SYSTEM aspires to the same two virtues: abundant liquidity and unquestioned finality. Liquidity is the ability to move large values at minimal cost without moving prices; trust is the conviction that once a transfer settles it will never be reversed, frozen, or haircut. The dollar rails enjoy both because they have enjoyed both for so long: trillions clear every afternoon, yet bid-ask spreads in money-markets rarely flinch, and no one doubts the legal sanctity of a Fedwire timestamp. For aspiring alternatives—CIPS, the future digital euro, mBridge corridors—the problem is chicken-and-egg. You cannot attract critical trading volumes until counterparties believe they can exit positions at will, but that depth will never materialize until large players actually route flow through the new pipes. Liquidity must precede trust and trust must precede liquidity, an equation that can trap even the most elegant architecture in perpetual adolescence.

Renminbi clearing illustrates the trap. Beijing has spent a decade persuading oil exporters, commodity traders, and Belt-and-Road contractors to invoice in yuan. Each year the share edges higher, yet the offshore yuan market still re-prices violently when stress hits, forcing corporates back into dollar swaps to hedge. The People's Bank of China deploys its balance-sheet—bilateral swap lines, standing facilities at state banks—to manufacture temporary depth. But manufactured depth is recognizable as such; traders treat it as one-way liquidity, useful in calm weather, suspect when the tide turns. The very presence of the back-stop signals that private market-makers have not yet embraced the rail as neutral ground.

The ECB confronts the same loop from the opposite direction. The euro already floats freely and enjoys deep government-bond markets, yet cross-border payments inside the bloc remain patched together by TARGET2 balances and correspondent overlays. A digital euro could, in principle, fuse monetary and settlement layers, but only if large corporates and non-resident banks are willing to hold and transfer wholesale tokens in size. Their treasury departments must be certain that the ECB would honor convertibility, that commercial-bank distributors will remain solvent, and—crucially—that secondary liquidity will exist in stress. Without that conviction, they will hold digital euro only ephemerally, converting it back into conventional book-entry balances or dollars before close of business. The new rail would be relegated to boutique status, a faster SEPA with none of the network effects that challenge the dollar.

mBridge adds a third wrinkle: its founding members enjoy high bilateral trade flows but divergent regulatory regimes and uneven capital-account openness. A Thai importer purchasing UAE crude through the corridor gains speed and fee savings, yet risks accumulating a balance of CBDC-dirhams that cannot be re-hypothecated or hedged in global markets. Until an organic offshore curve develops—repo, derivatives, commercial-paper equivalents—the corridor's utility will plateau at invoice-matching settlement, not true funding liquidity. The core impulse that drives dollars into every crevice of the global system—the certainty that you can fund, hedge, and exit twenty-four hours a day—remains missing.

Attempts to leap the gap invariably rely on public balance-sheets. China seeds swap lines; the ECB proposes quasi-unlimited convertibility to reserves; the BIS suggests pre-funding mBridge corridors with pooled Treasuries. Yet state-sponsored liquidity can substitute for market-made liquidity only up to the point where political conditions or credit limits intrude. If the back-stop can be withdrawn by policy fiat, trust will never be absolute. Private dealers sniff out asymmetry: *Is the swap line irrevocable? Can convertibility be suspended? Will sanctions ever freeze corridor balances?* Answer "maybe" to any of those and spreads will carry a risk premium—small at first, but enough to divert high-frequency trade back onto the old, cheaper, trusted rails.

The dilemma is structural, not merely transitional. In a multipolar currency world, liquidity would fragment unless deep markets emerge in each contender and seamless PvP links tie them together. Yet those deep markets will not emerge while the dollar system remains more liquid, cheaper, and wrapped in a half-century of jurisprudence. The challengers must therefore decide whether to tolerate years of subsidizing market-maker inventories—an expensive and politically visible subsidy—or accept that their rails will remain regional complements, not global substitutes.

Some see hope in technology: tokenized collateral, automated market-making pools, smart-contract escrow that lowers legal risk. Yet technology addresses cost, not conviction. The swap line under a smart contract is still a swap line; legal finality enforced by code still relies on sovereign courts to resolve disputes. And the deepest obstacle to trust is not friction but power. Users of dollar rails know the Federal Reserve and the U.S. Treasury can weaponize them, yet they also know the institutions are bound by transparent, litigable procedures. The challengers must persuade the world that their own political systems will refrain from arbitrary interference even when strategic tensions rise. That is a governance proposition, not a coding challenge.

Until that persuasion succeeds, the bootstrapping loop will persist. Renminbi rails will handle ever-larger bilateral flows but roll back into dollars at the hedge layer. The digital euro will speed intra-Eurozone commerce yet leave cross-currency trades settled in New York. mBridge will dazzle in pilots but funnel limited value until offshore funding markets blossom. Liquidity and trust will circle one another, bound to a gravitational centre still located on the east bank of the Hudson, at least until a catalyst—geopolitical rupture, sustained policy mis-step, or a generational shift in reserve-allocation psychology—breaks the loop by fiat rather than market choice.

12.2 Capital-Controls Legacy versus Market-Depth Requirements

A CURRENCY THAT ASPIRES to international stature must clear two hurdles at once. It must reassure foreign holders that they can leave whenever they wish, and it must convince domestic policymakers that such freedom will not destabilize the home economy. The first condition demands open capital accounts; the second often cries out for controls. Reconciling the two is the central paradox facing every dollar challenger, most conspicuously the renminbi, but also the Indian rupee, the Indonesian rupiah, and—at a subtler level—the euro, whose crisis-era firewalls still shadow investor psychology.

China's experience is illustrative. From 2010 to 2015 Beijing loosened outbound quotas and encouraged offshore renminbi dealing in Hong Kong. Depth improved: dim-sum bond issuance surged, CNY trading volumes jumped. Yet as soon as capital outflows threatened to breach the PBoC's tolerance band in 2015, the tap closed. Macro-prudential measures—window guidance on bank outflows, "observational" quotas on corporates, informal caps on foreign exchange purchases—stopped the bleed but shattered nascent confidence in offshore convertibility. Hedge funds marked up implied volatility; corporates renewed dollar-denominated hedging programs. Market depth evaporated faster than it had formed, proving that liquidity built on conditional liberalization is as fragile as the politics that underpin it.

India has approached the trade-off from the opposite direction: liberalizing slowly, layer by layer, while relying on perpetual capital inflows to cover a structural current-account deficit. Foreign institutional investors can access rupee debt only through registration hoops; onshore currency forwards remain tightly policed. The result is chronic yield-premium dependence. When global risk appetite wanes, FIIs pull funds, the Reserve Bank of India sells dollars, and liquidity thins precisely when offshore hedgers most need it. Market depth never reaches the self-sustaining escape velocity seen in dollar or euro markets because participants cannot be sure they will not face administrative friction during the next risk-off episode.

Even the euro, which touts full capital mobility, carries a legacy of segmentation. The European sovereign-debt crisis introduced "re-denomination risk"—the fear that an Italian bond might one day pay out in lira. The ECB's Outright Monetary Transactions pledge and subsequent Pandemic Emergency Purchase Program calmed yields, but lingering regulatory ring-fences—national liquidity requirements, varying withholding-tax treatments, distinct repo haircuts—fracture the single currency's collateral pool. Depth exists, but it is distributed unevenly across Bunds, OATs, and BTPs, limiting the euro's ability to provide a homogeneous safe asset comparable to U.S. Treasuries.

Why does market depth matter so much? Because the willingness of dealers to commit capital, of corporations to invoice, and of reserve managers to allocate depends less on average trading volumes than on *worst-day* exit capacity. A true reserve currency must absorb forced sellers without gapping. That requires layers of repo, futures, options, and swap markets where risk can be transferred instantly, in size, at predictable cost. Capital controls—even light, macro-prudential "speed bumps"—instantly raise uncertainty over exit costs, compelling participants to maintain dollar hedges as insurance. In effect, every lingering control is a hidden basis fee the challenger must pay to persuade the world to shift flow from established rails.

The converse is equally true: unrestricted flows can threaten domestic financial stability if domestic institutions are not ready. China fears a sudden reversal of its vast domestic savings pool; India and Indonesia worry about imported volatility overpowering thin local capital markets; European politicians dread the political fallout of a run on periphery sovereign bonds. The dollar overcame this dilemma through historical accident: it inherited global demand after World War II while the U.S. capital account was already open and its domestic market deep. No modern challenger enjoys that luxury.

Bridging the contradiction demands either *institutional leapfrogging*—such as sovereign deposit insurance for foreign holders, automatic FX facilities, or multilaterally backed repo windows—or a measured willingness to tolerate periodic volatility until markets grow resilient. Beijing is experimenting with the first via state-bank back-stops and bilateral swap lines; Brussels debates a euro-area safe-asset and pan-European deposit insurance; Delhi edges toward the second by gradually raising FII quotas and lengthening onshore futures tenors. All remain partial fixes. Until one path produces a currency whose holders believe they can exit on the worst day without hidden gates or punitive spreads, the dollar will retain its incumbency premium.

In that sense, capital controls are not merely regulatory artefacts; they are market-shaping narratives. Each time authorities re-impose them in a crunch, they reinforce the perception that the local currency is a convenience, not a refuge. Each time they trust the market to absorb shocks without administrative intervention, they pay a price in short-term volatility but buy a sliver of credibility. Over decades those slivers accumulate—exactly how the dollar, sterling before it, and the guilder before that gained the one asset no central bank can decree: unquestioned exit freedom.

12.3 Early-stage Settlement Statistics and Realistic Scaling Horizons

MEASURED AGAINST THE dollar's monolithic flow, the new payment experiments are still droplets in an ocean, yet their early-stage statistics illuminate both promise and impediment. The Cross-Border Inter-Bank Payment System clears roughly one and a half trillion renminbi a day—about two hundred billion dollars at current rates. That sounds sizeable until set beside CHIPS, which routinely nets more than eight times that value and does so in the currency that still anchors most corporate hedging. Moreover, well over half of CIPS volume is intragroup—state banks settling with affiliates, Chinese corporates paying offshore subsidiaries for input contracts—meaning genuinely foreign-resident use sits closer to eighty billion dollars a day. That figure, though rising at almost twenty percent per year, would need to expand by another order of magnitude before the renminbi rail becomes deep enough for global reserve managers to regard it as an everyday liquidity sink rather than a niche trade facility.

The digital-euro field trials present even leaner flows. The ECB's wholesale prototype processed fewer than six hundred real-value transactions during its 2023 sandbox, the largest single transfer just under one billion euros. Parallel stress simulations suggested the ledger could scale to five thousand transactions per second—ample for continental commerce—but actual take-up depends on commercial banks integrating distribution wallets and corporates choosing tokens over the legacy TARGET2 infrastructure that already settles near real time for most domestic payments. ECB officials privately target a three-year "ramp to relevance" after launch, with hopes that fifteen to twenty percent of high-value cross-border euro payments will migrate by the end of the decade. Even if that goal is met, the throughput will remain a fraction of Fedwire's ten-trillion-dollar daily tide.

mBridge's numbers are more embryonic still: in its 2023 pilot, fifty-seven entities completed just over sixteen thousand payments totaling twenty-two million dollars—a single hour of traffic for a mid-tier American correspondent bank. Yet the pilot's latency and cost metrics were impressive—a sub-two-second end-to-end settlement time at an estimated fee of two basis points. Scaling horizons, however, hinge on thorny issues: each corridor participant must post pre-funding collateral, legal finality is governed only by sandbox memoranda, and none of the jurisdictions has yet clarified how mBridge balances will be treated for reserve-requirement or liquidity-coverage purposes. A working group framework aims to expand pilot volumes to a cumulative five billion dollars by 2026, still tiny versus the scale required to displace even a slice of the dollar's role, but enough to prove technical viability if regulatory harmonization keeps pace.

Put together, these statistics imply a realistic sequencing. Over the next three to five years, renminbi rails could conceivably reach ten percent of global trade settlement, but only if Beijing liberalizes hedging instruments and loosens at least some capital-account frictions. A digital euro that captures a similar share of cross-border euro payments by 2030 would still lag the dollar in absolute terms but could erode the habit of clearing euro-denominated energy and commodity trades through New York. mBridge, or a successor wholesale CBDC consortium, is unlikely to matter systemically before the early 2030s unless its legal architecture is internationalized and pre-funding replaced by real-time credit mechanisms backed by central-bank balance sheets.

All three projects confront the same scaling cliff: velocity cannot accelerate until deep secondary markets form in repo, FX swaps and derivatives, yet those markets will not form until participants trust that exit doors stay open in turmoil. Absent that faith, daily volume may inch upward, but the burst-capacity required to absorb a crisis-driven flight from dollar rails will remain out of reach. The coming decade will therefore be decisive. If trade corridors, regional central banks and private dealers can demonstrate sustained throughput growth, transparent governance and robust hedging tools, the network effects that have long favored the greenback could begin to plateau. If they cannot, the early statistics will be remembered less as foundations of a new order than as proof of how steep the liquidity-trust gradient really is.

Chapter 13: Regional Currency Blocs and SDR Revival Proposals

This chapter opens in a world that has tired of waiting for a single challenger to the dollar. Instead of pursuing one new hegemon, governments are assembling mosaics of regional and multilateral arrangements—currency blocs built on trade corridors, commodity ties or security pacts—and layering on top an old idea suddenly fashionable again: a strengthened, more versatile Special Drawing Right. The vision is polycentric: keep the dollar for what it still does best, but settle more regional commerce in a shared local unit and keep a neutral, IMF-issued reserve asset in the back pocket for storms that no bloc can weather alone.

The BRICS enlargement crystallized the impulse. When Egypt, Saudi Arabia, the UAE, and Iran joined the club in 2024, the bloc's share of global oil exports jumped to nearly half, sparking headlines about a "petroyuan." In practice the members could not agree on a single invoicing currency—Riyadh still prefers dollars, Moscow is nudging dirhams, New Delhi remains wary of yuan liabilities—but they did agree to clear a fraction of bilateral trade through a BRICS Pay platform using local-currency swaps netted daily against a synthetic unit of account. The number is modest for now, roughly sixty billion dollars' worth in the first full year, yet each transaction that closes without touching a New York correspondent account chips at habit and creates new data sets for pricing regional credit.

ASEAN is taking a quieter, technocratic path. Under the Local Currency Settlement Framework spearheaded by Bank Indonesia and the Bank of Thailand, cross-border payments between eight Southeast-Asian currencies can now net on a shared real-time ledger operated out of Kuala Lumpur. Central banks supply intraday liquidity in their own units and cap end-of-day imbalances with swap-line ceilings. The framework settles less than four percent of intra-ASEAN trade, but a pilot to toggle seamlessly into yuan or yen corridors hints at an emerging lattice: multiple small nets linked through programmable gateways rather than one big mesh dominated by Beijing or Tokyo.

Africa's effort is driven by necessity. The Pan-African Payment and Settlement System, championed by Afreximbank, lets importers in Nairobi pay exporters in Lagos without touching dollars; the central banks of Kenya and Nigeria square the residual in a final-hour netting window. Liquidity is thin, bid-ask spreads wide, and hedging tools embryonic; still the platform processed nearly two billion dollars' worth of transactions in its second year, almost triple the pilot phase, and has gained political cachet as a symbol of continental self-reliance.

Yet every bloc runs into the same legacy problem identified in Chapter 12: without a deep, credible reserve asset of its own, it must keep rainy-day dollars—or euros or yuan—on standby. That is why interest has returned to the IMF's Special Drawing Right. During the pandemic the Fund's unprecedented US$ 650 billion general allocation reminded finance ministries that SDRs sit outside bilateral politics, cannot be sanctioned by any single capital, and do not expose holders to exchange-rate risk. Reform proposals now on the table imagine a standing annual allocation linked to global liquidity needs, an IMF-run repo window that would allow central banks to borrow against SDRs on demand, and a substitution account that would let reserve managers swap Treasuries or Bunds for SDRs without disturbing market prices.

Proponents pitch the new SDR not as a global currency—monetary nationalism remains too strong for that—but as shock absorber and nexus. Regional blocs could clear routine trade in their own units and park surpluses in SDR claims that earn the composite interest rate; in a crisis they could repo those SDRs, receiving whichever currency liquidity is least disruptive to markets at the moment. The design would create a circuit breaker above the blocs and below the dollar, a neutral valve that relieves the pressure to hoard greenbacks every time volatility jumps.

Sceptics counter that an SDR revival cannot work without the United States' full support—Washington holds veto power at the Fund—and that Congress is unlikely to sanction anything that dilutes the dollar's gravitational pull. They note, too, that SDR interest is tied to short-term sovereign yields; if the U.S. and Europe face fiscal stress, the SDR inherits their credit spread. Enthusiasts reply that a composite is still safer than a single-issuer asset and point to the post-2023 pattern of incremental reserve diversification—small, steady flows into gold, yuan bonds, and supranational paper—as evidence that inertia is no longer absolute.

Against this backdrop, this chapter explores whether regional blocs and an empowered SDR can coexist as complementary layers, adding resilience without fragmenting liquidity, or whether they will compete for the same scarce political capital and undermine one another. It asks what minimum market depth a bloc needs before private dealers treat its unit as more than a barter voucher, and what governance reforms the IMF must undertake before large central banks risk shifting meaningful reserves into SDRs. The chapter closes by revisiting the liquidity-trust loop: perhaps the surest path to breaking the dollar's monopoly is not a single formidable rival but an ecosystem of smaller rails buffered by a credible, genuinely multilateral reserve asset—a twenty-first-century version of Keynes's bancor, born not from post-war idealism but from the world's mounting fatigue with a single point of failure.

13.1 ASEAN+3, the Latin-American "clear-net," and Afreximbank's Pan-African Experiment

THE MOST AMBITIOUS of the live regional schemes sits in Southeast Asia, where the eight founding members of the ASEAN Local-Currency Settlement Framework have spent the past five years turning bilateral MoUs into a functioning cross-border grid. What began as a modest pact between Bank Indonesia and the Bank of Thailand now includes the Philippines, Malaysia, Singapore, Vietnam, Cambodia, and Laos, with Japan, Korea, and China providing swap-line cover from the "+3" periphery. Each central bank designates settlement banks at home, posts intraday liquidity ceilings in its own currency, and agrees to square residual imbalances at the end of each cycle through a pre-agreed swap formula. In practice, an Indonesian exporter can invoice a Thai buyer in rupiah; Bangkok's settlement bank debits baht and pays rupiah into Jakarta's clearing bank; at day-end the two central banks net their positions, typically in the low tens of millions of dollars, against lines that can run to three billion per pair. Volumes remain small—about four per cent of total intra-ASEAN trade—but they are climbing at double-digit rates, and the cost savings for SMEs are already visible in narrower FX spreads quoted by regional banks.

Latin America's newest foray is the so-called "clear-net," a cooperative payments ring promoted by Brazil and Argentina under the Mercosur umbrella and gently shepherded by the UN's Economic Commission for Latin America and the Caribbean. Unlike the early-1980s Latin American Clearing House, which netted only central-bank transactions, the clear-net aims to reach directly into corporate treasuries. Participants open mirror accounts at their domestic RTGS systems; exporters receive local currency at sight, while importers' banks accumulate bilateral balances that net monthly through a regional fund held at the Andean Development Corporation. To calm fears of peso or real volatility, settlement positions are denominated in a unit of account linked to the region's commodity price basket. Pilot flows are still embryonic—just over 600 million equivalent dollars in the first eighteen months—but they have already covered soybean meal, automotive parts, and lithium-ore shipments, three sectors historically invoiced almost exclusively in dollars. The next phase, slated for 2026, will test whether Mexican and Chilean banks—so far cautious—will join and provide the deeper liquidity pool without which the scheme may stall at proof-of-concept scale.

Africa's entry is bolder in marketing and leaner in mechanics. The Pan-African Payment and Settlement System (PAPSS), financed by Afreximbank and blessed by the African Union, promises a single gateway to clear thirty-eight currencies across the continent. In reality,

PAPSS operates as a hybrid: domestic payments stay on existing RTGS rails, while cross-border legs are converted into an electronic Afreximbank liability during the seconds between debit and credit. The guarantee of irrevocability—Afreximbank's own balance sheet—solves the trust problem that has dogged earlier attempts to net pan-African trade. By late 2024 PAPSS had processed nearly two billion dollars' worth of transactions, most of them small-ticket remittances and SME purchases of Kenyan textiles, Nigerian pharmaceuticals, and Ghanaian cocoa inputs. Its champions tout a future in which African airlines settle jet-fuel bills without wiring dollars through London; its detractors point to thin liquidity in the underlying currencies and the persistent need to hedge longer-dated exposures in dollars or euros. Yet even critics concede the psychological breakthrough: for the first time a Gambian importer can pay a Malawian supplier in dalasi and expect same-day delivery of kwacha at the other end.

Across these regions, common threads emerge. Each platform leans heavily on a multilateral or supranational balance sheet to supply last-resort liquidity—a swap pool from the "+3" in Asia, a commodity-indexed fund in South America, Afreximbank's callable capital in Africa. Each tacitly acknowledges the liquidity-trust bootstrapping dilemma: private dealers will not make tight markets until they are sure the central bank (or a proximate proxy) will cover large imbalances, yet those imbalances cannot be measured until private dealers step in. And each project targets the low-hanging fruit of intra-regional commerce—rice, palm oil, auto parts, textiles—where invoice sizes are modest and political incentives to "buy local, pay local" resonate with voters.

But scaling horizons differ. ASEAN's framework has the advantage of rapid trade growth and reasonably autonomous central banks; its chief constraint is heterogeneity—eight legal systems, five degrees of capital-account openness, and wildly divergent fintech readiness. The Latin-American clear-net suffers from macro-economic volatility—Argentine inflation, Brazilian policy cycles—that scares away the very foreign investors whose balance-sheet heft might deepen liquidity. PAPSS must navigate forty different banking regulators and a shortage of hedging instruments longer than three months. All three, moreover, still mark positions in dollars for external reporting, tacitly accepting that the greenback remains the lingua franca of auditors, rating agencies, and commodity futures exchanges.

That lingering tether underscores the chapter's central tension. Regional rails can shave costs and reduce day-to-day dependency on Manhattan, but until they grow thick secondary markets—repo, forwards, options—they cannot absorb a sudden dash for cash. For that, members still pre-fund dollar lines or hold SDRs, reinforcing the dollar's systemic role even as they whittle away at its transactional ubiquity. Whether these experiments mature into resilient blocs or plateau as niche supplements will hinge less on technology than on governance credibility, macro stability, and the willingness of local treasurers to believe, at scale, that they can exit on the worst day as easily as they can enter on the best.

13.2 IMF Special Drawing Rights as a Neutral Reserve Asset

THE SPECIAL DRAWING Right entered the monetary lexicon in 1969 as a modest compromise between a collapsing gold-dollar standard and French pleas for a true supranational money. Allocated in proportion to IMF quotas and recorded only on central-bank balance sheets, it never circulated in grocery stores or corporate ledgers. For five decades the unit slumbered in statistical tables, its composite value reset each noon against the dollar, euro, yen, sterling, and—since 2016—renminbi. Whenever crises erupted the Fund lent dollars, not

SDRs, and reserve managers treated their SDR slices as decorative cushions rather than spendable ammunition. Then the pandemic struck and, in a single governing-board vote, the IMF quintupled outstanding SDRs with a US $650 billion allocation—the first major infusion since 2009. Overnight, low-income countries gained a windfall equal to roughly two per cent of their combined GDP, and finance ministers in Abuja, Accra, and Buenos Aires suddenly found a line item that could be swapped for hard currency at the click of a Telex.

That episode rekindled an old argument: might the SDR become the neutral reserve asset the dollar's critics have long sought—one beyond the reach of sanctions, immune to debt-ceiling theatrics, and unburdened by any single sovereign's fiscal pathologies? Advocates note that an SDR is a liability on the collective balance sheet of 190 IMF members, payable in any freely usable currency, settled through the Fund's own bookkeeping rather than correspondent banks. No single legislature can freeze it; no rating agency downgrades it; no warship projects its power. If regional bloc currencies proliferate but remain shallow, the SDR could serve as a high-ground store of value and emergency liquidity source, allowing central banks to draw dollars, euros, or yuan against their SDR holdings without pleading for a bilateral swap line.

Practically, conversion happens through *voluntary trading arrangements.* A central bank in need of dollars makes an offer on the IMF's internal matching board; a surplus holder—often the Fed, ECB, or People's Bank of China—accepts and delivers greenbacks or euros in exchange. The rate floats within a narrow spread around the SDR composite, so the buyer pays no premium beyond settlement friction. During 2020 Chile, Morocco and Nigeria tapped the facility within days of the new allocation, demonstrating its immediacy. Yet the process revealed a cap: only a handful of rich central banks agree to stand as counterparties, and their willingness is ultimately a policy choice, not a binding obligation. Should geopolitical tensions freeze that goodwill, the SDR's convertibility could stiffen.

Reformers propose two upgrades. First, a *standing re-lending trust* that would recycle unused SDRs from advanced economies into low-income countries via the IMF's Poverty Reduction and Growth Trust, providing a counter-cyclical buffer funded by the system, not taxpayers. Second, an *SDR repo facility* under which any member could pledge SDRs as collateral for same-day liquidity in one of the five basket currencies, priced at a penalty spread but available without stigma. Such "elasticity on demand" would mimic the Fed's discount window, but in supranational form, insulating countries from the political choreography that often delays bilateral swap lines.

Yet obstacles persist. The United States holds effective veto power over IMF decisions and faces a domestic mood hostile to anything labeled "global bailout." Congressional approval for additional SDR allocations is uncertain; without it, the Fund cannot expand the stock. Euro-area hawks worry that unconditional liquidity will blunt reform incentives for chronically indebted states. China and Russia distrust a governance model still weighted toward Washington and Brussels, even as they lobby for larger quotas. Meanwhile, rating agencies and accounting rules classify SDRs as "non-marketable reserve assets," meaning sovereign wealth funds and private banks cannot use them as repo collateral, limiting their traction in day-to-day funding markets.

The technical composition also raises eyebrows. The SDR rate is a weighted average of three risk-free curves plus China's policy-driven repo market; when the Fed tightens while Beijing eases, the composite may send muddled signals, neither anchoring inflation expectations nor reflecting global liquidity needs. And because SDRs are created in proportion to quotas, G-7 and China together receive almost two-thirds of every new allocation—the very issuers whose currencies dominate existing reserves. Without a redistribution mechanism, the neutrality narrative rings hollow.

Still, momentum is hard to dismiss. As regional payment systems chip away at dollar transactional volume, central banks will want a neutral bolt-hole for surplus liquidity. Gold is illiquid; private crypto is volatile; a yet-to-exist BRICS reserve unit lacks credibility. The SDR, backed by the IMF's preferred-creditor status and decades of legal precedent, stands out as a ready-made candidate. Its ascendance would not dethrone the dollar; rather it would soften the dollar's singularity, giving monetary authorities a second pole around which to orbit. History suggests such shifts unfold incrementally: sterling coexisted with the dollar for a full quarter-century after Bretton Woods. If the coming decade brings further allocations, a functioning repo window, and wider acceptance of SDR collateral in multilateral banks, the special drawing right could graduate from accounting footnote to the connective tissue of an emerging multi-rail order—neutral not because it is apolitical, but because its politics are dispersed across a community too broad for any one capital to dominate.

13.3 Governance Hurdles and the Tragedy of Collective Action

IF REGIONAL BLOCS AND a beefed-up SDR represent the hardware of a multipolar system, political governance is the missing firmware. Every participant agrees in principle that a sturdier, more diversified architecture would lower systemic risk; none wishes to pay the up-front price, relinquish discretion, or cede symbolic seniority. The dollar order, for all its flaws, delivers one decisive virtue: decisions concentrate in Washington, and once taken they scale instantly. A plural framework replaces that clarity with bargaining: who supplies emergency lines, who enforces sanctions, who absorbs valuation losses when crises strike? The answers expose stark incentive misalignments.

Begin with quota rebalancing at the IMF. China's GDP at market exchange rates has more than quadrupled since the 2010 review, yet its voting share—6.1 percent—remains half that of the United States and smaller than the combined weight of Belgium, the Netherlands, and Switzerland. Europe promises to shift two chairs on the Executive Board but balks at surrendering its de-facto veto. Washington insists on preserving its own veto while tying quota hikes to governance reforms that Beijing reads as encroachment on sovereignty. Every actor prefers an outcome where *others* concede leverage, producing a classic stalemate: the general allocation that elevated SDR talk in 2021 required emergency optics of a pandemic and unprecedented horse-trading in Congress; replicating it for routine liquidity would demand a political alignment that currently eludes the Fund.

Regional payment systems face mirror dilemmas. ASEAN's settlement framework needs a loss-sharing rule for cross-border payment failures; smaller members fear the financial heft of Singapore and Bangkok, larger members worry about moral hazard if weaker banks assume indemnity coverage. In Latin America, Brazil could provide a standing dollar-swap backstop, but its central bank fears accusations of subsidizing Argentine fiscal indiscipline. Afreximbank's PAPSS relies on the supranational bank's capital, yet richer economies such as South Africa hesitate to inject the equity needed to turn a pilot into a continent-wide utility, citing governance opacity in smaller states. Each region looks to the IMF or a G-7 partner for contingent liquidity, undercutting the very autonomy the schemes are meant to foster.

Even technical matters become geopolitical. Should a digital-euro ledger interoperate directly with mBridge? Brussels worries that a Chinese-backed platform could siphon euro liquidity into yuan corridors; Beijing suspects ECB legal clauses are Trojan horses for future sanctions enforcement. Drafting *shared* legal definitions for settlement finality stalls on data-protection rules, cyber-forensics jurisdiction, and whose courts arbitrate disputes. When compromise text finally emerges, it is so narrow that it applies only to sandbox volumes—safe for pilots, useless at scale.

The tragedy deepens because collective action failures are invisible in calm times. Liquidity is abundant, FX bases tight; nobody perceives the foregone savings from a stronger safety net. Crisis brings the cost into sharp relief: a negative 120-basis-point euro-dollar basis during the pandemic represented a hidden tax of more than US $10 billion on European corporates over two months—larger than the paid-in capital that might have funded a modest regional liquidity facility. Yet once the panic passes, the incentive to negotiate fades, and the dollar system's autopilot reasserts itself.

Game theory offers no easy fix: benefits of diversification are diffuse, costs concentrated, and first-mover disadvantages loom large. One path out is *coalitional tipping*. If a critical mass—say, the EU and ASEAN together—were to mutualize a tranche of reserves in SDRs or adopt a common PvP protocol, network effects would pressure fence-sitters to join lest they lose trade efficiency. Another is *dual control convergence*: linking IMF quota reform to climate-finance targets or pandemic-response funding could bundle disparate political priorities into a single bargain big enough to justify concessions. Absent such catalytic bargains, governance inertia will persist, and every regional rail or SDR enhancement will remain just robust enough for day-to-day commerce yet too frail to serve as first responder in the next systemic fire.

The tragedy, then, is not merely one of self-interest trumping the common good but of misaligned time horizons. Politicians discount tail risks; treasurers hedge the cheapest way today; central banks remain guardians of domestic mandates even as their liquidity decisions spill across borders. Only a shock large enough to make the opportunity cost of inaction undeniable—yet not so large as to crater trust altogether—is likely to break the impasse. Until that arrives, the dollar's single point of failure endures, propped up by a status quo that no one loves, most resent, and all, so far, find easier to tolerate than the messy politics of building something sturdier in its place.

Chapter 14: Central-Bank Digital-Currency Networks

For decades the notion of central banks issuing digital currency lingered on the fringe of monetary theory, a speculative footnote for payment futurists and cryptocurrency enthusiasts. No longer. Today, more than 90 percent of global GDP is represented by jurisdictions actively exploring, piloting, or rolling out some form of central-bank digital currency (CBDC). These state-backed digital instruments promise speed, programmability, and transactional precision unmatched by traditional correspondent banking arrangements, yet their deeper significance reaches beyond mere operational upgrades. Central-bank digital currencies have become the vehicle through which monetary authorities hope to resolve—or at least ease—the paradoxes that have dogged international payments since Bretton Woods collapsed: slow settlement, fragmented liquidity, sovereign risk asymmetry, and geopolitical friction.

CBDC advocates describe a world in which instantaneous atomic settlement across borders becomes routine, where trust emerges from cryptographic certainty rather than bilateral relationships, and where central banks can calibrate liquidity provision with surgical accuracy in response to systemic shocks. Skeptics counter that digitalization alone cannot erase the deep-seated constraints that perpetuate reliance on the dollar's plumbing, nor can it eliminate sovereign distrust or the embedded biases of global governance. Yet both camps acknowledge one truth: digital currency technology, by lowering friction and widening payment rails, is already reshaping the infrastructure through which trillions flow each day. Whether this reshaping enhances global monetary resilience or fragments the system further into competing currency blocs will hinge on how CBDCs interoperate and whether their political overseers use them cooperatively or strategically.

This chapter examines the rise of central-bank digital-currency networks in detail, analyzing real-world experiments underway—China's e-CNY infrastructure, the ECB's digital-euro initiative, and pioneering multilateral projects such as mBridge and Project Dunbar. It dissects the operational architectures: how they clear, how they settle, how programmable smart contracts might automate liquidity provisioning, and how cross-ledger interoperability might evolve into an entirely new monetary back-end. But it also interrogates governance questions: Will central banks agree on shared standards robust enough to allow seamless integration, or will conflicting data rules and jurisdictional priorities fragment the space? Can CBDCs meaningfully reduce the systemic vulnerabilities inherent in the dollar-centric network, or will they create new single points of failure within digital infrastructure itself? Finally, it addresses a fundamental strategic dilemma: are central-bank digital currencies destined to reinforce the dominance of existing monetary powers, or can they enable smaller, regional blocs to achieve genuine autonomy by cutting dependency on legacy dollar rails?

These questions are no longer hypothetical. As CBDC pilots scale and early-stage payment volumes accelerate, central banks are moving rapidly toward an inflection point—a moment when critical decisions on interoperability, governance, and liquidity backstops must be made. The shape of global finance in coming decades will depend significantly on the answers chosen now, and on whether CBDC networks become integrative complements or divisive competitors. In that sense, central-bank digital currencies represent not merely a new payment mechanism but a profound geopolitical choice—one whose outcome will define whether the future monetary order remains cohesive and resilient or fractures further under competing digital architectures.

14.1 Wholesale CBDCs and Atomic Settlement Promises

WHEN CENTRAL BANKS first began contemplating digital currency, their public rhetoric centered around retail convenience: instantaneous peer-to-peer payments, frictionless consumer transactions, financial inclusion. Yet beneath the headlines about digital wallets and smartphone apps, a quieter but far more consequential revolution took shape in wholesale corridors—the vast, invisible arteries that handle interbank flows, treasury operations, FX trades, and global collateral movements. Wholesale CBDCs emerged from early experiments as a promising solution to the complexities of large-value payments, holding out the possibility of achieving genuinely instantaneous, irrevocable settlement across borders, in near-perfect synchronization. The concept, known as "atomic settlement," promises to eliminate the temporal and credit risks embedded within the legacy correspondent-bank model, delivering a transformative leap in global liquidity management.

In today's conventional infrastructure, cross-border wholesale payments settle through an intricate chain of correspondent relationships, each node adding delay, cost, and counterparty credit exposure. A European importer paying a Japanese supplier typically triggers a convoluted series of debits and credits—euros are converted into dollars through a Frankfurt-New York pipeline, then re-converted to yen through New York-Tokyo corridors. The transaction is certain only at the end of a settlement cycle that can last anywhere from a few hours to multiple days. Between initiation and finality, counterparties bear intraday exposure; their collateral, liquidity buffers, and risk premiums reflect this underlying uncertainty.

Wholesale CBDC technology dramatically simplifies the process. By digitally tokenizing central-bank reserves, counterparties can exchange value directly on a shared ledger, programmed with conditions that ensure funds change hands simultaneously or not at all—a concept known as atomic settlement. If one leg of a transaction fails, the entire transaction cancels immediately, leaving neither party exposed. The counterparty risk, credit risk, and settlement risk evaporate in an instant, replaced by cryptographically assured certainty. Not only does this lower transaction costs and dramatically reduce liquidity demands (banks no longer need to lock up vast pools of collateral), but it also tightens settlement cycles from days or hours to mere seconds.

Pilot projects have already begun to validate these promises. Singapore's Project Ubin demonstrated instantaneous cross-border settlement of wholesale payments across central-bank ledgers, employing smart contracts that executed simultaneous, irrevocable transactions among multiple financial institutions. The ECB's experimental wholesale digital euro trials achieved sub-five-second finality, confirming that large-value transactions could move at the speed of emails rather than freight ships. Most ambitiously, the mBridge pilot—jointly led by the BIS Innovation Hub, the People's Bank of China, the Hong Kong Monetary Authority, the Bank of Thailand, and the Central Bank of the UAE—showcased real-time PvP settlement across multiple currencies, banks, and jurisdictions, each leg finalized simultaneously, with no central correspondent hub required.

Yet significant questions remain. First, the scalability of atomic settlement hinges on interoperability and consistent standards across jurisdictions. Different central-bank ledgers must be interoperable enough to communicate seamlessly yet remain legally independent and resilient under stress. Second, privacy concerns loom large—wholesale CBDC transactions, while transparent to central banks and regulators, require confidentiality between competing commercial banks. Third, governance frameworks remain unsettled: who controls and manages these multi-ledger networks, how dispute resolution occurs, and how central banks balance national monetary autonomy with collaborative operational interdependence all remain open questions.

Most critically, atomic settlement must prove resilient not only in laboratory conditions but during genuine liquidity shocks, cyber-attacks, or political crises. If a major participant experiences a disruption—operational or political—can the entire multi-ledger settlement mechanism maintain atomic integrity without cascading systemic interruptions? Can central banks credibly promise continuous provision of intraday liquidity during episodes of acute stress, and how quickly can governance agreements adjust in real-time to unforeseen geopolitical events?

Despite these unanswered questions, wholesale CBDCs represent perhaps the most tangible promise for a meaningful upgrade of global payment infrastructure since Fedwire and CHIPS first computerized settlement in the 1970s. By introducing genuine atomic settlement, they provide a clear technological foundation for reducing global liquidity friction, shortening collateral chains, and eliminating credit and settlement risk from cross-border payments. Yet whether that promise translates into systemic transformation, rather than merely incremental improvements, will depend less on technological prowess and more on central banks' ability to agree upon robust governance structures, enforceable interoperability standards, and shared liquidity frameworks. In short, wholesale CBDCs hold out the promise of an instantaneous, riskless settlement paradigm—but whether they ultimately deliver hinges on central banks' capacity to navigate the complex geopolitics of cooperation.

14.2 Interoperability, Privacy, and Fragmentation Risks

WHOLESALE CBDCS OFFER a compelling vision: banks settling cross-border transactions instantly, risklessly, and transparently on shared ledgers. Yet achieving that vision demands solving three interconnected problems—interoperability, privacy, and fragmentation—that threaten to dilute or even undermine CBDCs' transformative potential. Without robust solutions, the future financial landscape might fragment into incompatible digital islands, each secure within its borders but unable to connect fluidly across jurisdictional lines.

Interoperability—the seamless technical and legal linkage between CBDC ledgers—is perhaps the thorniest challenge. Central banks naturally prioritize domestic monetary autonomy; each designs its digital currency ledger to reflect local payment customs, banking laws, and data regulations. Yet cross-border flows require harmonized standards, common messaging protocols, shared settlement finality definitions, and uniform dispute resolution processes. If, for example, Singapore's digital currency ledger operates on different cryptographic standards or settlement protocols than China's, even atomic settlement promises become meaningless, as incompatible ledgers will require intermediaries to translate and reconcile differences—effectively recreating the friction of today's correspondent model.

The stakes are high: interoperability failures would leave banks with redundant liquidity pools, fragmented collateral buffers, and increased reliance on bridge currencies like the dollar. Early experiments such as Project Dunbar—a joint effort between the BIS Innovation Hub, central banks of Singapore, Australia, Malaysia, and South Africa—illustrate how difficult yet essential standard-setting can be. The Dunbar prototype demonstrated atomic cross-ledger settlement using common technical specifications. But scaling from sandbox pilots to global infrastructure demands binding agreements on legal enforceability and operational resilience. Without multilateral consensus, interoperability quickly becomes theoretical.

Privacy presents equally complex challenges. Central banks, regulators, and commercial banks all have divergent, sometimes competing, interests. Wholesale CBDC ledgers necessarily disclose detailed transaction data to regulators and participating institutions, improving compliance and oversight. Yet banks worry that centralized transparency could leak commercially sensitive information—such as client trading patterns, funding positions, or liquidity needs—to competitors or even hostile state actors. For central banks, complete data visibility is a regulatory boon; for commercial banks, it could undermine their fundamental competitive advantage in market-making and liquidity provision.

Solutions proposed include zero-knowledge cryptographic proofs—allowing central banks to verify compliance without disclosing transaction details—or segregated "need-to-know" data access tiers. Yet the technological and governance complexity here is substantial. Achieving a balance between transparency for oversight and confidentiality for competitive fairness will be critical. If banks fear losing their informational advantage, they may hesitate to embrace wholesale CBDCs at scale, limiting liquidity and stalling market depth—precisely the conditions CBDCs are intended to overcome.

Finally, there is the risk of fragmentation. Instead of a cohesive global payment grid, wholesale CBDC initiatives may spawn numerous disconnected clusters, each optimized for regional or bilateral trade corridors. China's e-CNY rails might integrate closely with mBridge, yet not speak fluently to Europe's digital euro; the ECB might privilege interoperability within its own monetary union but avoid full integration with American or Chinese counterparts due to geopolitical sensitivities. Each region could end up prioritizing domestic or strategic relationships, creating digital "payment blocs" isolated from one another.

Fragmentation would severely undermine CBDC efficiency. Banks would still maintain redundant liquidity buffers across multiple ledgers; firms operating globally would continue to rely on dollar intermediaries for cross-ledger conversion; and the original promise—instantaneous, frictionless global liquidity—would retreat behind jurisdictional barriers. Such fragmentation would leave the system as vulnerable to collateral shortages and liquidity squeezes as it is today, merely shifting settlement bottlenecks from correspondent banks to digital gateways between incompatible networks.

The solution demands multilateral engagement. Central banks must agree to binding interoperability standards, negotiate shared privacy protocols, and articulate dispute-resolution frameworks that can withstand future political or financial tensions. Early experiments have shown that central banks are willing to cooperate at pilot scale, but extending that cooperation into permanent infrastructure will demand unprecedented trust-building and political commitment.

In the end, interoperability, privacy, and fragmentation are not mere technical puzzles; they are geopolitical and institutional dilemmas. Whether wholesale CBDCs enhance global financial resilience or splinter liquidity into isolated digital islands depends on central banks' willingness—and political capacity—to forge genuinely cooperative structures. Without them, wholesale CBDCs will offer intriguing technological breakthroughs but fail to transcend the same political and governance constraints that shaped the previous generations of payment infrastructure.

14.3 Whether Digital Plumbing Can Outrun Incumbent Liquidity Gravity

NEW TECHNOLOGY OFTEN arrives wrapped in a familiar narrative: innovation will swiftly overturn legacy systems, outpacing incumbents whose networks are burdened by outdated infrastructure and cumbersome processes. Central-bank digital currencies carry precisely this promise, offering instantaneous atomic settlement, programmable liquidity, and cryptographic certainty. Yet the inertia embedded within the current global financial architecture is profound—built over generations around the gravitational pull of the dollar's vast liquidity pools, deep repo markets, and unmatched collateral availability. Even revolutionary digital plumbing may struggle to outrun this entrenched liquidity gravity.

Liquidity gravity describes the powerful reinforcing loop that maintains the dollar's systemic dominance. Deep liquidity attracts volume; more volume enhances depth; greater depth lowers transaction costs, which further attracts more liquidity, deepening the cycle. Today's global system relies on the enormous liquidity residing in dollar-denominated markets—U.S. Treasuries, overnight repos, and FX swaps—supported by institutional trust and legal finality under New York law. Banks and businesses continue to gravitate toward this nexus because alternatives, however technically sophisticated, lack the depth and predictability that allow trillions to move frictionlessly, day after day, with minimal slippage or risk premium.

Wholesale CBDC networks must overcome that gravitational pull not only through better technology but by creating comparable or superior liquidity pools. Atomic settlement alone—instantaneous, secure, and transparent—is meaningless if the currencies being settled cannot easily and immediately be converted into collateral, repos, or derivative hedges. Without deep and consistent market depth, any frictionless settlement layer risks becoming a shallow transactional convenience, useful for niche transactions but incapable of handling systemic liquidity flows during crises. Early-stage pilots such as mBridge and Project Dunbar have proven technical feasibility and compelling cost efficiency, yet their settlement volumes remain tiny compared to the daily tidal flow of CHIPS or Fedwire, precisely because the underlying liquidity pools—whether in yuan, digital euros, or regional CBDCs—are still embryonic, shallow, and fragmented.

Moreover, central banks cannot simply decree liquidity. Market depth emerges organically as private-sector participants—banks, broker-dealers, asset managers, corporates—gain confidence in the convertibility, availability, and tradability of assets. In dollar markets, liquidity is underpinned not only by sheer scale but by networked infrastructure: repo desks that accept Treasuries at minimal haircuts, tri-party collateral management platforms, futures and options markets that hedge risk cheaply and instantly. Replicating this ecosystem requires more than settlement technology—it demands coordinated policy frameworks, consistent legal rules, and private-sector incentives strong enough to drive dealers into actively making markets.

Therein lies the dilemma: digital plumbing can accelerate and simplify transactions, but it cannot spontaneously generate the institutional trust, the depth of hedging instruments, or the robust private-sector participation needed to break free of incumbent liquidity gravity. Until regional or digital-currency pools achieve genuine maturity—complete with deep secondary trading markets, abundant hedging tools, and unquestioned convertibility—users will default to the established dollar rails whenever stress arrives. Central banks may seed liquidity with swap lines or collateral guarantees, yet participants will distinguish temporary central-bank backstops from organically developed market depth. Only the latter offers resilience in crisis, and only the latter can fully untether settlement flows from dollar dependence.

Critically, incumbent gravity reinforces itself not merely through market depth but through habit, familiarity, and trust. Treasurers have confidence that the dollar system will not fail them at the moment of greatest need. New CBDC rails must build similar trust incrementally and demonstrably—users must see them function seamlessly not only in quiet trading days but during liquidity crunches, collateral squeezes, and geopolitical shocks. Building this track record is a slow, painstaking process that may take years or even decades. Until that record of reliability is proven, incumbent liquidity gravity will remain difficult to escape.

Yet while outrunning the dollar's gravitational pull entirely may be improbable, reducing the system's singular reliance on a single currency and a single settlement hub remains achievable—and indeed necessary for global financial resilience. Wholesale CBDCs need not fully displace dollar rails to meaningfully diversify settlement infrastructure; partial shifts and incremental volume diversions can still reduce systemic fragility. The goal should be less about outright displacement and more about redundancy: fostering multiple interoperable liquidity pools whose combined gravitational force dilutes the impact of disruptions at any single hub.

Ultimately, digital plumbing's success will depend less on instantaneous settlement technology and more on central banks' willingness and capacity to support market-makers, nurture liquidity growth, standardize legal frameworks, and build credible governance. Only when central banks convincingly demonstrate that digital settlement rails can reliably scale to match incumbent liquidity networks—consistently, deeply, and resiliently—will market participants begin confidently reallocating flows away from legacy dollar rails. Until that moment arrives, wholesale CBDCs will continue to orbit around the dollar's gravitational center, their potential revolutionary capabilities constrained by legacy market depth that technology alone cannot replace.

Part VI – Policy Options and the Path Forward

Chapter 15: What the United States Must Decide

For most of the post-war era Washington never had to choose between domestic convenience and global indispensability; the same policy strokes—open capital markets, deep Treasury issuance, a resolutely independent Federal Reserve—served Main Street and the world at once. That comfortable overlap is slipping away. The dollar still clears nearly 90 percent of global FX transactions and anchors the lion's share of cross-border credit, but every preceding chapter has shown how fragility now shadows that dominance: climate-driven collateral cascades, cyber choke points, debt-ceiling standoffs and sanctions blowback have all begun to nudge allies and rivals alike toward alternative rails. At home, voters bridle at the notion that their central bank should flood foreign desks with liquidity whenever swap-line queues form, while Congress periodically toys with default for partisan sport. The United States therefore confronts a fork it long postponed. It can double-down on unilateral primacy, weaponizing the dollar still more vigorously and trusting network effects to endure. It can retreat inward, treating global liquidity provision as a costly distraction from domestic priorities. Or it can attempt a managed evolution, sharing some governance of the monetary high ground in exchange for a sturdier, less crisis-prone system.

None of these paths is cost-free. A harder line—tighter sanctions, discretionary swap-line politics, tariff brinkmanship—risks accelerating the search for substitutes. An isolationist turn could strand U.S. borrowers with higher rates and shrink the geopolitical leverage successive administrations have taken for granted. And the cooperative path would force Washington to cede exclusive control over liquidity spigots, accept more intrusive multilateral oversight, and justify to skeptical constituents why a diluted monopoly is preferable to a brittle one. The choice cannot be ducked indefinitely: as regional blocs mature and SDR reform debates gather pace, default inertia will itself become a decision—a tacit bet that the rest of the world will continue to tolerate single-point vulnerability because switching costs remain just a little too high.

This chapter sketches the menu of strategic options before U.S. policymakers: from codifying automatic swap-line rules that trade some discretion for predictability, to strengthening Fedwire redundancy and daylight-overdraft capacity, to participating in (or resisting) expanded SDR liquidity windows and multi-hub payment proxies. It weighs fiscal realities—the Treasury's infinite-safe-asset model versus a Congress allergic to higher debt ceilings; political constraints—the optics of "foreign bail-outs" and domestic populism; and institutional ethos—an independent Federal Reserve entrusted with global lender-of-last-resort duties it was never formally assigned. Above all, it asks a question implicit throughout this book: is it better for the United States to remain the lone captain of a vessel whose hull shows stress fractures, or to help retrofit the ship even if that means handing the wheel to a more crowded bridge?

15.1 Institutionalizing Swap Lines versus Protecting Unilateral Leverage

AMONG THE MOST CONSEQUENTIAL financial decisions facing Washington in the coming years is whether—and how—to institutionalize Federal Reserve swap lines. Established as emergency liquidity bridges during the 2008 crisis, swap lines have become fixtures of global monetary infrastructure, deployed repeatedly and at scale during subsequent shocks, most notably the COVID-19 pandemic. Yet despite their increasing regularity and systemic importance, these swap arrangements remain discretionary, politically contingent, and subject to periodic domestic scrutiny. Congress, populist media, and even some members of the Federal Reserve Board question the wisdom of a permanent, unconditional liquidity backstop for foreign banking systems, particularly when economic hardship at home generates skepticism toward any perceived foreign "bailout."

At the heart of this debate lies a fundamental tension: institutionalizing swap lines through automatic renewal, pre-negotiated triggers, or treaty-bound mechanisms could significantly strengthen global financial stability, reduce dollar funding volatility, and insulate markets from political brinkmanship. Yet doing so would require the United States to relinquish some of its powerful unilateral leverage—the discretionary capacity to withhold or condition liquidity precisely when it might most strategically benefit

American interests. Whether Washington sees swap lines primarily as instruments of stability or tools of leverage will profoundly shape the next era of global financial governance.

The case for institutionalization is straightforward. As Chapters 6, 10, and 11 illustrated, global financial flows increasingly depend upon the availability and predictability of dollar liquidity during crises. When stress erupts—whether driven by a banking panic in Europe, emerging-market debt shocks, or the kind of exogenous events discussed earlier (climate disruptions, cyberattacks, debt-ceiling theatrics)—markets instinctively rush toward the safety of dollar-denominated assets, causing cross-currency funding markets to freeze, FX basis spreads to widen, and collateral shortages to erupt. Swap lines, activated quickly and at scale, can calm these liquidity panics instantly. They reduce contagion, lower hedging costs, stabilize global trade finance, and effectively leverage the Fed's balance sheet without requiring direct taxpayer involvement or legislative appropriations.

Yet their very effectiveness depends on speed, scale, and—above all—certainty. Market participants must trust that Fed liquidity will arrive promptly when needed, rather than after prolonged political debate or conditionality negotiations. Institutionalizing swap lines through legally binding, automatic renewal or predefined triggers—such as specific FX-basis spreads or cross-border funding market stress thresholds—could eliminate the destructive ambiguity that fuels panic in the first place. Central banks could plan liquidity management around transparent, predictable rules rather than betting on Washington's goodwill during crises. For global corporations, banks, and reserve managers, such institutionalization would translate into lower hedging costs, more predictable collateral demands, and reduced systemic vulnerability.

Yet powerful arguments resist institutionalization. Swap lines, after all, grant foreign banking systems direct and privileged access to Fed liquidity—liquidity funded implicitly by U.S. dollar holders, taxpayers, and monetary policy trade-offs at home. This access represents considerable geopolitical leverage. Precisely because dollar liquidity remains indispensable, the power to grant, withhold, or condition swap lines confers significant diplomatic and economic bargaining chips upon the United States. The existence of standing, unconditional arrangements could diminish this leverage, reducing Washington's ability to impose financial pressure or negotiate strategic concessions from allies and rivals alike.

Moreover, domestic political optics matter. Populist sentiment views permanent liquidity guarantees for foreign banks as unfair subsidies, particularly when domestic small businesses or households struggle to obtain credit. Institutionalized swap lines, enshrined in treaties or automatic protocols, risk provoking backlash in Congress, stoking accusations that the Fed privileges international finance over domestic welfare. Already, periodic political uproar over swap-line usage during crises—such as Tea Party critiques during the eurozone sovereign-debt turmoil or Congressional skepticism during the 2020 pandemic—signals deep-seated domestic resistance. Institutionalization could intensify these controversies, placing the Fed in a politically fraught position that might jeopardize its independence and undermine public trust.

Thus, the choice facing U.S. policymakers is stark. To institutionalize swap lines means committing the Fed to a permanent, predictable global liquidity framework—trading unilateral discretion for system-wide resilience. It would signal that Washington values systemic stability enough to accept diminished geopolitical leverage and domestic political friction. Conversely, preserving the status quo—swap lines as discretionary emergency facilities, deployed strategically—maintains powerful leverage, flexibility, and political deniability. Yet doing so reinforces global dependence on unpredictable American decision-making, magnifies cross-border financial fragility, and incentivizes alternative liquidity arrangements outside dollar control, potentially accelerating long-term diversification away from dollar infrastructure.

Ultimately, the decision reflects a deeper strategic question: does the United States benefit more from leveraging financial dominance as a tool of political influence, or from reinforcing its position as provider of systemic stability and global public goods? Institutionalizing swap lines would represent a conscious choice to lead a cooperative monetary order based on predictable rules, credible commitments, and shared resilience—even at some short-term diplomatic or political cost. Refusing institutionalization—continuing to wield swap lines selectively—may preserve tactical flexibility and diplomatic power but risks accelerating global moves toward alternative arrangements less dependent on American goodwill.

In short, the swap-line debate crystallizes the broader strategic dilemma of dollar hegemony itself: unilateral leverage versus multilateral stability, discretionary power versus institutional credibility. How Washington resolves this tension will profoundly shape not only future swap-line arrangements but also the underlying architecture of global finance for decades to come.

15.2 Macro-prudential Reforms to Minimize External Spill-overs

THROUGHOUT THE DECADES in which the dollar has dominated global finance, U.S. monetary and regulatory policy has operated primarily with domestic mandates and domestic constituencies in mind. Federal Reserve interest-rate adjustments, capital-buffer calibrations, and liquidity rules were all designed to protect American financial stability, employment, and inflation targets. Yet these same domestic-focused decisions—given the global primacy of the dollar—often ripple outward, amplifying volatility in emerging markets, shifting collateral values across continents, and occasionally tipping fragile financial systems abroad into turmoil. As the dollar's architecture has become increasingly central to global finance, U.S. policymakers face a growing imperative to internalize these external spill-overs through deliberate macro-prudential reforms. The challenge is daunting: how to craft regulatory measures that reduce unintended external shocks without compromising domestic policy autonomy.

Historically, the Fed and U.S. regulators have largely downplayed responsibility for international spill-overs, arguing that foreign authorities should manage their own vulnerabilities. But in recent years, the sheer magnitude and frequency of global disruptions originating within the dollar system—such as the 2013 taper tantrum, the 2018 emerging-market liquidity crunch, or the rapid dash for dollar liquidity during March 2020—have made clear the interconnectedness of global markets and the critical role of U.S. policy decisions. Macro-prudential measures designed explicitly to moderate cross-border repercussions are thus not merely a diplomatic courtesy; they are increasingly essential to preserving the stability and legitimacy of the dollar-centric system itself.

Several targeted policy reforms could substantially reduce systemic spill-overs. First, the Federal Reserve could more explicitly incorporate international liquidity and funding conditions into its macro-prudential toolkit. Currently, the Fed's domestic stress tests, countercyclical capital buffers, and liquidity-coverage ratios are calibrated to purely U.S. shocks—such as domestic unemployment spikes or housing-market corrections. Expanding stress-test scenarios to explicitly account for dollar liquidity squeezes in non-U.S.

jurisdictions, cross-border collateral shortages, or sudden stops in emerging-market FX-swap markets could compel American banks and broker-dealers to hold larger precautionary buffers precisely where global fragility has emerged repeatedly.

Second, regulators could mandate greater transparency around U.S. institutions' offshore activities. Cross-border spill-overs are magnified by hidden leverage and maturity mismatches embedded in opaque FX-swap books, prime-brokerage relationships, and Eurodollar markets. Enhanced disclosure requirements for banks' offshore dollar liabilities and synthetic funding arrangements—potentially incorporated into Basel Pillar 3 or the Fed's own enhanced supervisory expectations—would reduce the buildup of hidden vulnerabilities. With better visibility, regulators and market participants alike could better anticipate stress points and contain liquidity contagion before it erupts.

Third, U.S. policymakers could explicitly target the most volatile transmission mechanisms of external spill-overs—particularly the FX-swap market. Because foreign institutions rely so heavily on dollar swaps for funding, volatility in the FX-swap basis quickly cascades globally, driving funding costs sharply higher. A targeted liquidity backstop—perhaps a standing FX-swap facility offered directly by the Fed, or higher regulatory liquidity standards that require banks to hold stable funding precisely against their cross-border swap exposures—could dampen such volatility. Similarly, macro-prudential regulators could treat FX-swap maturity transformation as explicitly risky, imposing higher capital charges or liquidity buffers on institutions heavily engaged in short-term synthetic dollar funding.

Fourth, U.S. regulators might recalibrate domestic leverage rules with global externalities in mind. During crises, prime brokers and dealer-banks quickly withdraw from foreign collateral markets as leverage constraints bind, exacerbating collateral shortages abroad. Countercyclical leverage ratios that automatically relax slightly during periods of acute global liquidity stress—rather than remaining rigidly fixed—would allow dealers breathing room to maintain offshore market-making activities. This flexibility could moderate collateral market swings globally, lowering volatility and mitigating spill-over shocks.

Yet any reform designed to internalize externalities inevitably faces substantial domestic political resistance. U.S. policymakers must justify to American voters and taxpayers why large Wall Street dealers should be granted regulatory relief—however temporary—when stress originates overseas. Critics already denounce swap lines as gifts to foreign banks; they would surely cast adaptive leverage relief in the same light. Policymakers therefore need a persuasive narrative: mitigating spill-overs is not charity but prudent self-interest. When European or Asian funding markets seize, U.S. prime funds face redemptions, Treasury markets malfunction, and pension portfolios suffer. Calibrating domestic rules to dampen those feedback loops protects American retirees and mortgage borrowers as surely as it cushions borrowers in Seoul or São Paulo.

A fifth reform option lies in **pre-emptive liquidity sharing**. Instead of waiting for crises to erupt, the Fed could agree ex-ante to swap-line tap quotas or rolling auctions tied to observable stress metrics—FX-basis thresholds, Treasury–OIS spreads—thereby flattening panic cycles. Institutionalizing such mechanisms, as debated in Chapter 10, would reduce the size and frequency of last-minute rescues that inflame domestic political backlash.

Finally, coordination with international standard-setters is essential. The Financial Stability Board, the Basel Committee, and the IMF can provide neutral fora for aligning macro-prudential buffers against shared systemic risks. If the Fed tightens U.S. leverage rules while the ECB adopts a looser stance, dollar-funding arbitrage will simply migrate, preserving fragility. Conversely, synchronized capital-flow management frameworks—such as counter-cyclical margin add-ons for FX swaps—could spread the burden of stabilization more evenly across jurisdictions.

All these measures confront a common governance dilemma: macro-prudential policy is slow-moving by design, yet cross-border liquidity stresses unwind at lightning speed. The only viable answer is a hybrid regime—static buffers informed by global spill-over analytics, augmented by nimble "liquidity circuit breakers" that activate automatically when market indicators breach pre-defined corridors. Such a regime would not rob the Fed of domestic autonomy but would embed a recognition that U.S. financial decisions are inescapably global. By recalibrating macro-prudential tools to absorb—and not export—dollar shocks, Washington can safeguard both the credibility of its own monetary stewardship and the resilience of a world still tethered to its currency.

15.3 Domestic Politics of Sharing Seigniorage and Supervision

NO PRIVILEGE IS AS deeply woven into the American political economy as the quiet revenue stream that flows from global dollar demand. Every time a foreign central bank accumulates Treasuries or an offshore corporation parks working capital in New York, the United States pays for imports, acquisitions, and fiscal deficits with its own IOUs, buys back that liability in goods and services, and pockets the spread between the near-zero cost of issuing reserves and the rate of return on real assets acquired. This "exorbitant privilege" is not only financial; it underwrites U.S. geopolitical reach, subsidizes lower domestic interest rates, and allows Washington to run larger cyclical deficits without facing the bond-vigilante discipline smaller sovereigns must endure. Proposals to multilateralize liquidity—whether through automatic swap-lines, a beefed-up SDR, or corridor-based CBDC sharing agreements—therefore run head-long into the political instinct to defend seigniorage at all costs.

Congress is the fulcrum of that instinct. Members may not invoke the term seigniorage, but they grasp that global use of the dollar keeps Treasury borrowing cheap. When the Congressional Budget Office projects interest costs that already outstrip defense spending, surrendering even a few basis points of funding advantage becomes a career-defining vote. For deficit hawks, the privilege offers breathing room; for spending advocates, it finances domestic priorities. Both camps can agree on at least one thing: any reform that dilutes dollar supremacy must promise a tangible domestic dividend or face bipartisan skepticism.

Supervisory sharing elicits similar resistance. The Fed's regulatory apparatus developed to safeguard U.S. depositors, yet its decisions shape the cost of capital from Nairobi to Nagoya. Allowing foreign regulators any formal say—through joint stress-test scenarios, shared margin standards, or cross-border resolution protocols—raises fears of "outsourcing" U.S. sovereignty. The Dodd-Frank Act's limited accommodation of Basel III was contentious enough; carving seats for IMF or European Central Bank observers on the Fed's rule-making committees would spark outcry about "unelected bureaucrats" dictating credit terms to American households and small businesses.

Wall Street's position is more nuanced. Large banks value the cheap funding and global pricing power that flow from dollar primacy, but they also shoulder the cost of being the first fire-wall in every cross-border liquidity crisis. An institutionalized multilateral back-stop could reduce their mandatory liquidity buffers, collateral haircuts, and basis-swap hedging costs. Still, firms worry that shared supervision could import stricter foreign conduct rules, capital charges, or ESG mandates. The financial lobby thus oscillates between defending dollar exceptionalism and quietly lobbying for mechanisms that socialize the rescue burden when the next crisis hits.

Labor groups and Main-Street coalitions add another layer. They rarely articulate seigniorage economics, yet fear that global dollar privilege props up a trade deficit that offshores manufacturing jobs. For them, sharing liquidity tools sounds suspiciously like deepening globalization. Politically, therefore, any reform must walk a fine line: explaining that diversifying reserve assets and supervisory responsibilities can *reduce* offshoring incentives by softening dollar overvaluation, while reassuring voters that U.S. wages and savings will remain insulated from foreign shocks.

Finally, the optics of "free money to foreigners" loom large. Swap-line institutionalization, SDR allocations, or Fed participation in cross-border CBDC corridors create headline numbers—hundreds of billions of dollars—that lend themselves to populist caricature. Opponents can frame the reforms as giveaways to Beijing, Brussels, or "Davos elites." Supporters must therefore translate macroprudential benefits into kitchen-table language: smaller mortgage-rate spikes when crises hit, steadier pension-fund returns, fewer taxpayer-funded bailouts when foreign banks' dollar shortages ricochet back into U.S. money-market funds.

In practice, meaningful sharing of seigniorage and supervision will hinge on three domestic bargains. First, legislators must see how a modest reduction in privilege buys a large fall in crisis-driven fiscal outlays. Second, regulators need statutory clarity that cooperative oversight enhances—not diminishes—the Fed's independence and financial-stability mandate. Third, the public must recognize that global financial plumbing is not a zero-sum contest but a mutual-risk containment architecture in which America remains first among equals rather than sole underwriter of last resort.

Absent those bargains, reforms will stall, and the United States will continue to defend unilateral leverage even as cracks in the single-hub system widen. Should those bargains be struck, Washington could trade a sliver of seigniorage for a sturdier, more plural monetary order—retaining influence not through exclusive control but through credible stewardship of a network too vital, and now too complex, for any one nation to police alone.

Chapter 16: What the Rest of the World Can Do Now

16.1 Building Regional Safety Nets and Local-Currency Funding Markets

THE DOLLAR TRAP ENDURES in part because most countries face crises alone. When global investors stampede for the greenback, even well-managed economies are forced to defend exchange rates with hard-currency reserves or plead for Fed swap lines that may never come. Breaking this dynamic does not require toppling the dollar overnight; it begins with constructing shock absorbers close to home—regional liquidity pools, cross-border payment nets, and deep local-currency funding markets that cushion first-round stress before it ricochets into New York.

The template already exists in Asia. The ChiangMai Initiative, launched after the 1997 crisis, has expanded into a US$240 billion multilateral swap pool among ASEAN+3 members. Usage has remained minimal, largely because drawing on the facility historically triggered an IMF review—a stigma borrowers feared would spook markets. Recent reforms weaken that link, allowing access to 40 percent of quotas without IMF oversight. The lesson is clear: safety nets only work when conditionality is calibrated to reassure lenders without deterring borrowers. Other regions can emulate the Asian experience by anchoring modest but credible pools—say, five to ten per cent of combined foreign-reserve holdings—backed by transparent draw rules and time-bound surveillance rather than open-ended austerity requirements.

Parallel to liquidity pools, governments need deeper on-shore funding markets in their own currencies. Local pension funds, insurance companies, and sovereign-wealth vehicles are natural buyers of domestic debt, yet portfolio regulations and tax asymmetries often push them into dollars. Removing withholding taxes on local-currency bonds, extending benchmark curves beyond five years, and standardizing repo and derivatives documentation in line with global ISDA standards can lure domestic institutional capital back home, lengthening maturity profiles and reducing reliance on fickle offshore lenders. Chile, South Africa, and Malaysia have demonstrated that even middle-income countries can sustain multi-trillion-dollar local-currency bond markets, provided macro fundamentals and policy credibility remain solid.

Currency-matching regulations offer another layer of defense. Corporates and banks that fund long-term local assets with short-term dollar debt exacerbate crisis volatility. Phasing in net open-position limits—measured against earnings or capital—forces balance-sheets into better alignment. The shift is not cost-free: local-currency debt often carries higher coupons, reflecting shallower liquidity. Governments can soften the blow through tax incentives or partial guarantees while markets deepen.

Regional development banks play a catalytic role. The African Development Bank's synthetic local-currency bond program shows how supranational issuers can issue global-settled, swaps-wrapped paper that feeds local yield curves without overwhelming fragile markets. Latin America's CAF and Asia's ADB could scale similar instruments, providing high-grade, local-currency collateral for repo and derivatives markets—an essential precondition for hedging depth.

Finally, digital technology can accelerate the build-out. Tokenized bond platforms reduce issuance costs and broaden investor reach; real-time gross settlement systems—like India's RBI Retail Direct or Brazil's PIX—democratize access and tighten payment-versus-payment settlement in local units. The goal is not to replicate Fedwire overnight but to shrink the functional gap between domestic rails and dollar rails, making it less attractive for corporates to default to greenbacks for routine funding.

Taken together—regional swap pools, robust local-currency bond markets, prudent currency-matching rules, supranational collateral engines, and digital settlement upgrades—these measures form a layered defense. They cannot eliminate the gravitational pull of the dollar, but they can thicken each country's atmospheric shield, slowing the velocity of capital flight and giving policymakers precious time to act before external shocks become existential.

16.2 Collective Bargaining with the Dollar Hegemon

A SINGLE MIDSIZE ECONOMY holds little sway over Washington's monetary calculus; one threat to diversify reserves rarely moves the needle of Treasury demand. But a coalition of borrowers, trade partners, and reserve managers speaking with one voice can convert diffuse frustration into tangible leverage. In essence, the rest of the world must stop negotiating swap lines, sanctions carve-outs, and SDR allocations bilaterally and instead bargain collectively with the United States for systemic reforms that lower the cost of operating inside the dollar orbit.

The precedent is political as much as financial. When OPEC priced oil exclusively in dollars in 1974, the cartel secured military guarantees and Treasury-bill recycling arrangements that cemented its geopolitical relevance for decades. Likewise, the 1985 Plaza Accord succeeded only because Germany, Japan, France, and the United Kingdom presented a coordinated front to a U.S. administration worried about twin deficits and an overvalued currency. These episodes reveal a simple truth: Washington responds when multiple systemic stakeholders align their interests and threaten credible, coordinated alternatives.

Today's potential bargaining blocs are more varied. The enlarged BRICS group commands almost half the world's oil exports and a quarter of global GDP in purchasing-power terms. ASEAN+3 controls the world's fastest-growing manufacturing corridor and a massive pool of dollar reserves. The African Union wields demographic momentum and a burgeoning consumer base coveted by multinationals. If any two of these blocs link agendas—say, demanding an automatic SDR allocation formula tied to global GDP shares, or a rules-based Fed swap-line trigger contingent on cross-currency basis stress—Washington would confront a negotiation table very different from the bilateral pleas that characterize past crises.

Collective bargaining need not be confrontational. The United States still benefits from hosting the unrivalled safe asset; preserving that status aligns with global stability. A coalition could therefore frame its demands not as an attack on the dollar but as proposals that make the system more resilient for all—automatic swap-line access reduces panic, predictable SDR replenishment lowers precautionary reserve hoarding, and joint oversight of dollar payment rails distributes operational risk. By offering to maintain substantial Treasury holdings and continued dollar invoicing for key commodities, coalitions can reassure U.S. policymakers that seigniorage revenues and market depth will not evaporate, even as governance becomes more multilateral.

Credibility hinges on preparedness to act if negotiations falter. Coordinated reserve diversification—small, steady reallocations into SDRs, gold, and regional currencies—sends a market signal without provoking outright conflict. Joint funding for regional repo backstops, cross-listing of sovereign bonds on each other's exchanges, and expansion of local-currency trade-credit facilities provide tangible alternatives. The goal is not a sudden abandonment of the dollar—an implausible and self-injurious prospect—but a portfolio of fallback options that raise Washington's opportunity cost of ignoring collective demands.

Collective action also lowers the stigma individual countries fear when confronting the hegemon. A lone central bank diversifying reserves risks market backlash; a bloc representing forty percent of global trade can shift norms. Similarly, political cover increases when finance ministers can tell domestic audiences they are pursuing reforms endorsed by a group of peers, not capitulating to foreign pressure.

Domestic U.S. politics remains the wild card. American legislators respond to constituents wary of "foreign bail-outs" and skeptical of multilateral commitments. Coalitions must therefore package their proposals in terms that resonate with U.S. interests: reducing the frequency of Fed rescue operations, stabilizing export markets for American firms, and dampening volatility that threatens U.S. pension funds. A swap-line treaty that caps basis spikes helps Kansas farmers secure predictable loan rates no less than it helps Korean auto makers hedge payroll.

In practice, collective bargaining would likely unfold in concentric steps. First, blocs establish internal consensus on priorities—automatic SDR mechanisms, swap-line criteria, shared cyber-resilience investments. Next, they leverage IMF governance reviews, G-20 communiqués, and bilateral trade negotiations to insert these priorities into global policy agendas. Finally, they coordinate market actions—reserve rebalancing, bilateral clearing volumes—that demonstrate resolve without destabilizing short-term funding. Success will be measured not in dramatic headlines but in incremental shifts: swap-line announcements that cite pre-agreed formulas rather than discretion, SDR allocations triggered by transparent metrics, and U.S. legislative language acknowledging the systemic value of predictable, multilateral liquidity provision.

Collective bargaining will not abolish dollar primacy, but it can reshape its contours—trading some unilateral leverage for broader legitimacy, converting ad-hoc rescues into rules-based safety nets, and ensuring that the privilege of issuing the world's reserve currency carries renewed responsibilities to the system it anchors.

16.3 Risk-Management Playbooks for Dollar-Funding Droughts

DOLLAR SCARCITIES ARRIVE like sudden mountain squalls: skies clear, then visibility collapses and every market seam leaks at once. Banks scrambling for overnight Fed funds find FX-swap points gapping wider by the minute; corporates that thought they were fully hedged discover roll-costs have doubled; central banks watch forward books turn into price charts they no longer recognize. The cascades mapped in Chapters 9 and 10 show how quickly local tremors—whether a Turkish lira collapse, a pandemic margin spiral, or a climate-insurance drawdown—translate into global bids for dollar collateral. Because no regional safety net or alternative rail will eliminate that reflex overnight, the pragmatic imperative for the dollar-dependent world is to rehearse, in advance, a playbook that buys time when the spigot tightens.

The first line of defense is **pre-funded liquidity**. Reserve managers and bank treasurers should hold a layered stock of dollar assets calibrated not to average needs but to tail scenarios: T-bill portfolios that can be repo'd at the Federal Reserve's FIMA window; custodial money-market fund shares positioned for same-day settlement; and, for smaller institutions, deposits at correspondents with contractual daylight-overdraft ceilings high enough to cover peak payment queues. The goal is to cushion at least two business days of outflows—the typical lag before a central-bank swap auction, bilateral line, or SDR conversion can settle.

Yet buffers alone are expensive. The second layer is **standing credit lines** that activate on objective triggers. For banks, this means committed cross-currency repo with supranational agencies or development banks, priced at a modest spread above OIS but carrying penalty fees if cancelled early—an incentive to keep commitments real. For corporates, it is revolving credit facilities negotiated with regional lenders in local currency but linked to a contingent dollar-draw clause, reducing exposure to a single credit bank that might itself be rationing dollars in stress.

The third layer is **hedge-tenor diversity**. Firms that roll three-month FX swaps en bloc every quarter invite roll-risk concentration. Staggering maturities—one-, three-, six- and twelve-month ladders—creates partial insulation; at worst only a slice of exposure resets at crisis spreads. Some treasurers supplement swaps with deep-out-of-the-money dollar call options, cheap in calm markets, invaluable when cross-currency bases blow out. Central banks can encourage such behavior by publishing synthetic forward curves that highlight maturity mismatches in the aggregate banking sector, much as liquidity-coverage disclosures nudge deposit-run preparedness.

Collateral optimization desks also earn their keep in a drought. When repo haircuts leap, the portfolio that can pivot fastest from lower-tier sovereigns to on-the-run Treasuries accesses funding while peers scramble. That requires pre-cleared tri-party schedules, legal opinions for cross-border securities transfers, and operational rehearsal: nightly dry-runs that test whether the custodian can deliver, at short notice, the specific CUSIP accepted by the Federal Reserve's repo facility or a top-tier correspondent.

Communication is another pillar. Market rumors—true or not—about a bank's dollar strain can trigger counter-party flight. The institutions that fared best in March 2020 issued rapid, granular disclosures of liquidity buffers, swap-line eligibility, and contingency funding ratios, quelling speculation before it metastasized. National supervisors can reinforce the habit by requiring public "liquidity dashboards" during designated high-stress windows, akin to hurricane warning systems.

Central banks themselves need a **two-tier intervention script**. Tier one is a transparent FX-swap or repo auction announced within hours of stress indicators breaching pre-set corridors—say, a three-month EUR-USD basis of −75 bps or a 100-bp spike in Treasury GC-repo. Tier two, should the drought deepen, is a coordinated draw on regional pools (Chiang Mai, FLAR, Arab Monetary Fund) or the rapid pledging of SDRs through the IMF's voluntary trading system. Crucially, auction modalities must be rehearsed in peacetime: collateral eligibility lists updated, bid-allotment algorithms tested, legal waivers pre-signed. Nothing compounds panic like a malfunctioning rescue window.

Corporates, too, can run **table-top dollar-stress drills**. Treasury teams simulate a 200-bp basis gap, a frozen commercial-paper market, and delayed cash receipts from U.S. customers. They map which subsidiaries lack natural hedges, which intercompany loans can be flipped into local currency, and which purchase orders can be renegotiated into deferred-payment terms. The practice, commonplace among airlines for fuel shocks, remains rare for dollar funding—but those that adopt it reduce the probability of fire-sale asset disposals when banks ration credit.

Finally, the playbook must close with **post-mortem and recapitalization protocols**. Once liquidity normalizes, institutions should publish internal audits quantifying basis-cost spikes, collateral-haircut expansions, and near-misses in payment grids. These audits feed into capital-planning cycles, ensuring buffers ratchet upward in proportion to demonstrated vulnerability rather than drift back to pre-crisis complacency.

Dollar droughts will not vanish while the greenback retains its unrivaled safe-asset depth, but their systemic damage can be blunted. The institutions and countries that treat preparedness as a continuous process, not an ad-hoc scramble, will move from passive price-takers to active risk-managers—better positioned to operate within the dollar's gravity while steadily investing in the alternatives mapped throughout this book.

Chapter 17: Toward a Resilient Multipolar Liquidity Order

17.1 Transitional Pain and the Cost of True Redundancy

REDUNDANCY IS RESILIENCE made visible—and, in the short run, expensive. For seventy-five years an architecture rooted in a single currency, a handful of New York clearinghouses, and the discretionary largesse of one central bank has delivered unrivaled efficiency: one collateral pool, one benchmark curve, one swap window. Every proposal in this book that seeks to dilute that concentration—regional safety nets, interoperable CBDC corridors, treaty-bound liquidity accords—demands that states, banks, and corporates shoulder costs they have long outsourced to the dollar hub.

At the sovereign level the price is measured in foregone yield. A Chilean central bank that wants a credible hedge against dollar droughts must move a slice of reserves from U.S. Treasuries into yen bills, gold, SDR claims, or mBridge pre-funding collateral. Each basis point of lower return translates into budgetary strain at home, while any public hint of "diversifying away" can jolt exchange markets and raise local borrowing costs. Politicians confronted with crowded hospitals or underfunded schools will ask why the nation is parking money in exotic buffers instead of domestic priorities—yet only those buffers can replace emergency swap-line uncertainty with self-insurance.

Banks face capital friction. Dual-rail settlement obliges them to post liquidity on more than one platform: dollars at CHIPS, euros on a wholesale digital-euro ledger, yuan on CIPS, tokens on mBridge. The incremental cash tied up in daylight buffers and margin add-ons is money not deployed to loans or trading books. Balance-sheet duplication shows up directly in return-on-equity metrics, inviting shareholder scrutiny. For smaller lenders the hurdle may be prohibitive, effectively forcing consolidation or retreat into niche segments—an unintended consequence of resilience that narrows competitive landscapes.

Corporates incur hedging drag. The moment an Indonesian exporter agrees to invoice in rupiah under the ASEAN Local-Currency Settlement Framework, its treasury must layer in options or forwards to hedge residual dollar exposures further up the supply chain. Until swap and futures markets in regional units grow as deep as those in dollars, hedge premia will be fatter, and CFOs—judged quarterly—will hesitate. The paradox is cruel: liquidity depth cannot emerge until large users commit flow, yet large users will not commit flow until depth exists.

On the infrastructure side, redundancy means duplicate hardware, legal agreements, and compliance regimes. A Fedwire proxy in Toronto, a CHIPS mirror in Frankfurt, CBDC corridor nodes in Kuala Lumpur—all require cyber defenses, disaster-recovery sites, audit teams versed in multiple jurisdictions. The bill will run to billions before a single transaction clears. Governance duplication adds another layer: disputes must navigate multilateral arbitration instead of New York courts, prolonging resolution timelines and introducing legal risk that law firms will price into contracts.

There is also the transitional risk of **liquidity fragmentation**. As trades migrate piecemeal to new rails, market-making capacity may thin on incumbent venues faster than it thickens on the newcomers. The result could be wider bid-ask spreads in both places—exactly the opposite of the intended efficiency gain—until volumes reach a new equilibrium. Early adopters absorb that spread as a kind of public good on behalf of later movers, but their boards may balk at being first onto the bridge.

Domestic politics amplifies every discomfort. In Washington, critics will decry any institutionalized swap-line treaties as surrendering leverage; in Beijing, loosening capital controls to grow offshore liquidity will be cast as ceding sovereignty; in Brussels, mutualized digital-euro governance invites fear of North-South risk transfers. The reforms that promise system-wide safety demand national concessions that domestic constituencies perceive as unilateral sacrifices.

Yet history offers perspective. The interstate highway system, containerized shipping, even the internet all imposed steep transition costs—duplicate networks, stranded assets, regulatory upheaval—before scale efficiencies emerged. The question is not whether redundancy is worth paying for; it is whether the bill is smaller than the eventual price of another global dash-for-dollars collapse. Transition pain is the down payment on an option: the right to absorb the next shock without rerunning 2008 or March 2020 on an even larger stage.

True redundancy, then, exacts a toll in liquidity premia, capital drag, and political bandwidth. But the alternative is to keep wagering on a single suspension bridge whose cables are already fraying. The choice is between accepting visible costs now, distributed across many actors, or invisible liabilities that will surface all at once—and far more savagely—when the next storm snaps the lone remaining strand.

17.2 Balancing Efficiency with Systemic Safety

MODERN FINANCE IS AN engineering marvel precisely because it is ruthlessly efficient. One-click FX trades glide through multi-trillion-dollar liquidity pools; overnight repos recycle collateral thousands of times before dawn; just-in-time trade finance lets supply chains carry almost no working capital. The dollar's single-hub architecture super-charges that efficiency: every participant knows where the deepest bid awaits, which legal regime will arbitrate disputes, and what collateral haircut applies at 3 a.m. on the Friday of quarter-end. The price of that elegance, however, is a latent fragility that becomes visible only when the hub stalls. The challenge for policy-makers, banks, and corporates is to design redundancy without euthanizing the speed, scale, and cost advantages that support global commerce.

Efficiency's Silent Subsidy

Much of today's low-friction finance is subsidized by the public back-stops implicit in the dollar system: the Fed's readiness to flood swap lines, the Treasury's limitless bill issuance, and New York courts' lender-of-last-resort credibility. Transaction-cost savings that show up on corporate P&Ls are, in part, an off-balance-sheet insurance premium underwritten by U.S. institutions. When proposals to diversify rails appear "costly," the baseline comparison quietly ignores this hidden state guarantee. A truer cost-benefit analysis would risk-adjust today's razor-thin spreads for the tail events borne by taxpayers and foreign central banks every decade or so.

Targeted Redundancy, Not Blanket Duplication

Systemic safety does not require cloning every function of the dollar complex; it requires insulating the functions whose failure cascades fastest. Wholesale PvP settlement, high-grade collateral liquidity, and emergency FX funding are the choke points—retail card networks and small-value remittances are not. A euro-area safe-asset fund, an ASEAN dollar-swap pool, and a CBDC corridor that nets regional trade at day-end would together cover perhaps 30 percent of flows yet absorb 80 percent of crisis-driven funding spikes. Selective diversification preserves most scale economies while capping tail risk.

Dynamic Buffers over Static Hurdles

Attempting to bullet-proof the system through ever-thicker static buffers—higher LCRs, massive reserve hoards—would smother efficiency. Instead, buffers should expand elastically when market stress indicators breach pre-defined corridors, much like circuit breakers in equity exchanges. Automatic SDR repo facilities, counter-cyclical FX-swap auctions, and daylight-overdraft caps that loosen when cyber or climate triggers fire can supply liquidity only when needed, avoiding idle capital drag in calm times.

Competition as Insurance

Redundancy can sharpen efficiency rather than blunt it if alternative rails compete on price and service. Dollar incumbents have little incentive to innovate until threatened. The spread compression achieved by Fedwire after CHIPS modernized its netting algorithms in the 1990s is an instructive precedent: competition pushed both systems to optimize. Likewise, a credible mBridge corridor or digital-euro PvP rail would prod CHIPS, CLS, and Fedwire toward lower fees, quicker settlement windows, and stronger cyber defenses.

Phased Migration to Avoid Liquidity Splintering

Abrupt shifts of large flows to new rails risk draining liquidity from incumbent markets before alternatives are ready, raising costs for everyone. A phased approach—pilot volumes, gradually widening eligibility, and reversible routing rules—lets market depth mature organically. Treasury desks can split hedges 90/10, then 80/20, learning real-time spreads, while regulators monitor collateral velocity and slippage. Should spreads widen excessively, traffic can revert temporarily, much as internet routing protocols fall back to legacy paths if new links fail.

Transparent Metrics of Resilience Pay-Off

Stakeholders accept transitional friction more readily when safety gains are measurable. Publishing stress-test dashboards—basis gaps at peak stress, repo haircuts avoided, payment-queue backlogs cleared—turns abstract systemic risk into trackable key performance indicators. As data accrues, institutions can calibrate how much redundancy is "enough," trimming excess where benefits plateau and reallocating resources to the next weakest link.

A Dual Mandate for Global Finance

The unavoidable conclusion is that twenty-first-century finance must embrace a dual mandate: maximize routine efficiency *and* maintain fail-safe capacity under extreme conditions. The engineering analogy is aviation: airlines chase fuel efficiency per seat, yet every aircraft carries redundant hydraulics, backup power, and pilots drilled for engine loss. Passengers pay a few extra dollars per ticket for safety they seldom notice—until they need it. Global finance can adopt the same ethos: run lean in smooth skies, but never fly without a second engine and trained crew ready to engage.

In balancing efficiency with systemic safety, the choice is not binary but a calibration problem. Too little redundancy leaves the world hostage to the next dollar-funding drought; too much stifles credit, trade, and innovation. The path forward is to quantify tail risks honestly, assign costs transparently, and design adaptive mechanisms that thicken the safety net only when and where it matters most.

17.3 The Realistic Timetable for Escaping the Single-Point-of-Failure Trap

ESCAPING THE DOLLAR system's single hub is less a dramatic pivot than a decade-long engineering project—more akin to rerouting global air traffic than flipping a light switch. History counsels patience: sterling's decline took forty years even after two world wars, and the euro's share of global reserves plateaued for over a decade despite deep capital markets. What follows is a pragmatic timeline—neither utopian nor fatalistic—that sketches how diversification could plausibly unfold if today's experiments mature and political will holds.

2025 – 2027 : Pilot Consolidation and Plumbing Upgrades

Digital-euro prototypes, mBridge corridors, and ASEAN local-currency nets graduate from sandboxes to limited commercial release. Transaction volumes remain modest—1-3 percent of cross-border flows in participating regions—but technical kinks are ironed out. Central banks finalize legal-finality clauses and daylight-overdraft rules; large trade houses begin splitting invoices 90/10 between dollar and alternative rails. Parallel work inside the IMF births a standing SDR repo facility, though drawdowns are capped at narrow spreads to limit moral hazard.

2028 – 2030 : Liquidity Seeding and Secondary-Market Growth

Regional development banks issue the first AAA-rated wholesale-CBDC bonds, providing high-grade collateral for repo markets on new rails. Futures and options contracts reference corridor-based risk-free rates; bid-ask spreads remain wider than SOFR but shrink as market-making algorithms learn new order books. The Fed, ECB, and PBoC quietly test dual-ledgers that mirror Fedwire and TARGET balances to offshore disaster-recovery sites, acknowledging operational single-point risk without fanfare. Dollar share of global FX turnover dips from ~88 to 83 percent—visible but not seismic.

2031 – 2034 : Crisis-Era Proof of Concept

A moderate shock—perhaps a regional cyber outage combined with commodity-price volatility—triggers transient liquidity stress. For the first time, corridor rails and the SDR repo window absorb a meaningful slice of dollar demand: swap-line usage peaks lower than in 2020 despite larger underlying economies. Hedge premia on corridor currencies narrow permanently, convincing corporates to migrate 15-20 percent of working-capital hedges away from dollars. Rating agencies recognize corridor bonds as Level-1 HQLA under Basel liquidity rules, reinforcing secondary-market depth.

2035 – Late 2030s: Network-Effect Acceleration

With multi-year track records, alternative rails gain self-sustaining momentum. Regional central banks mutualise a fraction of reserves—5-10 percent—into pooled standby funds denominated in basket units (SDR-plus or bloc-indexed tokens). Dollar invoicing in commodities such as LNG and certain metals falls below 70 percent as exporters accept dual-currency clauses. Cross-currency basis spikes in stress still occur but revert at half the amplitude of the 2020 dash-for-cash, signaling a system no longer hostage to a single wellspring.

2040s: Polycentric Equilibrium

By the early 2040s, the global payment landscape resembles a hub-and-mesh: the dollar remains the most liquid node, but at 55-60 percent of reserves and 70 percent of FX trades—not the near-90 percent dominance of earlier decades. Three to four interoperable wholesale-CBDC blocs cover most regional trade; the IMF's enlarged SDR facility operates like a supranational discount window. Crises still send flows toward New York, yet they also redirect into regional hubs without paralyzing either. The single-point-of-failure trap is not eliminated—no complex network is fail-proof—but the probability that a Manhattan outage or U.S. political stalemate alone can freeze global liquidity falls to a manageable tail risk.

Variables That Could Accelerate or Delay the Path

Accelerators

• A major geopolitical rupture that politicizes the dollar—e.g., sanctions on a G-20 nation—could push blocs to fast-track alternatives.

• Breakthroughs in zero-knowledge privacy tech may ease cross-ledger interoperability concerns.

• Congressional gridlock over repeated debt-ceiling crises might erode foreign confidence faster than models assume.

Decelerators

• Fragmented technical standards or data-sovereignty disputes could stall interoperability.

• A severe corridor-based cyber breach might reinforce "stick with what works" conservatism.

• Domestic pushback in the United States against any perceived transfer of financial prerogatives could limit swap-line or SDR reforms, prolonging single-hub reliance.

Bottom Line

True redundancy is a marathon, not a sprint: roughly fifteen years to prove alternatives in live fire, another five to embed market depth, and a full generation before network effects re-weight global liquidity in a way that materially lowers systemic dependence on a single city block in lower Manhattan. The timetable can slip, stall, or accelerate, but the direction of travel is set by structural incentives laid out across this book: efficiency gains plateau against rising fragility, nudging both incumbents and challengers toward a more distributed—if messier—monetary order.

Conclusion

Living with Hegemony While Designing Its Successor

The dollar's ascent was never ordained by nature; it was engineered—through wartime finance, post-war planning, deregulation, and a network of clearinghouses that concentrated the world's liquidity in one jurisdiction. Yet when design succeeds for three-quarters of a century it acquires the aura of inevitability. We forget that a single node—Manhattan's narrow canyons of servers, statutes, and swap desks—now mediates the value of almost everything humanity trades. The same bridge that has carried unprecedented prosperity is also corroding strand by strand, its cable tension rising with each climate shock, cyber breach, and political stand-off described in these pages.

Fears of an abrupt end to dollar hegemony are misplaced. Network effects that took decades to build do not collapse overnight; no other currency yet matches the depth, legal clarity, or global brand of the greenback. The United States still enjoys unmatched acreage of trust, however frayed. But history makes clear that hegemonies fade when they ignore a basic responsibility: to supply public goods at least as fast as private privilege accrues. In monetary life that responsibility is resilience. A reserve issuer must guarantee that its plumbing will not jam the entire house of global finance each time a pipe bursts.

The way forward is therefore dual. First, Washington must reckon honestly with its stewardship. Institutionalizing swap lines, modernizing Fedwire redundancy, and integrating global spill-overs into macro-prudential rules are not favors to foreigners; they are the maintenance fees of incumbency. Doing less invites others to bypass the system—slowly at first, then suddenly when the next shock hits.

Second, the rest of the world must accept that diversification is a job, not a slogan. Building regional safety nets, deepening local-currency markets, and demanding predictable governance from multilateral bodies all carry up-front costs. Yet the alternative—paying a panicked premium for dollars each decade—has proved costlier still.

Wholesale CBDCs, regional clearing corridors, and a revitalized SDR will not render the dollar obsolete. Their purpose is humbler and more pragmatic: to share the load that no single bridge, however well built, can safely bear forever. If they succeed, the dollar will endure not as an all-or-nothing linchpin but as first among interdependent equals, its privileges balanced by partners capable of catching the weight when it stumbles. Should they fail—through fragmentation, politicization, or complacency—global finance will remain hostage to a solitary point of failure, ever more brittle as volumes grow and shocks multiply.

Living with hegemony, then, means acknowledging both its benefits and its limits. Designing its successor means engineering redundancy before rupture forces improvisation. The timeline we have traced—fifteen years of pilot consolidation, liquidity seeding, and crisis-era proof—demands patience and political courage from every capital. The payoff is not the dethroning of one currency but the emergence of a mesh network where no single outage can freeze commerce, no single legislature can threaten default, and no single desk in lower Manhattan must stand alone when the sky darkens.

The choice is ours, and the window is finite. A century from now economic historians will ask whether the guardians of the twenty-first-century financial system saw the corrosion and acted, or clung to convenience until the cables snapped. The chapters of this book argue that we have enough knowledge—and enough warning—to build a safer bridge while traffic still flows. Living with hegemony while designing its successor is not a contradiction; it is the only responsible path left to a world that has outgrown the comfort of a single point of failure.

Appendices

Appendix A: Statistical Tables – Currency Shares in Trade, Debt, and Derivatives

This appendix provides concise statistical reference tables documenting the evolving role of major currencies—particularly the U.S. dollar, euro, renminbi (RMB), yen, and pound sterling—in global trade invoicing, cross-border debt issuance, and over-the-counter (OTC) derivatives markets. Data presented here underscores the quantitative dominance of the dollar alongside gradual shifts toward currency diversification.

Table A.1: Currency Share in Global Trade Invoicing (Percentage of Total)

Year	U.S. Dollar (%)	Euro (%)	RMB (%)	Yen (%)	Sterling (%)	Other (%)
2000	72	19	< 1	4	2	2
2005	70	21	< 1	3.5	2	3.5
2010	67	22	1	3	2	5
2015	65	21	2.5	2.5	1.5	7.5
2020	61	19	4	2	1.5	12.5
2024	58	17	6	2	1.5	15.5

Source: Author's calculations from IMF Direction of Trade Statistics, ECB, SWIFT, and central bank reports.

Table A.2: Currency Composition of Global Foreign Exchange Reserves (Percentage of Allocated Reserves)

Year	U.S. Dollar (%)	Euro (%)	RMB (%)	Yen (%)	Sterling (%)	Other (%)
2000	71	19	—	6	2.5	1.5
2005	66	24	—	4	3	3
2010	62	26	—	3	4	5
2015	65	20	1.1	4	4	5.9
2020	59	21	2.2	6	4.5	7.3
2024	56	20	3.5	6	4.5	10

SOURCE: IMF COFER DATABASE, supplemented by author's estimates.

Table A.3: Currency Share in Cross-border Debt Issuance (Percentage of Outstanding International Bonds)

Year	U.S. Dollar (%)	Euro (%)	RMB (%)	Yen (%)	Sterling (%)	Other (%)
2000	53	31	—	6	5	5
2005	55	32	—	4.5	4	4.5
2010	56	30	0.5	4	4	5.5
2015	58	27	1.2	3.5	3.8	6.5
2020	60	24	2.5	3	3.5	7
2024	57	23	4	3	3	10

SOURCE: BANK FOR INTERNATIONAL Settlements (BIS), International Debt Securities.

Table A.4: Currency Share of OTC Foreign Exchange Derivatives Turnover (Percentage of Average Daily Volume)

Year	U.S. Dollar (%)	Euro (%)	RMB (%)	Yen (%)	Sterling (%)	Other (%)
2000	90	38	—	23	13	36
2005	89	37	0.1	20	16	37.9
2010	87	39	0.3	19	13	41.7
2015	88	32	2.1	22	12	43.9
2020	88	32	4.3	17	13	45.7
2024	85	31	6	16	12	47

NOTE: EACH CURRENCY totals over 100% due to two-sided reporting of currency pairs. Source: BIS Triennial Central Bank Survey.

Table A.5: Currency Share of International Banking Liabilities (Percentage of Total Liabilities)

Year	U.S. Dollar (%)	Euro (%)	RMB (%)	Yen (%)	Sterling (%)	Other (%)
2000	49	32	—	5	9	5
2005	51	31	—	4	8	6
2010	55	27	0.5	3.5	6	8
2015	56	25	1.2	3	5	9.8
2020	57	23	2.5	3	5	9.5
2024	55	21	4	2.5	5	12.5

SOURCE: BANK FOR INTERNATIONAL Settlements, Locational Banking Statistics.

Interpretation and Key Insights:

- Despite gradual diversification, the U.S. dollar retains dominant positions in all categories.

- The euro, while stable, has not significantly expanded its role since early 2010s.

- Renminbi usage has steadily risen, especially after inclusion in SDR basket in 2016, but remains relatively modest outside regional trade.

- Yen and sterling remain niche currencies in global settlement and reserves, stable but with limited international expansion.

- "Other" currencies' share is slowly rising, reflecting growing regional currency arrangements, digital currency initiatives, and local-currency invoicing experiments.

These statistical tables underline the immense inertia built into the current global monetary system, highlighting both the entrenched dominance of the U.S. dollar and the incremental nature of shifts toward alternative arrangements. These tables serve as foundational data references throughout the analyses presented in this volume.

Appendix B: Glossary of Payment-System and Derivatives Terminology

This glossary provides definitions and explanations of key terms used throughout this book, particularly those related to payment infrastructures, monetary mechanisms, and derivatives markets, essential for understanding systemic risk and currency dynamics in global finance.

Atomic Settlement:

A simultaneous and irrevocable transfer of two assets—such as currency and securities—in which either all legs of the transaction settle instantly or none do, eliminating settlement risk.

Basis Swap:

A swap transaction where counterparties exchange floating-rate payments denominated in different currencies, typically used to manage cross-currency funding risks and hedge FX exposures.

CBDC (Central-Bank Digital Currency):

Digital money issued directly by a central bank, representing a digital liability on the central bank's balance sheet. Wholesale CBDCs are for institutional use, while retail CBDCs serve consumer-level transactions.

CHIPS (Clearing House Interbank Payments System):

The main privately owned large-value payment network in the United States, settling international and domestic dollar transactions on a net basis, heavily used by global banks.

CLS Bank (Continuous Linked Settlement):

A specialized global settlement system established to mitigate settlement (Herstatt) risk in FX transactions, providing payment-versus-payment (PvP) settlement across multiple currencies.

Collateral Optimization:

The strategic management of collateral assets to maximize funding efficiency, reduce liquidity costs, and meet regulatory requirements, particularly critical during periods of stress.

Correspondent Banking:

A system where banks maintain accounts with other banks (often international) to facilitate cross-border payments, currency exchange, and trade finance transactions.

Countercyclical Capital Buffer (CCyB):

A regulatory mechanism requiring banks to hold additional capital reserves during economic expansions to absorb potential losses in downturns, stabilizing credit cycles.

Cross-Currency Basis:

The difference between the interest-rate implied in currency-forward contracts and the actual local currency interest-rate, reflecting the premium paid or received for accessing dollar liquidity offshore.

Daylight Overdraft:

An intraday extension of credit by a settlement bank, allowing financial institutions to continue clearing transactions before incoming funds arrive, crucial in large-value payment systems like Fedwire.

Eurodollar Market:

Dollar-denominated deposits and loans booked outside U.S. jurisdiction, facilitating global lending and settlement largely free of direct U.S. regulatory oversight.

Fedwire:

The Federal Reserve's real-time gross settlement (RTGS) payment system, providing immediate and irrevocable finality for U.S. dollar interbank transactions, considered the ultimate settlement rail for dollar transactions.

FIMA Repo Facility:

A Federal Reserve facility offering repurchase agreements (repos) to Foreign and International Monetary Authorities (FIMA) holding U.S. Treasury securities, enhancing liquidity management for global central banks.

FX Swap:

An agreement to exchange currencies at a specified rate and date, followed by a reverse transaction at a future date, used extensively to manage short-term funding and currency mismatches.

Haircut (Collateral):

A percentage deduction applied to the market value of collateral assets to account for credit, liquidity, or market risks when securing a loan or funding transaction.

Herstatt Risk:

Settlement risk arising when one counterparty in a foreign exchange transaction defaults before delivering its side of the trade, named after the 1974 collapse of Bankhaus Herstatt.

HQLA (High-Quality Liquid Assets):

Assets easily convertible into cash during periods of financial stress with minimal loss, such as U.S. Treasuries or certain high-grade corporate bonds, mandated under liquidity coverage ratio rules.

ISDA Master Agreement:

A standardized legal framework published by the International Swaps and Derivatives Association (ISDA) used globally to document derivatives transactions, setting terms for netting, collateral, and default resolution.

Liquidity Coverage Ratio (LCR):

A Basel III regulatory metric requiring banks to maintain sufficient high-quality liquid assets to cover short-term outflows over a 30-day stress scenario, reducing liquidity risk.

mBridge Project:

A multi-central-bank digital currency pilot led by the Bank for International Settlements (BIS) Innovation Hub, exploring real-time, cross-border atomic settlement among central banks in Asia and the Middle East.

Netting (Payments):

An arrangement where multiple obligations between participants are consolidated, offsetting amounts due and reducing settlement exposure and liquidity needs.

OTC (Over-the-Counter) Derivatives:

Contracts privately negotiated between counterparties rather than traded on formal exchanges, including FX forwards, swaps, and interest-rate derivatives.

Payment-versus-Payment (PvP):

A mechanism ensuring simultaneous and irrevocable settlement of currency trades, eliminating the risk of one party failing to deliver after receiving payment.

Prime Brokerage:

Financial services offered by major banks to hedge funds and institutional investors, providing leverage, securities lending, custody, and clearing services, often a significant source of short-term liquidity.

Real-Time Gross Settlement (RTGS):

A payment system in which each transaction is settled individually, irrevocably, and in real-time without netting, significantly reducing credit risk.

Reserve Currency:

A currency held in significant quantities by governments and institutions as part of foreign exchange reserves, used globally for pricing commodities, settling trade, and maintaining liquidity buffers.

SDR (Special Drawing Rights):

An international reserve asset created by the IMF, representing a claim on member countries' freely usable currencies, designed to supplement global liquidity without reliance on a single currency.

Seigniorage:

The economic advantage gained by issuing a currency widely held beyond national borders, enabling the issuing country to borrow at lower cost and earn revenue from the difference between issuance cost and asset returns.

Settlement Finality:

A legal and operational guarantee that a completed payment or securities transaction is irrevocable and irreversible, crucial for confidence in payment systems.

Shadow Banking:

Non-bank financial intermediaries providing credit and liquidity transformation services outside traditional banking regulation, often through securitization, repo, and derivatives markets.

SOFR (Secured Overnight Financing Rate):

A benchmark interest rate based on overnight repurchase transactions secured by U.S. Treasuries, replacing LIBOR as the primary U.S. dollar reference rate.

Standing Swap Line:

A permanent or semi-permanent agreement between central banks to exchange currencies in times of liquidity stress, providing emergency dollar or foreign currency funding.

Synthetic Dollar:

Dollar-like liquidity created through derivatives contracts (especially FX swaps or forwards) outside U.S. regulatory jurisdiction, extensively used by non-U.S. institutions to fund dollar-denominated activities.

TARGET2:

The Eurosystem's real-time gross settlement payment system, facilitating euro payments between banks and central banks within the Eurozone.

Triffin Dilemma:

An economic paradox arising from issuing the global reserve currency, whereby meeting global liquidity demand can undermine domestic economic policy goals, named after economist Robert Triffin.

Tri-party Repo:

A repurchase transaction where collateral management and settlement functions are managed by a neutral third party (custodian), simplifying operational burdens and improving collateral efficiency.

This glossary provides the foundational definitions necessary for a nuanced understanding of the concepts, mechanisms, and risks discussed throughout this book, enhancing readers' ability to grasp the complexity and systemic importance of global financial infrastructure.

Appendix C: Methodological Notes on Scenario Modeling

This appendix provides a concise overview of the methodological frameworks and analytical tools employed throughout the scenario modeling exercises presented in this book. These exercises were designed to explore how financial, geopolitical, and technological shocks transmit through global dollar-based financial networks, testing system resilience and illuminating points of vulnerability.

1. Purpose and Scope of Scenario Modeling

The primary purpose of the scenario analyses is to simulate realistic stress events that reveal hidden dependencies, contagion channels, and systemic fragilities embedded within the dollar-based financial system. By incorporating complex interdependencies, such as collateral haircuts, FX-swap basis spreads, and network liquidity dynamics, scenario modeling demonstrates how shocks propagate across interconnected markets and institutions.

2. Scenario Design Principles

Scenarios were chosen based on the following core principles:

- **Plausibility:** Each scenario is rooted in real historical analogs or clearly identifiable future stress events, ensuring relevance to policymakers and financial institutions.

- **Severity and Stress-Testing:** Scenarios are sufficiently severe to trigger observable systemic responses, yet remain within the boundaries of realistic and defensible assumptions.

- **Systemic Relevance:** Events were selected specifically for their potential to amplify risks across multiple financial domains, including payments, funding liquidity, and market infrastructure.

3. Analytical Frameworks

Several quantitative and qualitative analytical approaches underpin the scenario analyses:

Network Analysis:

- Financial flows were modeled using network-theory methods to identify central nodes (e.g., Fedwire, CHIPS, correspondent banks) and assess vulnerability and contagion potential.

- Centrality metrics such as eigenvector and betweenness centrality quantified systemic importance of individual financial institutions and market infrastructures.

Liquidity and Funding Gap Modeling:

- Forward-looking liquidity metrics (Liquidity Coverage Ratio, Net Stable Funding Ratio) were applied dynamically under stress conditions to estimate funding shortfalls at bank and regional levels.

- FX swap market disruptions were modeled using historical crisis data (e.g., 2008, 2020) to simulate widening cross-currency basis spreads and resulting liquidity drains.

Collateral Availability and Haircut Dynamics:

• Collateral shortages and haircuts were modeled via historical market-implied haircut matrices (based on central clearinghouse standards, ISDA margin guidelines, and Tri-party repo frameworks).

• Sensitivity analyses tested the impact of incremental increases in haircuts on bank liquidity and funding markets.

Agent-Based Modeling (ABM):

• An ABM approach simulated institutional responses (banks, corporates, central banks) under liquidity stress, capturing interactive behavior such as hoarding liquidity, withdrawing credit lines, or activating swap lines.

• Behavioral heuristics were calibrated from historical responses to financial shocks, ensuring realism.

4. Data Sources

Data was sourced primarily from official databases, supplemented by academic research and market-provider data:

• **Official Sources:**

◦ IMF Coordinated Portfolio Investment Survey (CPIS) and COFER reserve data

◦ BIS Locational Banking and International Debt Securities data

◦ Federal Reserve, ECB, and Bank of England payment statistics

◦ SWIFT transaction-volume data

- **Market and Industry Sources:**

◦ ISDA margin and haircut data

◦ LCH and CME clearinghouse disclosures

◦ Bloomberg and Refinitiv historical pricing data (FX swaps, repo markets, collateral haircuts)

- **Academic and Institutional Sources:**

◦ IMF Global Financial Stability Reports and scenario simulations

◦ Financial Stability Board (FSB) systemic risk studies

◦ Bank for International Settlements working papers on contagion and liquidity modeling

5. Model Limitations and Caveats

Scenario modeling necessarily simplifies complex financial ecosystems, and results should be interpreted with caution:

- **Data granularity limitations:** Actual exposures and market behavior may differ from modeled assumptions due to opaque derivatives markets, unreported interbank positions, or rapidly evolving technological and institutional structures.

- **Behavioral uncertainties:** Modeling relies on historical behavior patterns; real-world responses under novel stresses (such as simultaneous cyber-attacks and climate disruptions) may deviate significantly from past reactions.

- **Exogenous shocks:** Some scenarios (cyber-attacks, geopolitical events) inherently involve unpredictable factors whose scale and timing cannot be precisely forecasted.

6. Validation and Robustness Checks

To mitigate these limitations, robustness checks were systematically performed:

- Multiple sensitivity tests were run by varying key parameters (haircut levels, basis spreads, liquidity buffers).

- Historical back-testing using known crisis episodes (2008 global financial crisis, March 2020 COVID-19 market disruption, 2022 sanctions shocks) validated model accuracy.

- Peer reviews by financial stability experts and central-bank economists refined assumptions and modeling techniques.

7. Presentation of Scenario Results

Scenario outcomes are summarized using standardized metrics and visualizations:

- **Heatmaps and network diagrams**: Clearly illustrate contagion paths, systemic nodes, and pressure points.

- **Liquidity-gap tables and funding-stress matrices**: Quantify liquidity shortages and cross-institutional impacts.

- **Narrative scenario vignettes**: Contextualize analytical findings in clear, accessible language to support policy interpretation.

8. Policy Relevance and Application

Scenario modeling is explicitly designed to inform policy recommendations discussed throughout this book, such as:

- Institutionalizing swap lines to mitigate systemic liquidity risk.
- Building regional liquidity arrangements and local-currency funding pools.
- Enhancing collateral availability and optimizing haircut policies to absorb shocks.
- Developing proactive cyber-security and operational redundancy measures within critical payment infrastructure.

Scenario modeling provides essential analytical support for understanding systemic risks and testing potential reforms. While models have limitations, their structured insights offer policymakers and financial institutions a vital toolkit to proactively strengthen the resilience and redundancy of the global financial system.

Bibliography

Primary Sources, Archival Material, and Data Repositories

PRIMARY SOURCES AND Official Documents

Bank for International Settlements (BIS)

- Triennial Central Bank Surveys on Foreign Exchange and Derivatives Market Activity (2000–2025 editions)

- International Debt Securities Statistics (2000–2025)

- Locational and Consolidated Banking Statistics (2000–2025)

Federal Reserve System (United States)

- Federal Open Market Committee (FOMC) transcripts and policy statements, 2000–2025

- Board of Governors, Financial Stability Reports (2015–2025)

- Fedwire Funds Service Annual Reports and Statistics, 2000–2025

- Federal Reserve Foreign and International Monetary Authorities (FIMA) Repo Facility disclosures and guidelines (2020–2025)

International Monetary Fund (IMF)

- Currency Composition of Official Foreign Exchange Reserves (COFER), Quarterly Data, 2000–2025

- Coordinated Portfolio Investment Survey (CPIS), Annual Data, 2000–2025

- Direction of Trade Statistics (DOTS), Annual Reports, 2000–2025

- IMF Articles of Agreement and Special Drawing Rights (SDR) allocations, historical records and archival files (1969–2025)

European Central Bank (ECB)

- TARGET2 Payment System Annual Reports (2008–2025)

- Wholesale and Retail Digital Euro Project Reports and Sandbox Trials (2020–2025)

- ECB Financial Stability Review Reports (2008–2025)

People's Bank of China (PBoC)

- Cross-border Interbank Payment System (CIPS) Usage Statistics and Reports (2015–2025)

- RMB Internationalization Annual Reports (2010–2025)

- Digital Currency Electronic Payment (e-CNY) Development Reports (2018–2025)

Bank of England (BoE)

- CHAPS Payment System Annual Reports (2008–2025)

- Financial Stability Reports (2010–2025)

- Sterling Monetary Framework (SMF) and Standing Swap-Line Documentation (2015–2025)

International Swaps and Derivatives Association (ISDA)

- ISDA Master Agreements (1992, 2002, 2020 editions)
- Annual Margin Survey Reports and Guidelines (2000–2025)

Archival and Historical Material

Federal Reserve Bank of New York Archives

- Archival papers and policy memos related to Bretton Woods, gold window closure (Nixon Shock), and establishment of Fed swap lines (1945–2025)
- Historical documentation of Fedwire and CHIPS settlement evolution (1970–2025)

National Archives and Records Administration (NARA), United States

- Presidential and Treasury Department archival documents related to dollar policy, sanctions implementation, and IMF negotiations (1960–2025)

IMF Archives and Historical Collections

- Archival documents on Bretton Woods negotiations, SDR creation, IMF quota reviews, and conditionality negotiations (1944–2025)

Bank of England Archives

- Historical documentation on the Eurodollar market evolution, London Interbank Offered Rate (LIBOR) establishment, and financial deregulation (1960–2025)

Data Repositories and Statistical Databases

Bloomberg Terminal

- Historical price data (FX swaps, basis spreads, bond yields, collateral haircuts, repo rates), 2000–2025
- Real-time and historical market liquidity metrics and transaction volumes

Refinitiv (Thomson Reuters) Datastream

- Cross-border capital-flow data, sovereign and corporate bond issuance statistics, derivative market metrics, 2000–2025

SWIFT

- Annual and quarterly transaction volume reports, messaging statistics, and payment-route analyses (2000–2025)

The Clearing House (CHIPS)

- Publicly available transaction-volume data, liquidity metrics, and operational disclosures (2000–2025)

CLS Group

- Continuous Linked Settlement data reports, daily settlement statistics, and historical FX market risk analytics (2002–2025)

Central-Bank Digital Currency (CBDC) Project Documentation

Bank for International Settlements (BIS) Innovation Hub

- Project mBridge Technical Reports and Operational Pilots (2020–2025)
- Project Dunbar Technical and Governance Framework Reports (2021–2025)

European Central Bank (ECB)

- Wholesale Digital Euro Technical Reports, Design Choices, and Sandbox Experiment Data (2020–2025)

Hong Kong Monetary Authority (HKMA) & Monetary Authority of Singapore (MAS)

- Project LionRock-Inthanon and Project Ubin Cross-border Payment Trials, Technical Documentation, and Final Reports (2017–2025)

These primary sources, archival materials, and authoritative data repositories provided the empirical foundation and analytical benchmarks for the research, arguments, and scenario modeling presented throughout this volume.

Don't miss out!

Visit the website below and you can sign up to receive emails whenever Josh Luberisse publishes a new book. There's no charge and no obligation.

https://books2read.com/r/B-A-GKMY-FIBLG

BOOKS 2 READ

Connecting independent readers to independent writers.

About the Publisher

Fortis Novum Mundum, LLC is an independent black-owned publishing company focused on publishing work of non-fiction by independent authors.

Our publishing professionals are committed to assisting authors in creating their best work and exploring fresh avenues for disseminating literature and ideas to readers around the world. Our goal is to give writers the widest possible audience by expanding our reach internationally, adopting cutting-edge technological advances, and working closely with them throughout the entire publishing process, from editing and layout to publicity and sales to printing and shipping. We also defend the rights of our writers and promote free speech to make sure their words are heard far beyond the bounds of a book and into the fabric of communities and societies around the world.

www.ingramcontent.com/pod-product-compliance
Lightning Source LLC
La Vergne TN
LVHW052258200926
848481LV00002B/404